Visiting Our Past

America's Historylands

Visiting Our Past

America's Historylands

National
Geographic
Society

VISITING OUR PAST: AMERICA'S HISTORYLANDS

PUBLISHED BY
THE NATIONAL GEOGRAPHIC SOCIETY

Editorial Consultant
DANIEL J. BOORSTIN
Librarian of Congress, former Senior Historian of the Smithsonian Institution. Pulitzer Prize-winning author of *The Americans: The Democratic Experience*

Chapters by Dr. Boorstin and
RICHARD R. BEEMAN
Associate Professor of History, University of Pennsylvania. Author of *Patrick Henry: A Biography*

RAY ALLEN BILLINGTON
Senior Research Associate, Huntington Library. Author of *America's Frontier Heritage*

JOE B. FRANTZ
Professor of History, University of Texas. Co-author of *The American Cowboy: Myth or Reality*

BROOKE HINDLE
Director, National Museum of History and Technology, Smithsonian Institution. Author of *Technology in Early America*

CHARLES PIERCE ROLAND
Professor of History, University of Kentucky. Author of *The Confederacy*

JAMES MORTON SMITH
Director, Winterthur Museum. Editor of *George Washington: A Profile*

WILCOMB E. WASHBURN
Director, Office of American Studies, Smithsonian Institution. Author of *The Governor and the Rebel: A History of Bacon's Rebellion in Virginia*

First edition 450,000 copies
Library of Congress CIP data page 399

A VOLUME IN THE
WORLD IN COLOR LIBRARY
PREPARED BY
NATIONAL GEOGRAPHIC BOOK SERVICE
JULES B. BILLARD, *Director*

Staff for this Book

ROSS BENNETT
Editor

CHARLES O. HYMAN
Art Director

ANNE DIRKES KOBOR
Illustrations Editor

CAROL BITTIG LUTYK
Chief Researcher

THOMAS B. ALLEN
SEYMOUR L. FISHBEIN
EDWARD LANOUETTE
DAVID F. ROBINSON
VERLA LEE SMITH
Editor-Writers

CONNIE BROWN
Design

MARY SWAIN HOOVER
SHIRLEY L. SCOTT
MARGARET SEDEEN
Researcher-Writers

MARY H. DICKINSON
KAREN H. VOLLMER
ELIZABETH L. WAGLEY
ANNE E. WITHERS
Editorial Research

ROBERT C. FIRESTONE
Production Manager

KAREN F. EDWARDS
Assistant Production Manager

LINDA B. MEYERRIECKS
BARBARA G. STEWART
Illustrations Research

SUZANNE P. KANE
Assistant

JOHN T. DUNN
Engraving and Printing

JOHN D. GARST, JR.
VIRGINIA L. BAZA
CHARLES W. BERRY
GEORGE E. COSTANTINO
ALFRED ZEBARTH
Map Design and Production

VIRGINIA THOMPSON
JESSICA C. TAYLOR
Index

WERNER JANNEY
Style

Contributions by
WAYNE BARRETT
ALICE J. HALL
NATHANIEL T. KENNEY
MAUREEN PALMEDO

Photographs by
MARIE-LOUISE BRIMBERG
COTTON COULSON
LOWELL GEORGIA
FARRELL GREHAN
DAVID ALAN HARVEY
JAMES L. STANFIELD
BILL STRODE
WILLIAM S. WEEMS *and others*

Map Paintings by
PAUL HOGARTH

438 Illustrations
413 in full color, 11 maps

Page 1, American eagle emblem; Pages 2-3, Independence Hall; Page 4, inkstand made by silversmith Philip Syng, used by signers of the Declaration of Independence, and preserved in Independence Hall; Page 6, New England whale weather vane; Page 7, Alexander Graham Bell's telephone; Page 9, military cartouche; all paintings by Paul Hogarth.

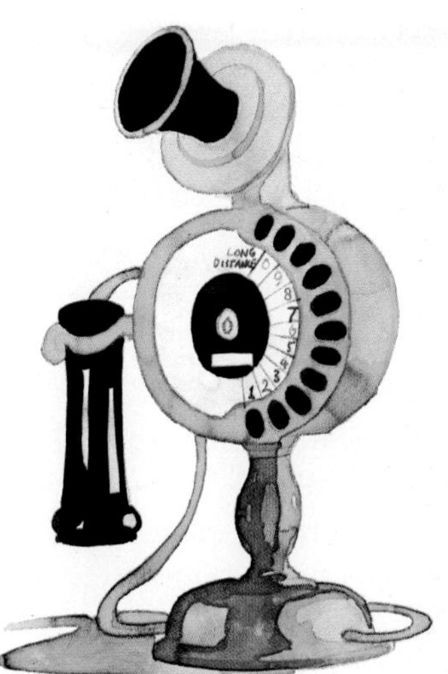

Foreword

I live beside the Potomac River, and every morning my eye falls upon a mysterious, man-made mound overlooking the stream. Someday an archeologist will probe it. Until then, I can only wonder what it hides—Indian artifacts dating from long before Columbus... a ruin left by our colonial ancestors... a hasty fortification marking some forgotten foray during the Civil War?

Each of us has his own counterpart of that mound, some constant reminder of our nation's past. A stroll through downtown Boston or Philadelphia brings you face-to-face with buildings that cradled the uncertain concept that became the United States of America. Plantation houses still stand in the South, colonnaded sentinels of a way of life that died at Appomattox. Missions in California speak of a Spanish past, and courtyard cottages in New Orleans recall early Creole life.

But history does not linger only in old structures. Dutch names still dot the Hudson River Valley; Mark Twain's sardonic spirit still haunts the Mississippi. And in Northern states, rivers remember the French voyageurs and explorers who dared swift currents in search of furs and adventure.

One of them, Pierre Esprit Radisson—who probably reached the upper Mississippi as early as 1660—encapsulated the experience of the first Europeans in the new, clean—and often dangerous—world that was 17th-century America: "We weare Cesars, being nobody to contradict us." Eager Indians relieved the newcomers of all labor in the hope "that we should give them a brasse ring, or an awle, or an needle." But the Caesars knew the terrors of the wilds and often had to "lye downe on the bare ground... the breech in the watter, the feare in the buttocks, to have the belly empty, the wearinesse in the bones, and drowsinesse of ye body...."

Radisson coursed his wild rivers, and each day I skirt my own tame one—the Potomac—as I drive to Society headquarters in Washington, D. C. From one vantage point during the short trip, memorials and monuments crowd the horizon. Marines frozen in bronze raise Old Glory at the Iwo Jima Statue. The stark shaft of the Washington Monument, the domes of the Jefferson Memorial and the Capitol on its Hill, the classic columns of the Lincoln Memorial—all vie for attention.

The city and its environs offer more than memorials to heroic figures and momentous deeds. Bits of real history are scattered throughout the area. In 15 minutes, for example, I can drive out 13th Street and stand on the parapet of Fort Stevens, a reconstructed earthen Civil War fortification now surrounded by houses and apartments. Heroic ghosts dwell here where destiny was delayed on July 12, 1864. Confederate Gen. Jubal A. Early had swept across Maryland and was advancing on the Capital, his skirmishers within rifle shot of the fort. To strengthen Union morale, President Lincoln rode out and insisted on standing atop the parapet as bullets whined around him. A young officer, Oliver Wendell Holmes, Jr.—later an Associate Justice of the Supreme Court—ordered him, "Get down, you damn fool!" And Lincoln did.

To the south of the city, a pleasant drive brings one to Mount Vernon. George Washington's estate, designed by himself, serenely commands the broad Potomac. His spirit still inhabits the tastefully beautiful house, and a visit there is a return to the simple self-sufficiency of our first citizens.

A few hours to the southwest, on a hilltop near Charlottesville, stands the home of Thomas Jefferson. Author of the Declaration of Independence, statesman, genius, he wanted his countrymen to remember him as the founder of the University of Virginia. From Monticello's terrace walk you can look down—as Jefferson did—upon the renowned educational institution that is his living memorial.

In New England, some original structures still stand after more than 300 years. For example, the house John Alden helped his son Jonathan build in Duxbury, Massachusetts, dates from 1653. Like most places featured in this book, the Alden house welcomes visitors at specified times and seasons. There you can look up at the original powdered clam and oyster shell ceiling, feel the "gunstock" beams, stand in the room where John Alden, sole surviving signer of the Mayflower Compact, breathed his last at the age of 88 in 1687.

Interest in the American past does not confine itself to historical sites. Young people have turned to old-fashioned handicrafts with enthusiasm, and the country is blessed with a resurgence of weaving, candlemaking, silversmithing. In Virginia's Colonial Williamsburg such honored trades thrive, and scholarly musicians have even rediscovered the airs that regaled our forefathers. The Indians of New Mexico and Arizona have rekindled a sense of pride and independence through skills perfected by their ancestors. Their finest rugs command thousands of dollars; their exquisite pottery and jewelry reach markets throughout the world.

For the preservation of America's cultural riches we owe a debt of thanks to private groups and individuals as well as to state and local agencies and the federal government. The National Trust for Historic Preservation, which maintains such treasured sites as The Shadows-on-the-Teche antebellum mansion in Louisiana, encourages public participation in the work of guarding our heritage. Through the National Park Service, the federal government administers such disparate historic areas as Fort Laramie, Wyoming, haven for wagon trains on the Oregon Trail, the 23-room house of Thomas A. Edison in West Orange, New Jersey, and the Saugus Iron Works in Massachusetts. The federal government is the custodian of thousands of other sites, both private and public, and lists some 13,000 in a national register of historic places.

Visiting Our Past: America's Historylands distills the essence of those myriad places, focusing on cherished representative shrines to portray our collective past. A handy supplement describing selected sites accompanies the book and highlights, state by state, places where you may find a link with your own past.

Turn the page now for a commentary by prize-winning historian Daniel J. Boorstin, Librarian of Congress. Then begin a tour of those visible landmarks that chronicle a great civilization.

Gilbert M. Grosvenor

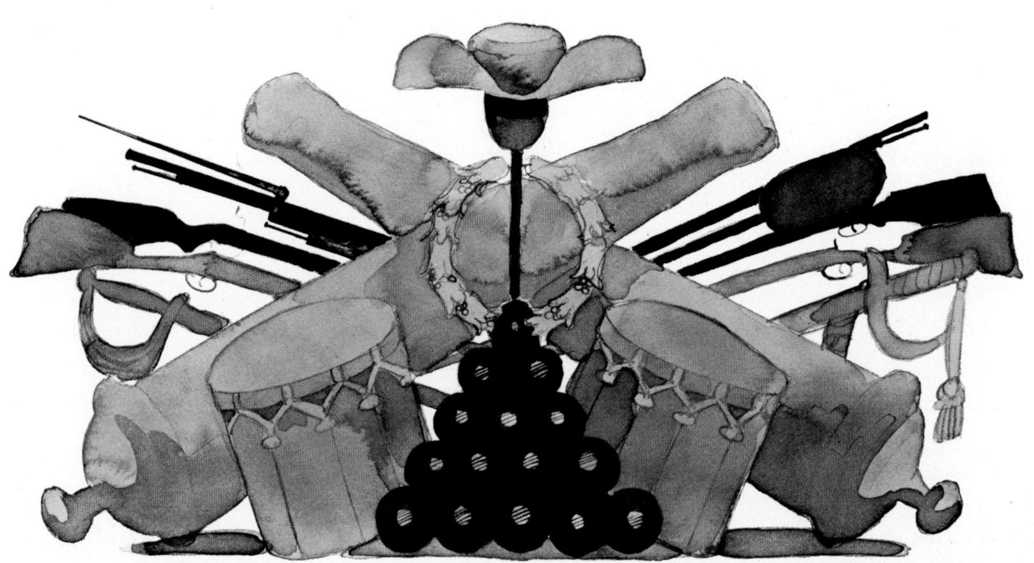

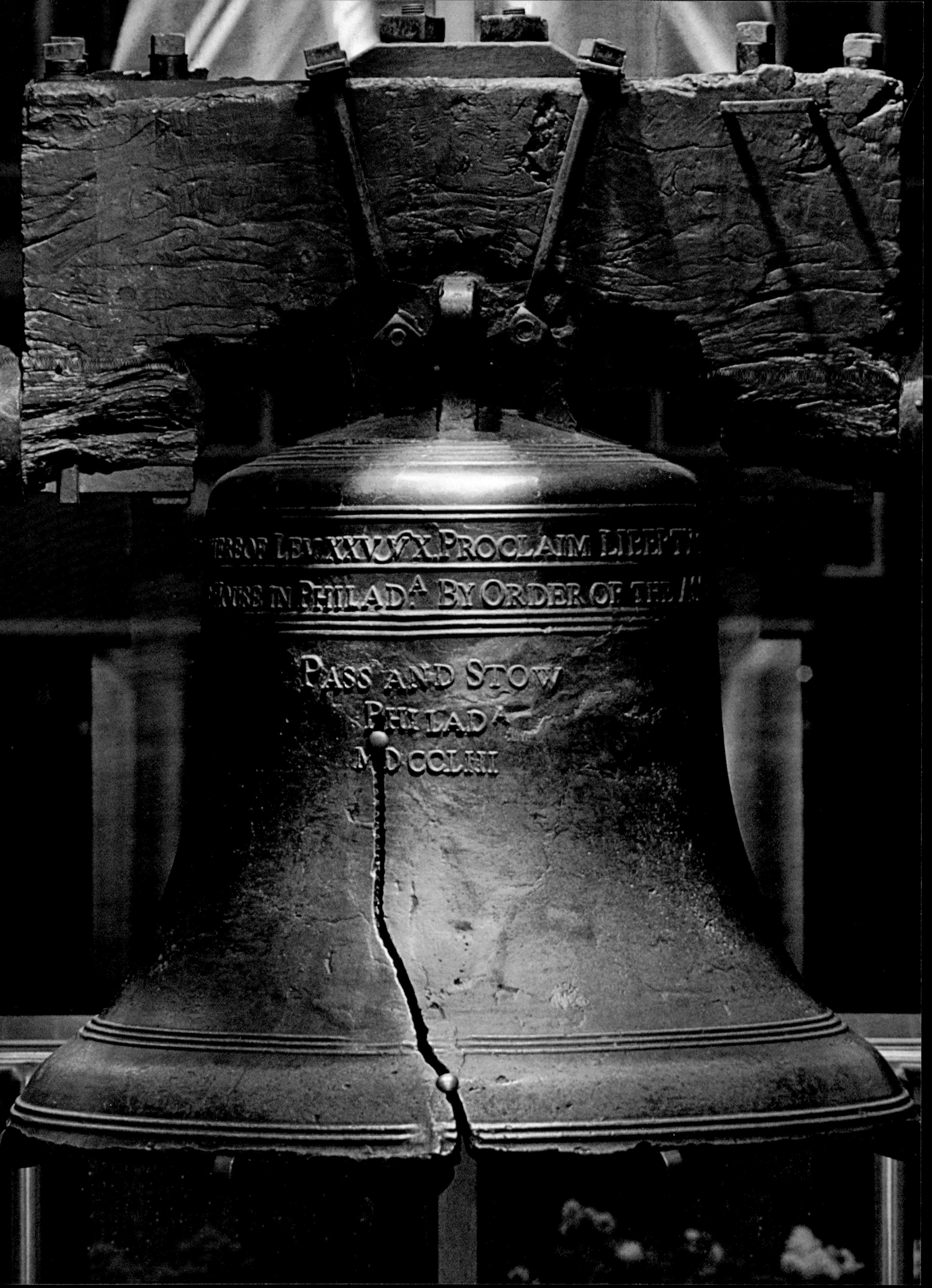

PASS AND STOW
PHILADA
MDCCLIII

The Landscape of American History

DANIEL J. BOORSTIN

Each of us has become an everyday television visitor to the remote corners of our country. Any evening, if we wish, we can have a glimpse of New York or San Francisco, San Diego, Denver, or Tampa. We can share vistas of open desert, sheltered forest, or glaciered mountain. Our magical reach across space has inevitably dulled our sense of wonder at the varieties of our cities and our countrysides. With our TV-vision we range instantly across the continental space. But our technology has done little to help us reach across time, to glimpse the distant century. It has become easy to visit our present—in all its varieties of landscape and catastrophe. Drowned in the televised present, we are tempted to confine our historical imagination to the post-photographic era.

Visiting our past may actually be more difficult today than ever before. Our "audiovisual aids," in the very act of extending, have also limited our vistas, and given earlier decades a new ambiguity. The vividness with which we can see the living gestures and hear the voices of Presidents since Theodore Roosevelt somehow makes earlier Presidents seem figures of an ancient history. The past seems to become more inaccessible precisely because of the institutions and the forces that have helped us make the most of our New World. The computer can, of course, help us classify and catalog and retrieve our legacy of documents and objects, books and furniture and paintings. But our main highways to the past remain what they were in the pre-electronic age before photography, before radio and television: our books and our landscape.

Books, like this one you hold in your hands, remain our principal resource for learning about all earlier times. TV can never displace them. If we want to know what earlier Americans—Pilgrim Fathers, Founding Fathers, soldiers in the Civil War—were thinking and doing, we must turn to the printed page, to our libraries and to our bookstores. The *New England Primer,* the Declaration of Independence and the Constitution, the Emancipation Proclamation and the Gettysburg Address—these bring us messages which can come in no other way. We cannot know our past, or begin to feel at home there, unless we read.

But there are some things that we cannot learn from the printed page. These we must experience in our landscape. This landscape includes, of course, the enduring features of our continent—oceans and lakes and mountains—as well as all the human relics which we find about us: trails and roads, canals and railroad tracks, streetcars and cog railways, monuments and cemeteries, churches and houses and public buildings, furniture and paintings, and countless other items which exist only because they were put there by our ancestors. They speak to us from the past in a language that all of us can learn. The more we become familiar with them, the more they tell us.

LIBERTY BELL, IN ITS PAVILION ON INDEPENDENCE MALL, PHILADELPHIA; MARIE-LOUISE BRIMBERG

Some of these relics we can see by traversing the outdoors. Some we can find in museums, in lovingly preserved family mansions, in scrupulously restored houses, in antique shops, in whole towns such as Old Sturbridge or Colonial Williamsburg. Our past is also casually preserved in junk shops, on trash heaps or garbage dumps, among the neglected or despised debris of the past. Other relics we try unsuccessfully to forget in the once-charming but now run-down houses of inner cities or in the obscene jungles of car-cemeteries. All these are "documents" of the past, raw materials with which every citizen can become his own archeologist, his own historian. Such are the pieces of a puzzle which we must fit together if we are to share the experience of those who lived here before us, and those who helped make our nation what it is.

The effort of visiting our past in books is sedentary, and usually lonely. Visiting our past by exploring our landscape requires a very different sort of effort. This requires the energy to go places, the vehicles to get us there, the time to look and wander and reflect on where we are, where we have been, and what we have seen. Such visiting is far from sedentary, and is anything but lonely. It can be costly and troublesome, but it can also be convivial and refreshing. Even if it were not more economical to travel with others, it is immeasurably more rewarding to have companions beside us when we go visiting the past to share our own awe and delight and dismay. Our companions will help us see things that neither you nor I would see if left to ourselves. Children are some of the most perceptive and awakening and stirring of such companions. Since their imaginations have not yet got into our adult ruts, they imagine flights through time as easily as we imagine flights through space. The impatience of our children pushes us on.

If we are lucky enough to have the money and the vehicle and the time, we still need to sharpen our vision to learn what we can about our past. Just as every nation develops its own political institutions, its poetry and folklore, so every nation develops its own archeology. American history left us an archeology all our own with our own ways of preserving and destroying the relics of our past.

This is the archeology of democracy. It is a New World archeology, shaped by a people who insist on moving up in the world as well as around the world, people with an insatiable appetite for the new, always infatuated with this year's model. Our landscape bears the marks of mixing peoples and cultures, of a standard of living never before seen. I will list a few peculiarities of our special American archeology. You will discover for yourself the suspense and the reward of your personal visits to our past. The adventure of visiting our past, then, is not only the opportunity to find what we were already looking for, but the chance to encounter what we had never expected to find. In this way we discover clues to a past which speaks to you or to me. There is no substitute for going.

History spread out and not piled up. To discover our American history in our landscape we must travel far—across rivers, deserts, plains, and mountains. By contrast we can sample the main stages of history in any country of Western Europe within the radius of a few hundred miles. Over there, relics of the outposts of the Roman Empire are buried under the buildings of the Middle Ages, which in turn have become rubble or substructure for architects of the Renaissance. Beside these we find factories of the Industrial Revolution and hovels of a 19th-century proletariat. The Old World historical landscapes are more often vertical than horizontal. Their pasts are buried in one level after another. But our history is scattered across a vast land.

To explore our colonial history we must traverse the thousand miles that separate the Plymouth haunts of the Pilgrim Fathers from General Oglethorpe's Georgia. We must travel three thousand miles to follow the course of settlement of the farther West. The story of the American farmer stretches across Western states, many as broad as England is long. The rise of American commerce and industry, the growth of American cities, is embedded in the story of a continent. Since we are a two-ocean nation, our history is a transcontinental story. For the most part, when our history is visible it is spread thin and near the surface.

Fourth of July fireworks burst over the Mall and three of the most visited shrines in Washington, D.C.: the Lincoln Memorial, the Washington Monument, the U.S. Capitol.

WILLIAM S. WEEMS

JULY
IV
DCCLXXVI

People move away from their past. The fifty million immigrants who have come here since colonial times came to get away from their past. Again, as they moved across the continent they moved away from their first American locale. They, like us after them, left ancestral homes behind. Many of us have never seen the house where our grandfathers lived. In the United States, keeping an ancestral home and treasured relics of family history has been the privilege of the very rich or the penalty of the very poor. Children and grandchildren seldom remain on premises where they could keep up the old homestead to pass on to their children. Even among farmers this has become difficult or impossible.

Toward the disposable and the renewable. The progress of our standard of living has taken us from the durable and the immovable toward the temporary and the disposable. The annual-model contagion has touched houses, churches, and everything but tombstones. We Americans, then, measure our progress and our well-being not by what we can preserve from our past, but by what we can displace or leave behind. We have few incentives to preserve the everyday apparatus of our fathers. Every year new technologies give us new incentives to turn in last year's model.

This enthusiasm for the latest thing breeds an indifference to some of our most interesting relics. "Urban Renewal" has tended to detach us from our history, every year making the task of visiting our past more difficult. It is often easier and cheaper to tear it down for something new than to restore it so we can recapture the old. Bulldozers every day clear away foundations of interesting and solid buildings so they can be replaced by flimsy, uninteresting boxes which may not outlast a generation. State and local historical societies, energetically aided by the National Trust for Historic Preservation, supported by city ordinances and state and federal laws, can all help us preserve the avenues to our past. In a country so blessed as ours with wealth and technological progress, we need a special effort of self-restraint, of private philanthropy and public investment, to preserve reminders of our history.

Beacon of freedom and hope, the Statue of Liberty tends the gateway to New York City, journey's end for millions of Europe's "huddled masses yearning to breathe free."

JOHN VELTRI

Everybody's history is our history. In the more homogeneous countries of Western Europe, when people travel across their land they trace the story of people most like themselves. In our country, however, the landscape of our past exacts a double feat of imagination. We must not only put ourselves back in time, we must put ourselves into the ways of thinking, speaking, and worshiping of people much different from your ancestors or mine. To feel one with American history, each of us must adopt a motley past. We must try to understand people who, when they came, were as different from Americans already here as were the peoples of the different Old World nations.

Along with these features of our American archeology, which complicate our trip into the past, are others which can make our task easier.

The continuity of our history. The story of most other nations is one of ups and downs: of dark ages, renaissances, revolutions, invasions, epochs of flowering, and centuries of decay. When you tour Greece or Italy or Turkey you find yourself being guided among ruins, relics of the greatest periods, remains of the most impressive monuments of their civilization. But the "classic" eras of their past—of Plato's Greek Republic, of Caesar's Roman Empire, of the Ottoman Empire of the sultans—have no counterpart in our national history. For us the present seems the climax.

The history of our civilization in the United States, while briefer than that of other continents, has also been strikingly continuous. Except for the early encounters of Europeans with the American Indians, and except for the Revolutionary and Civil Wars, we have experienced no national trauma of violence on our land. Of course, some people in some regions look back with a special nostalgia or romantic regret—to the age of John Winthrop in New England, of Benjamin Franklin in Philadelphia, to Jefferson Davis's Old South, to the mission times or the gold rush era in California. But the more intimately we visit those pasts, the fewer of us regret that we did not live then. And each of these pasts fits into a remarkably unbroken national story.

Our nation, unlike others with longer history, is not a land of ruins. Since the Civil War, the great wars which our nation has fought have luckily not been fought on these shores. Few other modern nations have enjoyed so remarkably continuous a national political life. In recent decades the people of Germany or of Russia have busied themselves first putting up, then removing, the signs that named their buildings, their streets—even their cities—after Hitler or Stalin. Meanwhile, we still proudly commemorate our Washington and Jefferson and Adams, our Jackson and Lincoln, our Grant and Lee, our Wilson and Theodore Roosevelt and Franklin Roosevelt, our Eisenhower and Kennedy. In our democratic civilization, it is public buildings, not feudal castles or noble palaces, that contain and continue our history. Schools and universities, libraries and museums—joint products of community spirit, of public and private philanthropy—mark a tradition still very much alive in our time.

In each of the United States we can see continuity also in the most deliberate and artificial of our political intrusions—our county seats and state capitals. Each of our 3,000 county seats is not only a place where records of our past can be visited, but also a visible symbol of continuity: a federal representative government in a landscape of changing communities. In these county seats we glimpse the special meaning that a nearby political center once held for a nation of farmers without automobiles.

In our state capitals, too, we find clues to both the continuities of our federal system and the mobility of the American people. Even before the War of 1812, nine of the original thirteen states already had a different capital from that at the date of the Declaration of Independence, some 35 years before. In several cases the new capital had not existed as a town, but was conjured up to become a capital, to meet new needs of moving population, of shifting commercial or political balance. New Hampshire's capital moved from Exeter to Concord, New York's from New York City to Albany, New Jersey's from Burlington and Perth Amboy to Trenton, Pennsylvania's from Philadelphia to Lancaster to Harrisburg, Delaware's from New Castle to Dover, Virginia's from Williamsburg to Richmond, North Carolina's from New Bern to Raleigh, South Carolina's from Charleston to Columbia, and Georgia's from Savannah to Augusta to Louisville to Milledgeville and eventually to Atlanta. As recently as 1910 Oklahoma moved its capital from Guthrie to Oklahoma City. All these capitals remain signs of the continuing political and emotional meaning of states in American life.

A national capital made to order. It suited the hopes of our Founding Fathers to build a grand Capital City for their grand new republic. Of course the location of the city in what is now Washington, D. C., between the old settlements of Alexandria in Virginia and Georgetown in Maryland, was the result of compromise—which made it the more fitting symbol of a nation that would thrive on federal compromises. The new Capital was placed in the borderlands of the South, in a bargain between New Yorker Alexander Hamilton and Virginian Thomas Jefferson in return for fiscal arrangements which benefited the Northern states.

If we take the city of Washington and its many beauties for granted, if we think of it simply as a government center, we are undervaluing ourselves—and missing one of the most delightful and most instructive of all possible excursions into our past. Each of us should visit our Capital City, should walk through the houses of our Congress, the White House, our Supreme Court, our Library of Congress, our Smithsonian Institution, and the scores of other living monuments that belong to us. Today we reap dividends from the vision, the compromises, and the necessities, which put our national Capital in a new place. Washington, D. C., remains our prime place of pilgrimage. Here past meets present. In buildings that reach back to the early decades of our republic, we see our representatives using the Constitution which first brought our nation together. We see people trying to keep our historic national institutions in working order, and we can count ourselves among them.

Although our history is briefer than that of European nations, when we Americans go visiting our past, we do have a strenuous, puzzling task. We must seek out the pieces strewn across a continent. We must make ourselves one with many varieties of earlier Americans. In this search for our shared history we will rediscover our nation and ourselves.

American "soldiers" re-enact the defense of Baltimore's Fort McHenry during the 1814 British bombardment. Francis Scott Key watched, then wrote "The Star-Spangled Banner."

ROBERT W. MADDEN, NATIONAL GEOGRAPHIC PHOTOGRAPHER

Footholds in a New World

To the shores of a new-found Eden, fraught with peril and promise, sailed conquistadors searching for gold and glory, refugees pursuing utopian dreams, down-and-outers hungering for land, and pious venturers seeking freedom of worship.

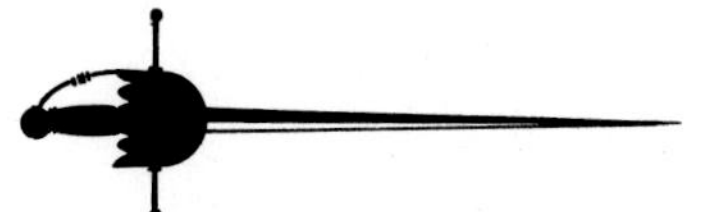

WILCOMB E. WASHBURN

Deep within Chesapeake Bay, two small ships skimmed the silvery-blue waters, gliding past forests crowded thick "with great Curiosity of woods." By night the 250 English colonizers aboard gazed at Indian signal fires blazing along the banks. On a March day in 1634 the travelers anchored the *Ark* and *Dove* and waded ashore—a damp finale to their four-month-long journey across the Atlantic.

After meeting with the "Emperour" of the Piscataway Indians, this goodly company settled on the east bank of the St. Marys River. Here English folk of both Catholic and Protestant persuasions, of high and low birth, founded St. Marys City. They swapped cloth, axes, hoes, and knives for land and Indian huts, into which the colonists moved. Nearby, they erected a palisaded fort, then a wooden house for Governor Leonard Calvert, and, gradually, thatched cottages, a gristmill, and a brick chapel where everyone worshiped.

In an age when Protestants and Catholics took turns persecuting each other, the little "Mariland" settlement experimented in religious liberty. In 1649 the general assembly passed the Toleration Act guaranteeing freedom of conscience to Christians, and although five years later the growing number of Puritans forced repeal of the act, it had been an expression of a new hope.

A certain liberation of women even glimmered. Mistress Margaret Brent, executor of Leonard Calvert's estate, demanded a seat in the assembly. Although her request was denied, the legislators noted that the estate was better managed "in her hands than in any man's else in the whole Province."

Faint outlines of the first settlement are all that remain in the sleepy little village today. But the spirit of those early days is captured by St. Marys State House, a replica of the original two-story brick manor built in the shape of a cross. One can envision the assembly—Catholics and Protestants—gathered in the massive room on the first floor to enact laws. A climb up the oak stairs ends in the chamber where the governor and five councilmen considered bills for approval.

A stroll through the graveyard outside leads to the foundations of the original building and to a monument on the site where Calvert signed a treaty with the Indians in the shade of a mulberry tree. A limb from that tree is preserved as a communion rail in nearby Trinity Episcopal Church.

On summer weekends history comes alive under the river bluff where the early settlers scrambled ashore. There, the drama *Wings of the Morning* re-creates the struggles of this Maryland community in a setting nearly as quiet, uncluttered, and unhurried as it was more than 300 years ago.

St. Marys City today is a tangible reminder of the past. With Jamestown and Plymouth—the first major English footholds in the New World—it

SHIP MODEL, MARINERS MUSEUM, NEWPORT NEWS, VIRGINIA; DETAIL OF A PAINTING BY BIRNEY LETTICK; PHOTOMONTAGE BY JAMES L. STANFIELD, NATIONAL GEOGRAPHIC PHOTOGRAPHER

ROBERT W. MADDEN, NATIONAL GEOGRAPHIC PHOTOGRAPHER

exemplifies the embryonic colonies that emerged after many unsuccessful attempts at settlement.

More than six centuries earlier, Norse adventurers had left an imprint at L'Anse aux Meadows in Newfoundland, earliest documented European site in the New World. Vikings wintered there on the edge of a grassy meadow about the year 1000. They lived in turf-walled houses, lounged in a steam bath, and forged nails from local bog iron.

Nearly 500 years passed before other European mariners braved the Atlantic and again probed the New World. Christopher Columbus, coasting Cuba and Hispaniola in 1492, gazed upon lofty mountains that "seem to reach to the sky" and palm trees "wondrous to see for their beautiful variety." Convinced that he had discovered a new sea route to the Orient, the admiral spun tales of an exotic realm of gold and pearls, of strange herbs and fruits, and of even stranger copper-skinned natives who "go as naked . . . as when their mothers bore them."

Columbus's four voyages inspired a generation of explorers who searched in vain for a passage to Asia. John Cabot, a Venetian sailing for England's Henry VII, scouted Newfoundland and Nova Scotia. Portugal's Gaspar Corte-Real followed in his wake, and Cabot's son Sebastian cruised from Labrador to Delaware. The Florentine Amerigo Vespucci, after whom the Americas were named, skirted Brazil. Such discoveries touched off bitter rivalries among Old World powers hungry for the riches of the new land.

During the half century after Columbus's first voyage, the Spanish conquered the islands of the West Indies, poured into Central and South America, and raised massive harbor fortresses. Even today we see impressive evidence of Spain's iron-fisted grip on the New World. In Puerto Rico, San Juan's original bastion, La Fortaleza, sheltered the little settlement from roving European corsairs. A second fortress, El Morro, star attraction of San Juan

Atlantic waters split against the prow of El Morro, massive citadel at San Juan, Puerto Rico. Oldest fort in United States territory, it symbolizes Spain's might in the Americas. From its concrete walls, four tiers of cannon could sweep the waterline planking, hulls, decks, or rigging of enemy ships.

National Historic Site, towers above the harbor entrance, no longer a menace to ships of any flag.

Sir Francis Drake, the swashbuckling English sea dog, swooped into San Juan's harbor in 1595 with 3,000 men but failed to capture the 35 tons of silver and gold stored in La Fortaleza—today the governor's residence. Three years later the Earl of Cumberland attacked El Morro by land. His troops routed the Spaniards but were soon forced to withdraw because of an epidemic of dysentery.

To choke off the Spanish treasure route, the French planned to harass the Spaniards from a base on the Florida peninsula. Ponce de León, who had sailed with Columbus, claimed the "island" of Florida for Spain on his 1513 quest for gold and a fountain of youth. Half a century later, on a bluff overlooking the St. Johns River, Jean Ribaut planted a stone column bearing the arms of France. Much to the pleasure of Huguenots who returned two years later, Indians had carefully tended the shaft and decorated it with flowers. The Frenchmen raised a sod-and-timber fort and named it Caroline in honor of their young king, Charles IX. Where sentinels once kept a wary lookout, the stockaded earthwork has been reconstructed near Jacksonville.

To Philip II, Florida seemed a sword pointed at Spain's lifeline to her colonies, so he dispatched the ruthless Don Pedro Menéndez de Avilés to root out the Huguenots. In August 1565, Menéndez sighted Florida on almost the same day his arch rival, Jean Ribaut, returned to Fort Caroline with French reinforcements. Each sought to surprise the other. Ribaut sailed down the coast to attack the Spanish fleet, anchored in a sheltered harbor 30 miles away. But a hurricane wrecked Ribaut's ships and scattered the survivors up and down the coast.

Implanted at journey's end, the first footholds clung to the untamed shores of a vast new land. Spanish conquistadors whipped the French in Florida, Dutch folk penetrated the Hudson Valley, Swedish settlers peopled the Delaware, and English colonizers dug in from Maine to the Carolinas. Rivers hindered north-south journeys but sped the restless westward.

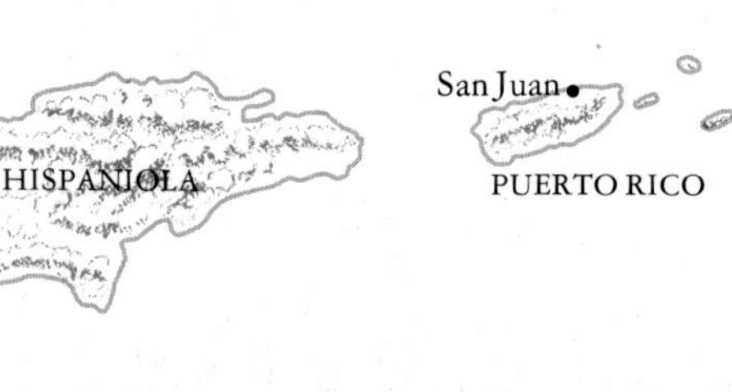

Now it was Menéndez's turn to attack. With 500 soldiers he slogged overland through the stormy darkness, across swollen streams and swamps waist-deep in muck. At dawn on the fifth day the Spaniards pounced on Fort Caroline and butchered 132 "heretics" without losing a man. Menéndez then rounded up the shipwrecked French soldiers, stranded on a sandbar. He marched the prisoners, ten at a time, behind the dunes. As each group crossed a fatal line drawn in the sand, the Spaniards fell upon them with pikes, swords, and knives at what became known as Matanzas (Spanish for "slaughters") Inlet. Spain's toehold in Florida was secure and would remain so until the early 1800's.

With the French threat dispelled, Menéndez settled at an Indian village he renamed St. Augustine—oldest continually inhabited city of European origin in what is now the United States. For more than a century the Spanish capital barely survived neglect by her motherland and raids by privateers and Indians. Finally, growing pressure from England prodded Spain into constructing a massive citadel to shelter as many as 1,500 townspeople.

The Castillo de San Marcos proved impregnable to all attackers; it still broods over old St. Augustine. Along the narrow streets, shaded by overhanging balconies, reminders of two centuries of Spanish life abound: the humble wooden dwellings of soldiers and laborers, elegant houses with sun-dappled patios, the scent of hand-dipped bayberry candles, a thick-walled inn with latticed windows. An ivy-covered chapel marks the site of St. Augustine's first mission, Nombre de Dios. Under the stars each summer, *Cross and Sword,* a symphonic drama, reenacts the city's bloody beginnings.

American history is usually seen as a progression from east to west, yet European contact in the 16th century was almost as early from the Pacific side as from the Atlantic. Juan Rodríguez Cabrillo, the Spanish "Columbus of California," dreamed of finding the fabled Strait of Anián, a waterway through North America linking the Atlantic with the Pacific. In 1542-43 his two caravels sailed from Mexico and probed the California coast as far north as Oregon, but failed to discover a shortcut to the Orient.

Francis Drake, on his piratical voyage around the world in 1577-80, swept up the west coast of the continent almost as far as the present Canadian border. But cold forced his ship back down the coast, through "thick stinking Fogs," until he fell in with a "convenient and fit harborough." Drake dubbed his California landing place Nova Albion ("New England") and promptly claimed it for Queen Elizabeth. Scholars still debate the exact point, but it is most likely Drakes Bay at Point Reyes National Seashore, just north of San Francisco Bay. Visitors to the area know that, in summer, fog and mist keep temperatures cool and skies overcast. Drake recorded this experience: "Notwithstanding it was in the height of summer, and so neere the sunne, yet were wee continually visited with like nipping colds as we had felt before...." Any chance of a California empire for England evaporated with Drake's departure five weeks later. Spain gradually extended her power into California from the south, creating the string of missions that still stretch from San Diego to Sonoma.

The Spanish also were the first Europeans to stake their claim in the Southwest. Gold-hungry conquistadors, accompanied by Indian guides and porters, settlers, and black-robed priests, filtered in from Mexico. In 1540 Francisco de Coronado, a 30-year-old grandee, trudged across sun-glazed desert and trackless plain as far as central Kansas, searching in vain for the legendary golden cities of Cíbola.

Those who know the western United States appreciate its peculiar fascination. The distances appear to be greater than in the East, the views longer, the sky bluer, the valleys deeper, the mountains higher. Outcroppings of eroded rock plateaus, such as El Morro National Monument in New Mexico, dot the horizon and guide travelers. The haughty conquistador Don Juan de Oñate camped at El Morro on one of his expeditions. Visitors can still see the inscription he recorded on the soft sandstone bluff: "Passed by here... from the discovery of the Sea of the South on the 16th of April 1605." Disillusioned, Oñate and his soldiers were marching back from the Gulf of California, which they had hoped to find overflowing with pearls.

The Spanish had circled the globe, conquered much of Mexico and South America, and probed the North American wilderness before the English

thought seriously about setting up "plantations" in the New World. Armchair chronicler Richard Hakluyt spurred English colonization with narratives of Elizabethan exploration. Another exuberant stay-at-home, Samuel Purchas, enticed colonizers with his florid discourse, bidding readers to "looke upon Virginia; view her lovely lookes... her Virgin portion nothing empaired, nay not yet improoved... she is worth the wooing and loves of the best Husband...." Interest in America blossomed, especially since viable settlements there would create a Protestant bulwark against Catholic Spain.

An English America soon emerged in the wonderfully fertile tidewater plains bordering Chesapeake Bay. On Roanoke Island the English planted their first American colony. A product of the vision and energy of Sir Walter Raleigh, the tiny settlement lay inside the far-flung "outer banks" of the North Carolina coast, protected from direct naval assault as well as from potential inland enemies. But the disappearance of the men, women, and children who settled there in 1587 dispelled that illusion of safety. The mystery of the "Lost Colony" still haunts historians and visitors to the restored star-shaped earthworks at Fort Raleigh National Historic Site near Manteo, North Carolina.

A marshy, mosquito-infested fist of land in the James River to the north marks the 1607 birthplace of the first permanent English settlement in the New World—Jamestown, Virginia. The tiny outpost struggled through a feeble infancy but eventually prospered. Modern-day visitors can relive those grueling days by wandering about the reconstructed huts, fort, and ships at Jamestown Festival Park.

Unlike the Chesapeake Bay settlers, the first colonizers of New England found a harsh and forbidding terrain. In 1604 the French planted a short-lived colony near the mouth of the St. Croix River, now the Maine-Canada boundary. Three years later Englishmen led by George Popham planted a fishing settlement on the Maine coast at the mouth of the Kennebec River, but Indian attacks, a bitter winter, and the "malice of the Divell" forced them to leave.

Separatist Pilgrims tackled the wooded coast of New England in 1620. They had withdrawn from what they regarded as a "pudle of corruption" in the English church and, after 12 years of self-imposed exile in Holland, embarked for a more isolated place where they could worship according to their beliefs. The small ship *Mayflower,* crammed with 102 "saints and strangers," sighted southern New England just before the onset of winter. Rebuffed from a more southerly landing by dangerous shoals, the leaky ship reached its final anchorage at Plymouth Harbor, north of where the arm of Cape Cod joins the mainland. William Bradford, later governor of Plymouth Colony for 31 years, movingly expressed the feeling of the voyagers: "Being thus passed the vast ocean, and a sea of troubles before in their preparation... they had now no friends to welcome them nor inns to entertain or refresh their weather-beaten bodies; no houses or much less towns to repair to, to seek for succour."

Scurvy, pneumonia, influenza, and tuberculosis wiped out half the colonists that first miserable winter. The survivors leveled the ground over the

Conquistadors once trod where Florida visitors now savor St. Augustine's colonial past along St. George Street. In the Oldest House, built on a site occupied since the early 1600's, hand-hewn cedar beams support low ceilings. Portraits of the Apostles gaze down on a refectory table dating from 1650.

NICK KELSH

burials "lest the Indians should know how many were the graves." But the Pilgrims never lost faith. The old town of Plymouth memorializes their courage and endurance; nearby Plimoth Plantation recreates the small Pilgrim settlement as it might have appeared around 1627.

Perhaps the challenge of a hostile environment motivated the early Pilgrims and Puritans to dig in and build a new society. In the spring of 1630 John Winthrop led his flock of nearly a thousand Puritans from England to Salem. Searching for a better site, they pressed south and eventually settled on the Shawmut Peninsula—today's Boston.

About 200 of the first Bostonians perished under winter's bitter onslaught. But the Puritans, like the Pilgrims, overcame the wilderness and recorded their accomplishments in books and sermons which, even as they gave primary credit to divine providence, reflected honor on themselves. While piety does not automatically die in more languorous climes, a stern commitment to a Calvinist God is easier to sustain where the bounty of the land does not shower itself upon man.

St. Augustine's fortress, Castillo de San Marcos, bristles with cannons above the Matanzas River. Walls of resilient coquina limestone—seashells cemented by lime—withstood the cannonballs of British troops who leveled the city in 1702.

JAMES L. AMOS, NATIONAL GEOGRAPHIC PHOTOGRAPHER

NICK KELSH

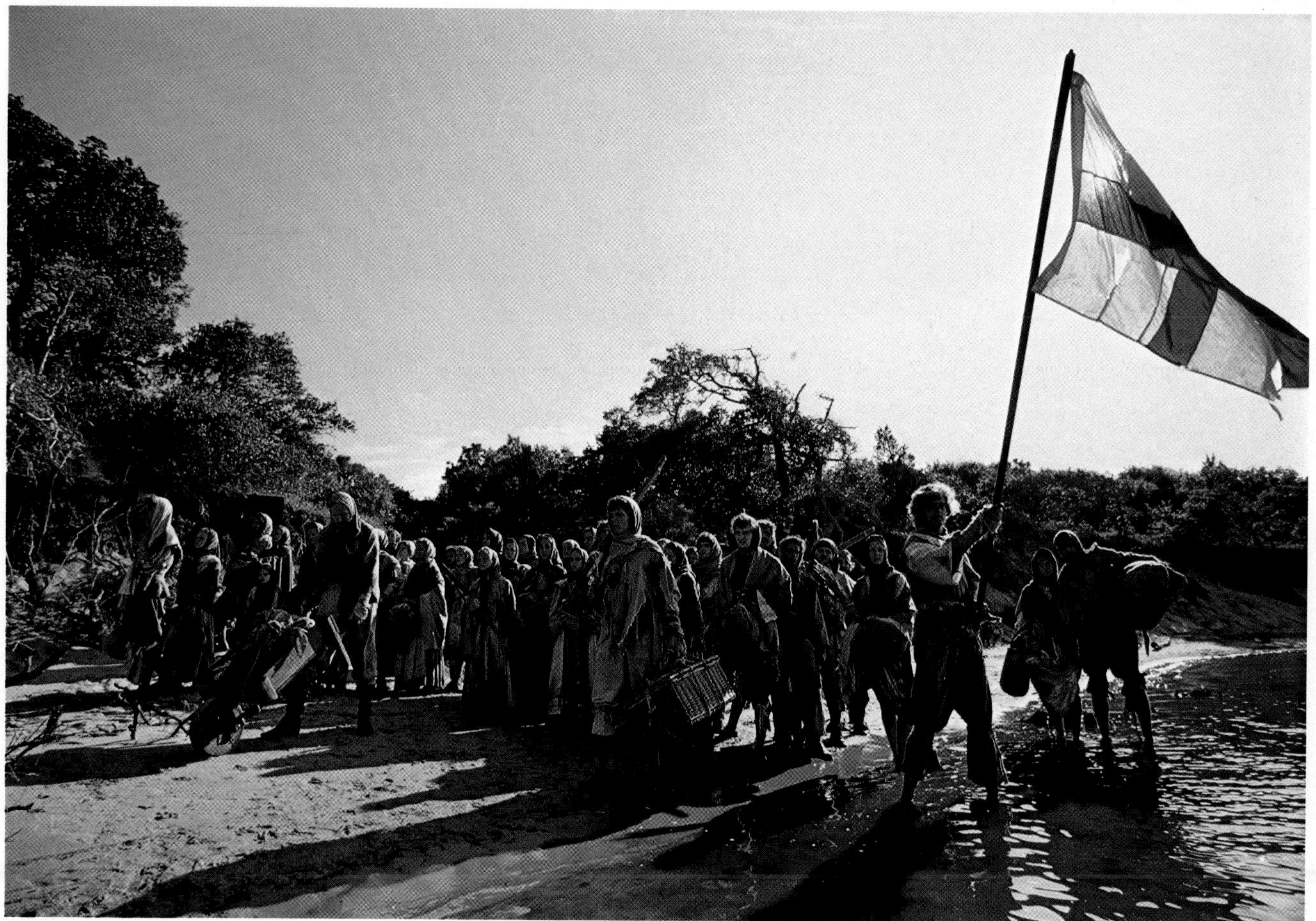

The Puritan sect, a dissenting group in England, became the established church in New England. Puritan ministers, the intellectual leaders of the community, recognized their "mission in the wilderness." They wanted to create an ordered society rigorously controlled by the elect. But the new orthodoxy spawned dissent. Little did Puritan leaders recognize at first the lure of the American forest, the fertility of the land to the west. While hunger for more land drove many farther into the wilderness, the desire for self-government and religious freedom impelled others to leave the stifling orthodoxy of the compact settlements along the coast. Plymouth's Governor Bradford feared that this breaking away "will be the ruin of New England, at least of the churches of God there, and will provoke the Lord's displeasure against them."

Sectarian bitterness and exclusivity were more characteristic of the 17th century than of our own day. Tolerance was not then championed as a principle; it was regarded more as a disagreeable alternative to community discord. Every sect preferred that dissenters find some other place to worship. On Boston Common, Puritans hanged four Quakers who had returned after being expelled. Roger Williams—for unorthodox beliefs that included doubts about the king's right to grant Indian lands to Englishmen—escaped deportation to England by fleeing south, where he founded Rhode Island. The colony became noted for being as tolerant of unorthodox persuasions as Massachusetts was intolerant. A year later, in 1636, Thomas Hooker moved a more orthodox group of believers from the Boston area to the fertile Connecticut River Valley and founded Hartford. Most of the colonies, however, established an uneasy truce with those who believed differently from the majority.

Colonial America's most persistent mystery, "The Lost Colony," reappears each summer as an outdoor drama on Roanoke Island, North Carolina. An actor portrays Manteo, the young chieftain who befriended Raleigh's ill-fated colonists.

The New World seemed vast enough for all who sought its untamed shores. Once the Virginia and Massachusetts settlers had demonstrated that communities could survive, even thrive, others sought to establish themselves in the new setting.

Visitors crossing the Verrazano-Narrows Bridge linking Staten Island and Brooklyn can look north to the Hudson River and Manhattan Island, heart of the Dutch empire in North America. Early exploration of the gateway to America's greatest commercial city illustrates the cosmopolitan nature of European discovery. Giovanni da Verrazano, an Italian navigator sailing for the king of France, cruised into New York Harbor in 1524. But the area was not fully explored until 1609 when Henry Hudson, an English mariner employed by the Dutch, sailed up the river that would bear his name.

The Dutch, after throwing off the Spanish yoke at home, forged into all parts of the world where Spain and Portugal had reigned supreme. When the Dutch set up Hudson River trading posts at present-day Albany and at New Amsterdam on Manhattan, they established themselves as a leading claimant to the emergent wealth of North America.

Perhaps the most feeble European foothold in North America was that of the Swedes around Delaware Bay. Visitors to Wilmington can find few remnants of the Swedish occupation of Fort Christina, erected in 1638. More lasting in America's physical inventory and storehouse of images is the log cabin, introduced by the Swedes (although often mistakenly attributed to the English).

Lt. Col. John Printz, "a man of brave size, weighing over 400 pounds," governed New Sweden for a decade. Called "Big Guts" by the Indians, he monopolized the fur trade and erected forts to secure his domain. But four years after the Dutch raised Fort Casimir (now New Castle) in 1651, New Sweden surrendered to the Dutch, who in turn fell prey to a resurgent English expansionism.

Cruising up the Delaware River in 1681, the first settlers dispatched by Quaker William Penn passed the log cabins of Swedish, Dutch, and English colonizers. At the mouth of the Schuylkill River, Penn's surveyor laid out Philadelphia, and by 1685 more than 7,000 immigrants had streamed into the city. A replica of Penn's sumptuous country retreat, Pennsbury Manor, sits on a gentle rise above the thickly wooded Delaware River near Morrisville, Pennsylvania. Pebble pathways lead past vineyards and orchards to Penn's stately manor house and a row of brick outbuildings—an icehouse, plantation office, smokehouse, and a large bake and brew house.

Though they look secure in retrospect, the American colonies remained tenuous footholds until the power of the Indians was broken. Red men rolled back tidewater settlements as late as Bacon's Rebellion in 1676. Mutual Indian-white murders ignited the frontier. Disagreeing with Governor William Berkeley's cautious efforts to repress the violence, Nathaniel Bacon and 200 frontiersmen massacred friendly Indians along Virginia's southern border. The rebels then stormed into Jamestown and forced the assembly to empower Bacon to wipe out all Indians. A civil war flared: The rebels burned Jamestown to the ground. They held the upper hand at first, but Berkeley eventually trounced Bacon's forces.

King Philip's War, named for a native chief, secured New England against Indian attack. But more towns were ravaged and more settlers killed in proportion to the population than during any subsequent American war. The conflict cost the white man 100,000 pounds sterling, but it cost the red man even more—he lost his homeland.

America's spirit derives largely from the challenge of a wilderness filled with both difficulties and opportunities. In the 16th and 17th centuries the perilous voyage across the "vast sea" was a frightening and educating experience. But as the memory of the ocean crossing faded, the lure of the land exerted a growing attraction. Confronting a wilderness they hardly knew how to exploit, Europeans faced unknown terrors: poisonous snakes and plants, strange beasts. It took courage to stay. Not all colonists had that courage, nor the luck, nor the intelligence. But enough did, and remnants of the first fragile footholds, though obscured by time, still endure to remind us all of those trying years.

The splendor of life in the country lingers on at Pennsbury Manor, reconstructed plantation of William Penn. From his beloved refuge on the Delaware, Pennsylvania's founding father commuted 25 miles to Philadelphia in a six-oared barge.

GARY FRIEDMAN

Jamestown

"Fire!" The terrifying cry rang through James Fort. Frightened men ran from their huts into the biting cold, pulling on their clothes.

A brilliant glare lit the area within the fort's palisade. The timbered storehouse was ablaze. Frantically the settlers worked to beat out the fire. But flying sparks nested in the thatched roofs; wooden beams fed the flames. Church, guardhouse, log fence went up in smoke.

Within hours, the tiny Jamestown settlement lay a smoldering ruin. Arms, bedding, clothing, food—nearly all were gone. Only three huts remained to shelter some 150 men from the "Great Frost" that January of 1608.

Once again, the settlers bitterly faced disaster. They would rebuild. But their infant Virginia colony seemed fated to suffer "a ghastly epic of misfortune."

Today, James Fort, its sturdy log palisades 11 feet tall, stands boldly above the James River where three ships are moored. Reconstructed at Jamestown Festival Park, a mile upriver from the original site, the fort is shaped "triangle wise, having three Bulwarkes, at every corner, like a halfe Moone, and foure or five pieces of Artillerie mounted in them." Within the enclosed acre, visitors can easily imagine colonists walking purposefully from church to storehouse, wondering nervously if the palisades will protect their wattle-and-daub huts from Indian attack. Guards in Elizabethan costumes man the ramparts.

Bound for Virginia, 105 English colonists braved the Atlantic in tiny ships. Replicas Susan Constant, Godspeed, *and* Discovery *lie at Jamestown. The largest measures 110 feet.*

FARRELL GREHAN

FARRELL GREHAN

The vessels at the dock are reconstructions of the three English merchant ships, *Susan Constant, Godspeed,* and *Discovery,* that brought the colonists to Virginia in April 1607. Their sponsors, the Virginia Company of London, directed them to establish a permanent settlement away from the coast. Choosing a tributary of Chesapeake Bay, the settlers—skilled craftsmen, laborers, four boys, and some 50 gentlemen—sailed slowly up the James River, seeking a favorable site.

About forty-five miles upstream, the colonists came upon a pleasant wooded peninsula. Though investigation showed it was marshy and humid, the position could be defended easily against Spanish raid or Indian attack. Best of all, the waters were so deep that even large ships could anchor close by. After some

Jamestown colonists hacked their first huts from Virginia's raw wilderness. Pine and oak timbers, shaped with a sash saw, framed walls woven of saplings and plastered with mud. Marsh reeds tied with vines thatched the roofs.

colonists needed not gold, but food, shelter, and security. Organizing labor details, he "set some to mow, others to binde thatch, some to build houses." When these tasks were finished, the resourceful Smith took to the waterways to negotiate with the Indians, commandeering corn if they refused to trade.

Wholly dedicated to the colony's success, Smith exploded with rage when he returned from one expedition to find the deposed president and his followers trying to escape with stolen provisions in the only ship. Turning the fort's cannon on the deserters, he ordered them to "stay or sinke." They stayed.

By December, the colony was stable enough to permit Smith's absence on an extended exploration of the Chickahominy River. Again trouble overtook him. While separated from his party, he was captured by Pamunkey Indians.

A rush-matted Indian longhouse at Festival Park recalls this adventure. In a simple structure framed with saplings and tied with rawhide, the wily Powhatan, ruler of a large confederation of Chesapeake tribes, sentenced Smith to death. But just as the braves raised their clubs, Smith later wrote, the chief's young daughter darted forward. Cradling Smith's head in her arms, Pocahontas pleaded for his life. Powhatan relented. Smith not only went free, but in the Indian maid he gained an important friend for Jamestown.

Even with support from Pocahontas, the first years at Jamestown were hard. Disaster chased every advance. Rats ate a hard-gained store of grain. The fire of 1608 swept newly built huts. More settlers arrived in "supplies" from England, only to die of typhoid, malaria, and dysentery. The ambivalent Indians alternated help with harassment.

Though anxious to protect its investment, the Virginia Company was out of touch with the colony's needs. Instead of hard-working farmers and builders, noted Smith, they shipped over "unruly gallants." From their distant London offices came impractical and naive instructions: Crown Powhatan king of Virginia. Discover a passage to the South Sea. Spend more time searching for gold.

Then tragedy struck. A gunpowder explosion injured John Smith, forcing his return to England. Discipline dissolved. "For want of providence, industrie, and governement,"

the colonists faced a grim survival test. The winter of 1609-1610 became known as the "starveing Tyme."

When Lt. Gov. Thomas Gates arrived in May, Jamestown appeared "as the ruins of some auntient [for]-tification . . . the Indian as fast killing without as the famine and pestilence within." Of 500 settlers, only 60 were alive to greet him.

Appalled, Gates decided to abandon Jamestown. "But yet God would not so have it." En route down the river, the departing ships met a boat from Lord De La Warr's fleet, arriving from England with men and supplies. The colony was saved.

Under rigid military discipline, the settlement stabilized and began to prosper. On Jamestown Island, foundation ruins some 360 years old suggest the little town that grew up outside the walls of the fort. Land grants attracted more settlers; boatloads of women arrived "to make wifes to the Inhabitantes."

The Virginia Company, always hoping to wring some profit from Jamestown, introduced a variety of industries: silk-making, iron-smelting, lime-burning. Visitors today watch potters and glassblowers at work using 17th-century methods.

But it was "a confirmed smoker," John Rolfe, who hit on a money-making product for the colony. He developed a mild, hybrid tobacco, and demand for the new Virginia leaf soared in England. Within five years, the colony was exporting the "golden weed" by the ton. By 1619, when a ship captain traded the first blacks into service, tobacco growers were already complaining about the shortage of laborers to work their vast holdings.

Family, land, tobacco, servants—these strands wove the patterns of the tidewater plantations. But the patterns did not include Jamestown. Virginia became an agricultural province, its population dispersed on self-sufficient farms. Scattered along the creeks and rivers of the Chesapeake region, planters could trade directly with Europe, by-passing Jamestown as a marketplace.

In 1619, Virginians elected the first representative legislature in America, which met in Jamestown's little church. Yet even as Virginia's capital, Jamestown remained a small town, its brick homes and taverns busy mainly when the lawmakers convened. Attempts to increase business failed; its citizens never numbered more than 500.

Indians, disease, and fire periodically devastated the town until 1699, when the capital moved to Williamsburg. Unhealthy, unlucky Jamestown, England's first foothold in America, gradually declined, reverting to wilderness. But its job was done; the English were here to stay.

ANNE E. WITHERS

Tobacco fever raged when Jamestown found a cash crop; colonists planted yards and streets to meet demand for the "joviall weed." The plantation system, sustained by slavery, anchored Virginia's economy for two centuries.

FARRELL GREHAN. ABOVE: ARENTS COLLECTION, NEW YORK PUBLIC LIBRARY

Dutch on the Hudson

Come sit beside the millpond at Philipsburg Manor as the drowsy warmth of a late-summer sunset falls over the Hudson River Valley. Fat geese chatter under the weeping willows. Tawny cows, heavy with milk, plod back to the barn. Inside the oak-timbered gristmill, ponderous millstones grind to a halt.

In the early 1700's, about 200 tenants worked Frederick Philipse's 90,000-acre estate and industrial-commercial complex—the most important, if not the earliest, in the colony. Farmers carted grain to the mill to be ground into flour, which was packed into barrels made from Philipse lumber, then shipped on Philipse sloops manned by Philipse sailors. Tenants paid rent and bought goods—and perhaps a draft of rum—at the Philipse trading post.

Follow a pathway of crushed oyster shells (gravel was scarce in Dutch days) to the whitewashed stone house Frederick built in what is now North Tarrytown, New York. Inside its two-foot-thick walls, servants once roasted heath hens on a spit in the huge kitchen fireplace. Sweet-smelling preserves bubbled in smoke-darkened caldrons, and samp porridge—meal with meat and vegetables—simmered three days until it formed a thick, crusty chunk.

A secret passage enabled the lord of the manor to eavesdrop on his servants. During Indian raids, cattle were hidden in a basement large enough to hold a dairy, slave kitchen, and a year's supply of food.

Frederick Philipse, first lord of the manor, chose furnishings as stout and sturdy as the folk who used them. The massive wooden *kas,* or storage chest, held the household silver, fine china, and glassware. Curtains encircled beds for warmth. Rugs, considered a luxury, covered tables, while clean sand carpeted the well-scrubbed floors.

Frederick Philipse's estate—with its lush valleys and spacious coves—was truly what Henry Hudson's officer had deemed "a very good Land ...and a pleasant Land to see." In 1609 Hudson, an Englishman commissioned by Dutch merchants, left "the mayne ocean" and sailed slowly up "the great River of the Mountains." Although shoal water forced the *Half Moon* to turn back near present-day Albany, Hudson had established Dutch claim to the "great streame" that bears his name.

Seventeen years later, Canarsie Indians outsmarted the Dutch West India Company by selling land they held no claim to—Manhattan Island. There Hollanders living in bark hovels founded New Amsterdam.

The tiny colony, treated like a stepchild by the West India Company, matured slowly under the rule of its profit-hungry founder and inept governors. To spur immigration, the company directors offered vast tracts of river frontage to any member who could "plant there a Colonie of fifty souls." The patroon, in turn, would administer his holdings as "a perpetual hereditary fief." But Old World fiefdoms did not suit the raw frontier. Only Kiliaen Van Rensselaer's 700,000-acre patroonship—larger than today's Rhode Island—flourished during those formative years.

In 1647 peg-legged Peter Stuyvesant, newly appointed governor of New Amsterdam, thumped ashore and took on a town torn by strife, terrorized by an Indian war, and almost bankrupt. Near today's Battery Park, tiny thatched houses huddled around the worm-eaten palisades of

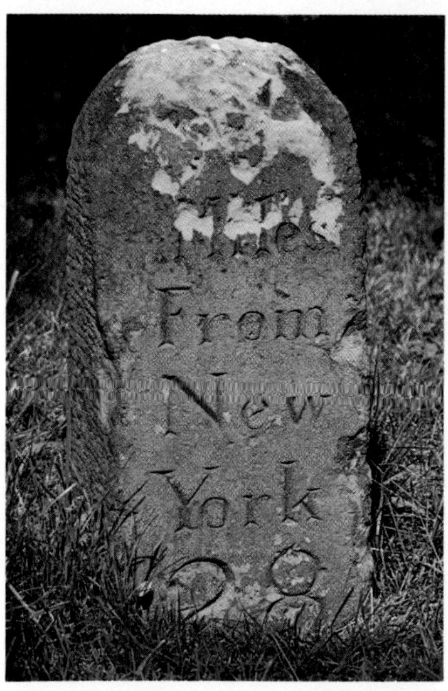

Spirits of the past haunt the Old Dutch Church of Sleepy Hollow: the Headless Horseman hurling his pumpkin head at Ichabod Crane, Dutch folk worshiping inside its stalwart walls. Bricks came from Holland as ballast. Built by Frederick Philipse in 1697, the church stands on the old Albany Post Road. Philipse and his wife owned the silver baptismal bowl and beakers.

REGENE RADNIECKI

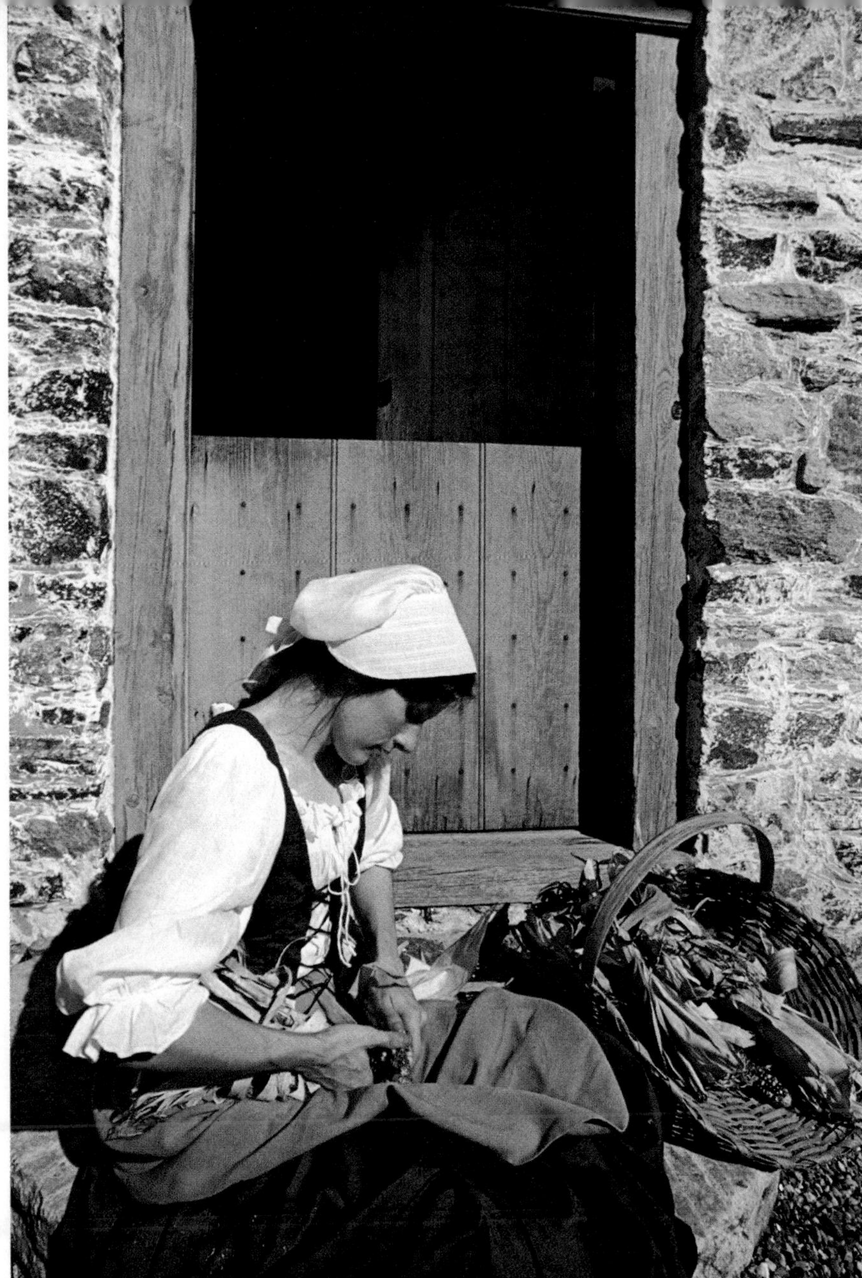

REGENE RADNIECKI

Fort Amsterdam. Rotting garbage, rubbish, and dead animals littered the dirt streets. Beyond the "good stiff Fence," the protective barrier where Wall Street runs today, only a few *bouweries,* or farms, supplied the colony with food.

In 1664 the British seized New Amsterdam in a bloodless take-over and gave the city its present name. Under Stuyvesant's tyrannical rule, this "brave place" had grown from a rowdy fur post to a miniature Amsterdam of step-gabled brick houses. Frederick Philipse had grown too, from a shrewd carpenter to a prosperous landholder, merchant, and, some said, New York's wealthiest

A Currier and Ives setting comes alive at Philipsburg Manor as the miller carts stone-ground cornmeal across a 200-foot oak dam to waiting customers —today's tourists. In Frederick Philipse's day, hourglasses sifted away the time as graceful sloops freighted flour to Europe, Africa, and the West Indies. Painted chests stored the riches from such profitable ventures. At the manor, servants shelled corn on the stoop for the gristmill and ground spices or crystallized chemicals with a mortar and pestle —this one crafted in Holland by Henryck Ter Horst. With wooden mallets, Dutch artisans fashioned sturdy barns as well as finely detailed furniture.

REGENE RADNIECKI

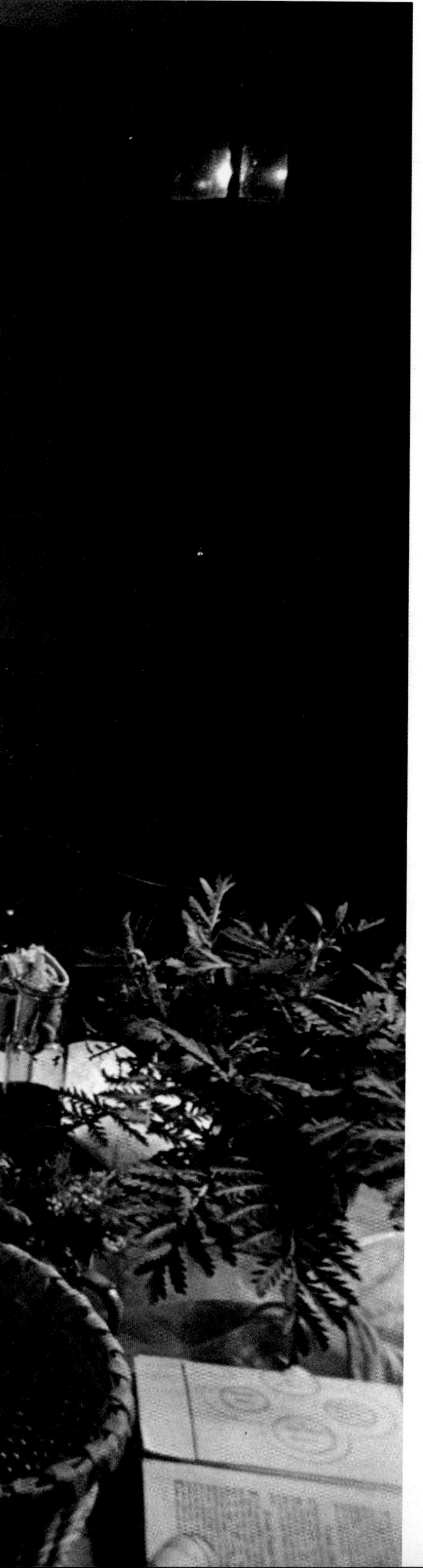

resident. His is one of colonial America's first success stories.

Under British rule, Philipse and other entrepreneurs converted the Dutch patroonships into freehold English manors. Frederick often stayed at Philipse Manor Hall in Yonkers (named for a *jonker,* or nobleman). As the Philipse family increased in number and power, the small farmhouse there grew into a grand Georgian mansion. Inside, elegantly carved woodwork and delft-tiled fireplaces can still be seen.

Families and fortunes merged when Frederick married the sister of Stephanus Van Cortlandt, a wealthy fur trader, first native-born mayor of New York, and founder of Van Cortlandt Manor, an 86,000-acre estate adjoining Philipsburg Manor. Fortress-like walls protected the manor houses from the flaming arrows of Indians, who destroyed thousands of homes along the Hudson and Mohawk rivers during the 1700's.

Early in the 1800's, a century after Frederick was buried inside his church at Sleepy Hollow, Washington Irving journeyed up the Hudson. Wandering through sheltered hollows and drowsy villages, he found these scenes little changed.

Near Tarrytown, Irving raised the roof of an old Dutch cottage to create an eclectic stone mansion "as full of angles and corners as an old cocked hat." Today ivy and gnarled wisteria vines, more than a century old, climb Sunnyside's walls. Irving's collection of 3,000 books is housed in the library, where the author spent long hours reading, writing, and receiving callers.

With his pen Irving captured the rich Dutch lore that stirs in every cove and crag from Spuyten Duyvil to Rensselaer. Acquaintances and friends became characters in his fanciful tales. He patterned Ichabod Crane, the lanky schoolmaster of Sleepy Hollow, after a local pedant. Ichabod courted the "ripe and melting" Katrina Van Tassel, who was reportedly the belle of the Van Alen family. Her portrait hangs in their brick farmhouse, with its brightly painted trim, steep roof, and parapet gables, near Kinderhook.

A terrified Ichabod, fleeing the Headless Horseman one moonless night, tumbled from his steed near Frederick Philipse's church. In its shaded grounds rest the church's founder and Ichabod's creator, amid the spirits of the Hudson River Valley they knew and loved so well.

CAROL BITTIG LUTYK

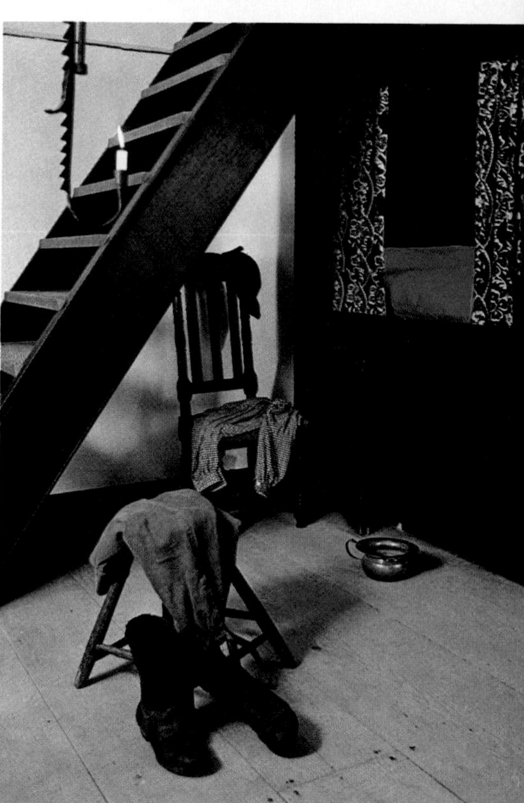

The flavor of old Dutch ways lingers on at Van Cortlandt Manor. Following "receipts" 250 years old, costumed guides prepare gooseberry tansy—herb-flavored cakes fried over a crackling wood fire. In the Ferry House Kitchen beside the Croton River (above), an adjustable candleholder lights the alcove bed where the manor's ferryman slept.

The Hudson: A Dutch Treat

A timeless air of magic and mystery swathes the Hudson River Valley, where elegant manors and modest dwellings of Dutch folk still stand. Pieter, only son of Jonas Bronck (after whom the Bronx was named), built a gabled fieldstone house around 1663. During the Revolution the local Committee of Correspondence met here secretly and, more than a year before the signing of the Declaration of Independence, pledged "never to become slaves."

The Senate House hosted New York's first elected Senate, the "government on the run," which adjourned hastily upon learning that redcoats were approaching. During some of the war's quieter days, George Washington found respite at the DeWint House, where he signed Major John André's death warrant for spying. Philip Schuyler entertained Washington and other notables at his elegant Georgian mansion, The Pastures.

Dutch customs live on at the Voorlezer's House, where a layman led services and taught school. Dating from the 1690's, the clapboard house is part of the Richmondtown Restoration.

Homes built by descendants of early Dutch settlers welcome visitors to New York City. The Georgian style of the 1748 Van Cortlandt House, erected by a nephew of the first lord of Van Cortlandt Manor, reflects English influence. The Lefferts Homestead, a Dutch colonial house, was partially burned in 1776 and rebuilt with salvaged timbers. Family heirlooms fill the 1783 Dyckman House.

Upriver, British sympathizer States Morris Dyckman designed Boscobel, a gracious "Mansion house," during the early 1800's but did not live to see his dream fulfilled. In the 1890's, financier Frederick Vanderbilt created a grandiose Italian Renaissance mansion at Hyde Park—a 54-room "royal palace" that cost more than two million dollars to build and furnish. A few miles away, Franklin Delano Roosevelt grew up in a comfortable 35-room house overlooking the majestic Hudson River—beloved by FDR and his Dutch ancestors.

Mohawk River
Albany
Rensselaer
SCHUYLER MANSION
Kinderhook
Coxsackie

PIETER BRONCK HOUSE
Coxsackie

SENATE HOUSE
Kingston

Kingston
Hyde Park
VANDERBILT MANSION
FRANKLIN D. ROOSEVELT HOME
Hudson River
BOSCOBEL
Garrison
Croton-on-Hudson
NEW YORK
NEW JERSEY

SUNNYSIDE
Tarrytown

North Tarrytown
Tarrytown

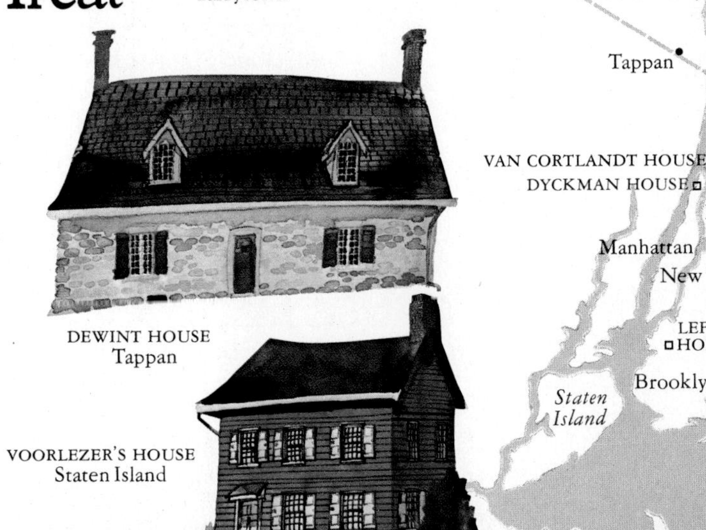

DEWINT HOUSE
Tappan

VOORLEZER'S HOUSE
Staten Island

PAINTINGS BY PAUL HOGARTH

VAN ALEN HOUSE
Kinderhook

VAN CORTLANDT MANOR
Croton-on-Hudson

OLD DUTCH CHURCH OF SLEEPY HOLLOW
North Tarrytown

PHILIPSBURG MANOR
North Tarrytown

PHILIPSE MANOR HALL
Yonkers

Plymouth

Tension fills the air as the men gather in the cramped and gloomy Great Cabin of the *Mayflower* on November 11, 1620. After more than two months "beating at sea," the ship will not, after all, be arriving at her supposed destination in the Hudson River area—"Northern Virginia" as the region then was known. Instead she has anchored off the wild coast of New England, some 225 miles northeast of where her Pilgrim passengers had intended to establish a "plantation."

Ever since their attempt to sail south around Cape Cod ended in near-disaster on the shoals off Monomoy Island, some of the passengers have been grumbling about the change in destination. Several have talked of splitting off from the rest of the group and going their own way when the ship puts ashore.

Alarmed that the colony might die aborning, Pilgrim leaders such as John Carver, William Brewster, and William Bradford have argued at length with their disaffected companions. Meetings have been held and an agreement has been drafted to "combine ourselves together into a civil body politic."

Now, on a bright Saturday morning, as the *Mayflower* swings at anchor in Provincetown Harbor—then called Cape Harbour—the voyagers gather in the cabin. They examine the document, discuss it, and, one by one, nearly every male passenger signs it. Thus the Mayflower Compact records the first instance of self-rule by Europeans in the New World.

John Carver, a prosperous merchant who has invested in the venture, is promptly elected governor.

For the *Mayflower*'s 102 passengers—men, women, and children—it has been an arduous, 67-day crossing from Plymouth, England. The voyagers have been crowded below decks amid the stench and darkness of a leaky wooden vessel, with little more to eat than hardtack, dried fish, cheese, and salt beef. Storms, at times so fierce [illegible] they could not bear a knot of sail," have threatened to pound the ship into oblivion. But only one passenger, a young servant named William Butten, has succumbed to the rigors of the voyage—and a baby, Oceanus Hopkins, has been born.

Visitors to the Plymouth, Massachusetts, waterfront can appreciate the hardships faced by those early voyagers by stepping aboard *Mayflower II,* a reproduction of the kind of stubby merchantman that brought the Pilgrims to these shores. The smell of tar and salt, the creak of hawsers, and the slap of waves against the hull lend a touch of vividness to the experience. The ship is open for inspection spring through fall.

Of the passengers aboard the original *Mayflower,* only 40 or so called themselves "Saints"—religious dissidents who had cut all ties to the Church of England they regarded as hopelessly corrupt. The rest were "Strangers"—as the Saints called them—humble folk recruited to fill out the lists. The Strangers simply hoped to better their lot in the New World. Later generations, influenced by 19th-century romanticists, would lump them all together as "Pilgrims."

The Saints had fled from England in 1608 to avoid harassment for their radical religious views. They lived in Holland a dozen years, their worship unmolested. But foreign customs, a desire to better themselves, and the realization that their children

Mayflower II, *a modern representation of her illustrious namesake, spreads a tracery of spars and rigging against a Plymouth sky. The sterncastle bears the May-blooming hawthorn flower from which the vessel took her name. Built in England, the 180-ton ship sailed the Atlantic in 1957; she now lies berthed near Plymouth Rock (below). Historians debate whether that venerable boulder actually served as a stepping-stone to the New World.*

Three-time governor of the colony, Edward Winslow once saved the life of Chief Massasoit, cementing the respect and friendship of his powerful tribe.

FARRELL GREHAN (ALSO OPPOSITE). PILGRIM SOCIETY, PLYMOUTH

FARRELL GREHAN

might grow up more Dutch than English prompted them to look afield. A group of English "merchant adventurers," sensing profits from an overseas colony, eventually agreed to back their journey.

The Strangers included among themselves a powerfully built young cooper named John Alden and a professional soldier, Myles Standish, hired to take charge of the colony's defenses. Both would become pillars of the Pilgrim community, as would other Strangers named Eaton, Hopkins, and Mullins. Still others would prove to be nettlesome citizens. One of these, John Billington, was eventually hanged for murder.

Excited passengers lined the bulwarks as the *Mayflower* dropped anchor and rode safely in a "pleasant bay . . . compassed about to the very sea with oaks, pines, juniper, sassafras, and other sweet wood."

On Monday, after observing the sabbath aboard ship, the women went ashore to scrub the accumulated grime of nine weeks from clothes and bedding—thereby establishing the pattern for Monday washdays throughout much of New England. Children romped on the beach. The shallop, a large open boat stowed between decks, was floated ashore for badly needed repairs. The Pilgrims gorged themselves sick on mussels. Plans were made to explore the coast for a suitable habitation—a task that took nearly four weeks.

Shore parties saw Indians—usually fleetingly and at a distance. But once, at a beach the Pilgrims named The First Encounter, a brief bloodless skirmish erupted. Today a stone marker at the foot of Samoset Road near Eastham marks the site.

Indian encampments, some obviously abandoned in haste, were found. On a knoll near present-day Truro the Pilgrims unearthed bushels of Indian corn, "some yellow, and some red, and others mixed with blue." The explorers called the spot Corn Hill—a name that still endures.

On one sortie the explorers found a grave containing the bones of a man and a child. The man wore mariner's gear; his skull bore traces of "fine yellow hair." Who he was and how he met his end puzzled the Pilgrims—and modern historians.

On December 8 a party of men in the shallop rode into the mouth of Plymouth Harbor on the wings of a gale that smashed the boat's rudder and mast. The beleaguered crew suffered a rain-drenched night on the lee shore of a heavily wooded island they later named Clark's Island in honor of the *Mayflower*'s mate.

The explorers spent the next two days here, and on Monday, December 11 (December 21 by the Gregorian calendar adopted in 1752), they stepped ashore at Plymouth. Detailed contemporary accounts of the event make no mention of Plymouth Rock. About 120 years later an elderly villager, recalling stories his father told him about the *Mayflower* settlers, would point to the boulder as their landing place. On such scanty evidence rests the enduring legend of Plymouth Rock as the cornerstone of the republic.

Once on shore the explorers found a "goodly land" of thick forests, deserted cornfields, "and little running brooks, a place very good for situation." Patuxet Indians had lived here, but a "pestilential sickness" three years earlier had all but wiped out the tribe.

"Try your match! . . . Present! . . . Give fire!" With a roar and a belch of smoke, musketeers flanked by pikemen enact a 17th-century drill within the palisades of Plimoth Plantation, set up in 1947 as an educational organization. At hilltop rises a re-creation of the Pilgrims' fort-meetinghouse, "built of thick sawn planks stayed with oak beams."

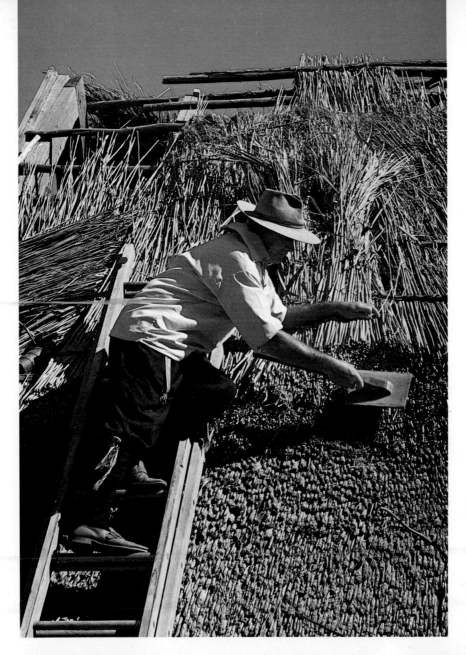

The exploring party returned to the *Mayflower* only to learn that Bradford's young wife, Dorothy, had fallen or jumped into the sea and drowned during his absence.

Several days later the *Mayflower* arrived off Plymouth. The first work parties went ashore to begin erecting the crude huts that would shelter the Pilgrims during their first terrible months.

The winter of 1620-21, although comparatively mild, blew wet and miserable. Crew and passengers, weakened by crowding, exposure, and improper diet, sickened and died in alarming numbers—six in December, eight in January, seventeen in February. Of March, Bradford wrote: "This month thirteen of our number die. . . . scarce fifty remain, the living scarce able to bury the dead." Entire families perished—the Martins and

Keeping old-time skills alive, craftsmen at Plimoth Plantation thatch an unfinished house. Reeds gathered nearby are bound into bundles and lashed to roof purlins in overlapping courses. Comb-like leggets (left and below) "beat up" reed ends into an even finish. Such a roof may last 50 years.

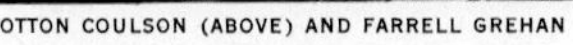
COTTON COULSON (ABOVE) AND FARRELL GREHAN

Glimpses of Pilgrim life: a woman weaves untarred hemp into a fishing net; glowing coals roast a cod Indian style—trussed to a rack of green wood and stuffed with oysters; in the Warren House, staff members of Plimoth Plantation dine on Early American fare prepared and cooked by them that day. Scenes such as these, based on records, journals, and archeological findings, reflect the Pilgrim world of 1627—at a time when the colony enjoyed a reasonably secure foothold. Guides encourage questions and even invite visitors to try their hand at colonial tasks. A summer encampment nearby demonstrates how Indians lived.

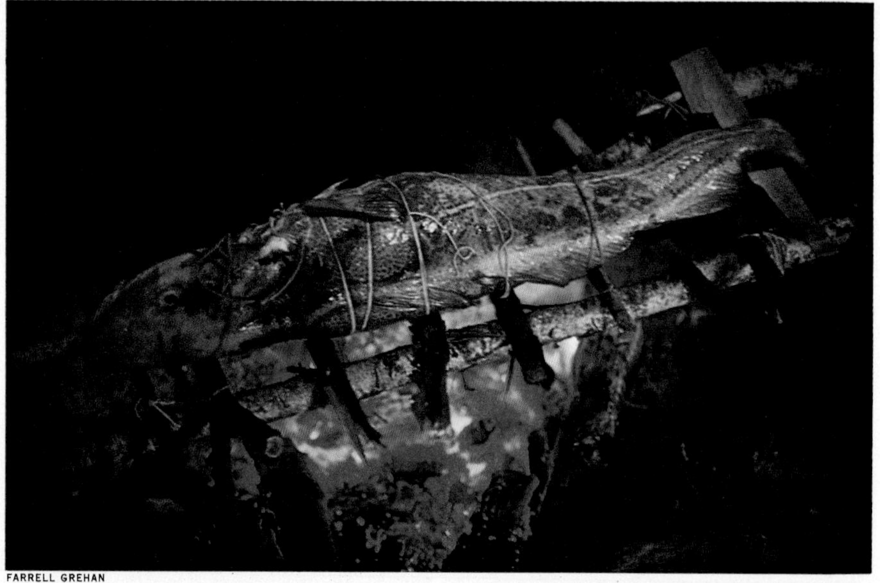

FARRELL GREHAN

Tinkers, Turners and Rigdales. Of the eighteen married women who landed at Plymouth, only three survived. Baby Oceanus died.

To keep Indians from learning of the colony's plight, survivors placed the dead in concealed graves under cover of dark. The burying ground, today called Cole's Hill, overlooks Plymouth Rock and the harbor. A large stone sarcophagus at the top of the hill bears the names and remains of those who died that winter. A wax museum and a statue of Massasoit, the Indian chief who befriended the Pilgrims, also occupy the hilltop.

Misfortune continued to dog the struggling colony. Mary Allerton gave birth to a son—stillborn. She, too, died several weeks later. Chimney sparks twice ignited the thatched roof of the Common House sheltering the sick—and the colony's store of gunpowder. The fear of Indian attack caused concern, and wolves and wildcats bedeviled the settlers. In February an unseasonable rain accompanied by "the greatest gusts of wind that ever we had" melted the mud-daubed walls of their dwellings.

But warm weather brought with it a change of luck. The "great sickness" tapered off; a week after the settlers started their gardens, an Indian strode into the encampment and announced, "Welcome."

This was Samoset, a visiting subchieftain from the future state of Maine who had learned English from roving fishermen. Soon afterward he introduced the Pilgrims to Massasoit, sachem of the neighboring Wampanoags, and to Squanto, the last known surviving Patuxet.

Squanto, too, spoke English. He had been kidnaped and had lived for a time in England. He soon became a valuable member of the community, teaching the Pilgrims where to trap eels and how to plant corn. Friendly relations were established with surrounding tribes.

Autumn brought a season of plenty. "Our harvest being gotten in, our governor sent four men on fowling, that so we might after a special manner rejoice together." A single day's shooting yielded the hunters "as much fowl as . . . served the company almost a week."

Massasoit arrived with some 90 tribesmen, contributed five deer, and for three days red man and white celebrated "the fruit of our labors" with feasts, marksmanship contests, and games of skill and chance.

A hungry winter followed—made leaner by the unexpected arrival in November of 35 ill-provisioned settlers aboard the *Fortune.* The colonists tightened their belts and went on half-rations.

Gradually conditions improved. Plimoth Plantation became New Plymouth Colony, stretching from Cape Cod to Narragansett Bay, from Scituate to Nantucket Sound. Pilgrim traders founded outposts from Maine to the Connecticut Valley, matching wits with French, Dutch, Indian, and fellow English traders.

Today the old town of Plymouth preserves many relics and memories of its colonial ancestry. Plymouth Rock, broken when part of it was hauled to a nearby site and further reduced by souvenir hunters, again lies at tide's edge—this time sheltered by a classical colonnade. Pilgrim Hall, one of the nation's oldest public museums, houses documents signed by Governors Bradford and Winslow, a painting of Winslow—the only known portrait of a *Mayflower* passenger—as well as Myles Standish's swords, a chair owned by Bradford, and other artifacts.

One of Plymouth's oldest dwellings, the Sparrow House, completed in 1640, probably never was occupied

Gateleg table and wainscot chair reveal an era's taste for dignity over comfort in furniture. Herbs and drying sunflowers grace a cottage interior. Storage casks and bottle-shaped eel traps line the Common House wall.

FARRELL GREHAN

by original settlers. Its low-ceilinged rooms contain a round-cornered fireplace and carved paneling. The heavily buttressed front door was built "to withstand tomahawk blows."

But *Mayflower* passengers John and Elizabeth Howland probably did live in the Howland House on Sandwich Street. Built in 1667 by Jacob Mitchell, it was later bought by the Howlands' son Jabez and presumably sheltered his parents.

Harlow House, completed in 1677, contains some of the hand-hewn beams originally used by the Pilgrims in their fort-meetinghouse. Here costumed guides demonstrate spinning, candlemaking, and other 17th-century household arts.

The Jenney Grist Mill, a modern reproduction on Town Brook, occupies the site of a Pilgrim mill built in 1636. A fish ladder enables alewives to swim upstream to spawn in April and May—just as they did in colonial days.

Across Summer Street from the mill rises Burial Hill. The Pilgrims knew it as Fort Hill and here, stretching from the southern slope to the waterfront, they established their community. A tablet on Leyden Street marks the site of the Common House. The fort-meetinghouse, built in 1622, occupied the crest of the hill until the structure was dismantled in the late 1670's. The old graveyard here offers a sweeping view of the countryside. Weatherbeaten headstones dot the grassy slopes and, at dusk on a clear evening, the distant Gurnet Light blinks across the expanse of Plymouth Harbor. On the west slope may be seen the grave of *Mayflower* voyager John Howland, and Governor Bradford is believed to lie near his son, Maj. William Bradford.

Plimoth Plantation, three miles south of town on Route 3A, recreates Pilgrim days with a stockaded community and also maintains *Mayflower II* and a shallop at State Pier on Water Street.

Nearby Duxbury also holds close Pilgrim associations. Here lived Philippe de La Noye, an ancestor of Franklin Delano Roosevelt, and here stands the John Alden House, built by John and his son in 1653. It has been in the Alden family for three centuries and is now a museum. John Alden died in this house and so too, probably, did Priscilla. They are thought to lie in the Old Burying Ground, not far from the grave of Myles Standish, odd man of Longfellow's fanciful poem, *"The Courtship of Miles Standish."*

EDWARD LANOUETTE

Garlanded dancers celebrate October's Harvest Home festival in step to an old English tune called the Nonesuch. Pilgrims found joy in living. They delighted in clothes as colorful as natural dyes could make them. They enjoyed music, frolic, and the pleasures of a bountiful table—including "beere" and "strong water," or liquor. Thanksgivings were celebrated whenever the occasion demanded.

Rounding up recalcitrant livestock requires nimbleness—so does spearing a swiveled target without a clout from the bag in a game called quintain.

FARRELL GREHAN

New England Puritans

Puritan. Rightly or not, the word evokes somber images: work . . . self-denial . . . sermons laced with threats of everlasting fire . . . grim-faced men sitting in judgment . . . scarlet letters worn in shame. And witches.

Salem, Massachusetts, is not proud of Gallows Hill where, during the witchcraft hysteria, nearly a score of men and women were put to death in 1692. Today tall apartments and a water tank overshadow the hill, its crest an unkempt playground. No marker calls attention to the tragedy that took place here.

But Salem does preserve several of the houses associated with those nightmarish months. The so-called Witch House near the heart of town belonged to Judge Jonathan Corwin. Its chambers, used for preliminary hearings, witnessed the anguish of those accused of witchcraft.

Across town, a secret staircase in the House of the Seven Gables entices so many visitors that the treads need frequent repairs and replacement. The narrow, twisting passage, entered through a closet next to a first-floor fireplace, leads to a third-floor bedroom—"Clifford's chamber" in the Nathaniel Hawthorne novel that gave the house its name. No one knows why the stairway was built—perhaps as a hiding place for household members accused of consorting with the devil, or to conceal goods smuggled from China aboard the owner's ships.

At nearby Danvers may be seen the home of Rebecca Nurse, a 71-year-old woman of exemplary character who was hanged as a witch. To the modern visitor all these old houses seem dark and foreboding—haunted by memories of the past.

Salem's witchcraft frenzy began in the home of the Reverend Samuel Parris. Here his aged West Indian slave Tituba enthralled a group of girls with tales of sorcery and magic. Soon Parris's daughter Elizabeth and some of her older friends fell into paroxysms of madness, shrieking, writhing, contorting their faces and limbs. Encouraged by a clergy that believed implicitly in possession of the soul by the devil, the girls began naming their supposed tormentors. And so began the mass hysteria that rippled outward to other towns. By the end of the witch-hunt era, 32 victims had been executed throughout New England and scores had suffered imprisonment.

Salem, whose name derives from the Hebrew word "shalom," meaning peace, began as an Indian village. In 1626 Plymouth defector Roger Conant led a group of Englishmen there and set up a community. Two years later John Endecott, a staunch Puritan, arrived and took command of the settlement. He and his contingent of some 40 colonists had been sent from England to pave the way for later Puritan arrivals.

The Puritans, those "great grim earnest men," as Ralph Waldo Emerson called them, were, like their Pilgrim neighbors, disenchanted with the "corruptions" of the Anglican church. But, unlike the Pilgrims, most of them wished to remain inside the church—to "purify" it from within. "We do not go to New England as Separatists," intoned one of their ministers, "we go to practice the positive part of Church Reformation, and propagate the gospel in America."

This burning sense of mission, coupled with deteriorating economic conditions at home, the growing despotism of Charles I, and a feeling that the mother country was doomed

New England Gothic: Echoes of a Puritan past linger on a Concord headstone and on a hilltop in Salem. The winged "soul effigy"—evolved from earlier death's-head carvings—signified the soul's flight to heaven. An overweening fear of Satan led otherwise level-headed Puritans to hang 19 men and women on Salem's Gallows Hill (above)—and to bury them there in unmarked and unhallowed graves.

FARRELL GREHAN

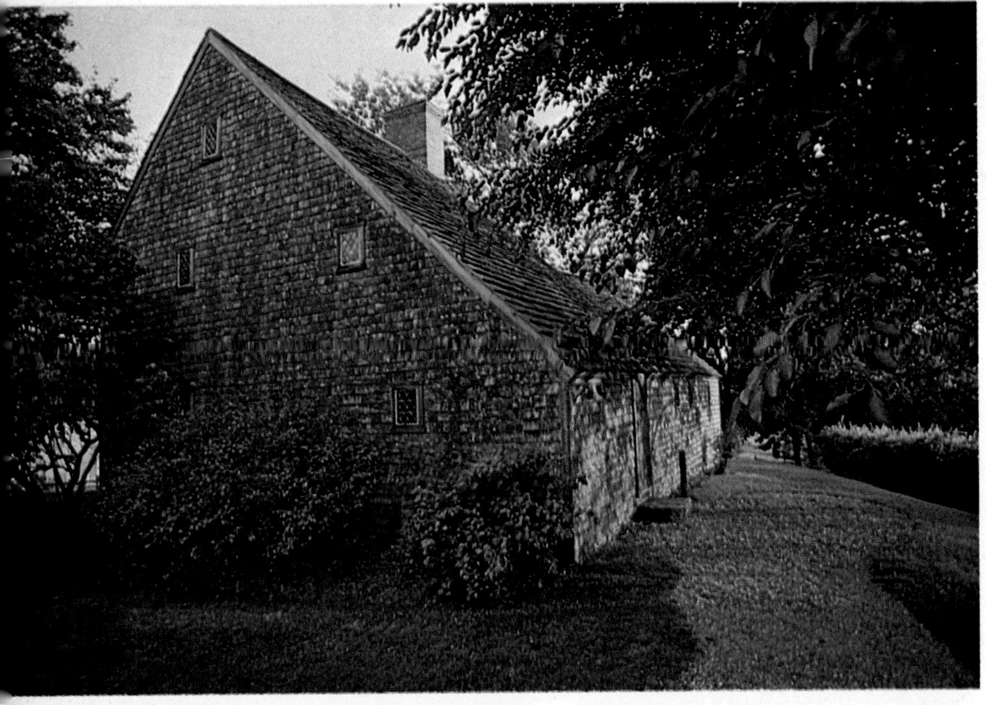

Bowered in tranquility, relics of a colonial heritage beckon the wayfarer in Massachusetts. Sturdiness and simplicity mark the Hoxie House (above) in Sandwich. Built in 1676 for one of the few Puritan ministers to tolerate Quakers, it shows the steep roof of the New England saltbox dwelling.

Topsfield's Parson Capen House (below), erected in 1683 and noted for its overhanging second floor and gable ends, reveals an Elizabethan influence.

The House of the Seven Gables in Salem belonged to a cousin of Nathaniel Hawthorne. His frequent visits there may have inspired the novel about a curse put on Colonel Pyncheon and his descendants ("God will give him blood to drink!") after the grasping colonel denounced a man as a warlock.

FARRELL GREHAN

to "generall calamity," led many Puritans to risk the Atlantic.

Visitors to modern Salem can see how its earliest white settlers lived by strolling through Pioneers' Village in Forest River Park. Here are sod-roofed dugouts, bark-covered "English wigwams" resembling Quonset huts, and roughhewn frame houses. Here stands the "Governor's Faire House," there a thatched cottage with catted chimney of logs and clay. Saltworks, a brick kiln, sawpit, forge, and fish-curing "flakes" recall pioneer occupations.

When Governor John Winthrop arrived at Salem on June 12, 1630, followed by a straggling fleet of ten ships, Endecott warmly welcomed him with "good venison pasty and good beer." But, as one of Winthrop's assistants succinctly put it, "Salem... pleased us not."

Continuing down the Massachusetts coast, Winthrop chose the mouth of the Charles River as a "place for our sitting down." But they didn't "sit" long. Lack of fresh water soon drove Winthrop's party to hilly Shawmut Peninsula across the river. They met the Reverend William Blackstone, survivor of a defunct trading-post venture. Blackstone, an Anglican minister, had lived alone about five years. His house, complete with a library of 200 books, nestled close to a bubbling hillside spring. Blackstone offered to share his water with the new arrivals. They accepted, made the cleric a reluctant member of their congregation, and presented him with 50 choice acres of his own land.

Soon afterward Blackstone sold back his holdings to the Puritans and decamped to the hinterlands. The newcomers set aside part of Blackstone's tract as a town pasture and training field — Boston Common.

On September 7, 1630, the Puritans named their settlement Boston after the Lincolnshire town many

FARRELL GREHAN

had left behind. Soon the peninsula bristled with clustered huts and "a fort which can command any ship as she sails into the harbor."

By late autumn several communities dotted the area—Salem to the north, Dorchester to the south, and between them Boston, Charlestown, Medford, Watertown, Roxbury.

Winter set in with "many snows and sharp frost." Scores of settlers "afflicted with the scurvy" died before a relief ship in February slowed the toll with fresh supplies.

Spring brought new hope, and the colonists came to realize that prosperity lay in the sea: fishing—especially for cod—trading, shipbuilding. In 1631 the Puritans launched their first ship, the 30-ton *Blessing of the Bay.* Others followed, some as large as 400 tons. Soon Bostonians proclaimed their city "the chief place for shipping and Merchandise."

By 1650 dozens of towns had sprung up, from Hingham to Saugus, site of America's first complete ironworks. At Saugus, just north of Boston, the original ironmaster's house still stands. A reconstructed furnace, forge, and rolling and slitting mill re-create the ironworking community the Puritans named Hammersmith. Imagination supplies the churning waterwheels, the panting bellows, and sweat-stained workmen in leather aprons who hammered hot metal into wrought-iron "merchant bars."

Located near plentiful bog iron and a seemingly endless forest of hardwood (for the charcoal-burning furnace), America's forerunner of a company town provided housing and

Clack, clack goes the batten as a weaver works his loom at the Whipple House in Ipswich, a task colonial housewives often delegated to itinerant artisans. In the hallway lies a volume written by Puritan zealot Cotton Mather.

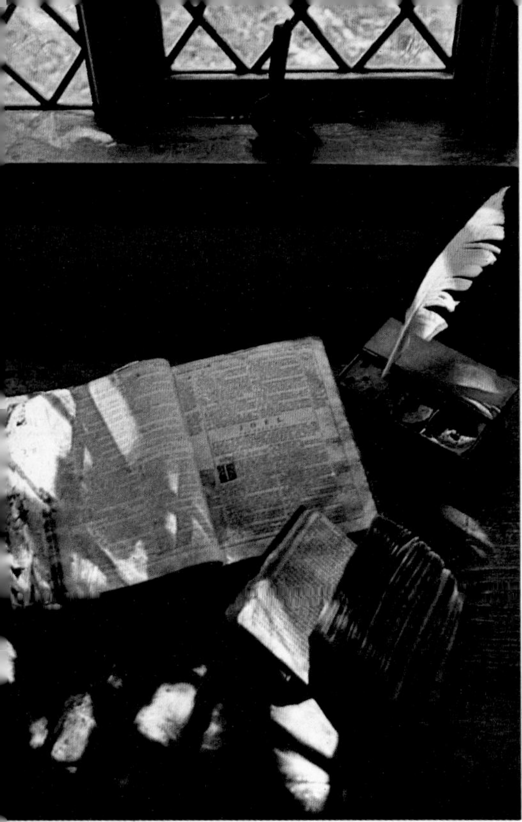

a store for its workers—who included about 35 Scotsmen captured at the Battle of Dunbar, Scotland, and transported to the colony. The company operated some 20 years, until mismanagement and cheaper imported iron forced it out of business.

However much the Puritans railed against intolerance at home, they imposed orthodoxy with a vengeance in their "Wilderness Zion." Thundered one minister, " 'Tis Satan's policy to plead for an indefinite and boundless freedom." Another denounced freedom of worship as the "first born of all abominations."

Puritan ministers, like Old Testament patriarchs, laid down the law from the pulpit—and woe betide the miscreant who failed to live up to rigid moral codes.

One ship captain, returning after three years at sea, spent two hours in the stocks for kissing his wife on Sunday in public—the doorway of

Four-poster beds, like this one in the Whipple House, wore drapes in winter to cut drafts. Six generations of the family lived in the house—and kept a family Bible similar to the Geneva edition (above) favored by Puritans.

FARRELL GREHAN

his own house. Idleness and frivolity on the sabbath were sins to be rooted out with admonitions, fines, or whippings "not exceeding five stripes for ten shillings fine."

Harsh as life was for Puritans, it was grim for Quakers, Baptists, and other "heretics" who sought to disrupt the established order. Four Quakers went to the gallows; three had their ears cut off; forty were banished; forty were flogged, one man until the flesh of his back "was beaten black as into a jelly."

And even the Puritan establishment itself occasionally harbored a maverick. In 1635 Roger Williams, pastor of the Salem church, was banished from Massachusetts for denying the king's right to give away Indian land and for preaching that civil authorities had no right to meddle in spiritual matters. Fleeing to Narragansett Bay to escape deportation to England, he eventually drew up America's first document separating church and state.

Anne Hutchinson, a woman of "nimble wit and active spirit," was banished for publicly doubting the sanctity of certain clergymen. The Reverend Thomas Hooker, pastor of the Newtown (later Cambridge) congregation, who believed that all men—not just church members—should have the right to elect magistrates, also found life in the Bay Colony untenable. His belief that "the foundation of authority is laid . . . in the free consent of the people" today stands as one of the nation's guiding principles.

Gradually, with the rise of Boston as a hub of international commerce, the clergy's hold began to give way to civil rule by laymen. "Puritanism," remarked James Russell Lowell two centuries later, "believing itself quick with the seed of religious liberty, laid, without knowing it, the egg of democracy."

EDWARD LANOUETTE

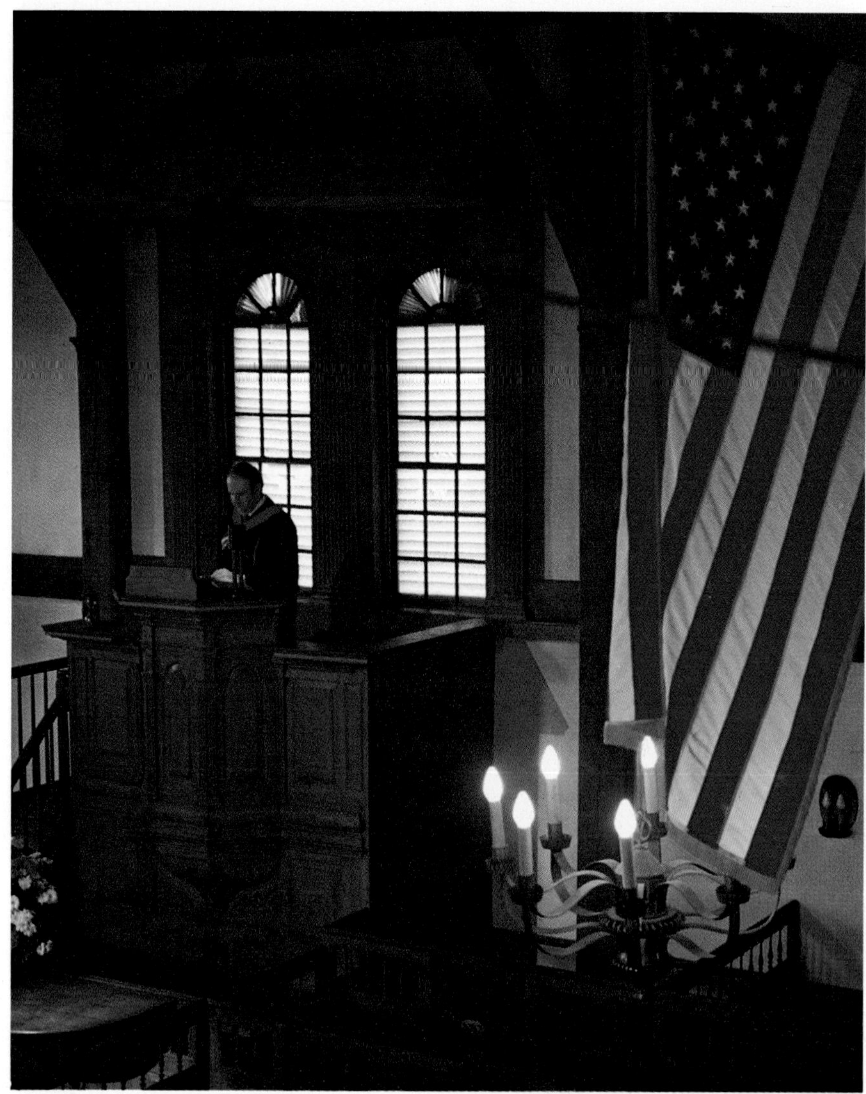

FARRELL GREHAN

Old Ship Church in Hingham has echoed to Sunday prayer since ships' carpenters raised its beams in 1681. Puritans shunned altars, focused instead on the pulpit. Box pews began to replace backless benches in the mid-1700's. Part of one pew (right) now serves as a choir-loft bench. Hourglass beside minister (above) recalls days when sermons rumbled on for hours. A tithingman kept nodders awake—feathered end of his pole tickled noses. The blunt end poked mischievous boys.

At the last hymn (opposite), the congregation traditionally turns to the choir at the rear of the church.

The Colonial Frontier

Under Britain's flag the New World colonies flourished from New England to the Deep South. Regionally, the settlers constituted a diverse people, even though they shared a common Old World heritage. But as they subdued the raw land and built their cities, they emerged as a nation of "Americans."

RICHARD R. BEEMAN

Colonial Americans were a widely varied lot. On those rare occasions before the Revolution when people from New England, the middle colonies, or the South met one another, what impressed them most were their differences. A visitor from Boston in 1773 wrote that in Virginia the small farmers were "a vastly more ignorant and illiterate kind... than with us." And a Pennsylvania mother, exasperated by a disobedient daughter, threatened to give the child to the Yankees if she didn't behave.

Yet those same provincial Americans had a good deal in common. With the notable exceptions of the Africans and Indians, most 18th-century Americans—whether of English, German, Scotch-Irish, or French Huguenot origin—shared a Western European heritage geared to land and family and the rhythms of an agricultural economy.

Shared cultural traits and goals would eventually bind these diverse people together as a nation. But in the 18th century, regional distinctions persisted—and grew stronger as patterns of life developed in each colony. In the North, people generally lived in tightly knit, self-governing communities. In the South, families lived on widely dispersed plantations. Both systems depended on a factor unique to the Americas—the easy availability of arable land.

Deep in the rolling hills of western Massachusetts lies the town of Deerfield, a typical early New England village. Visitors who stroll its streets today enjoy many sights that greeted 18th-century travelers. A score of pre-Revolutionary houses still stand, many open to the public: Frary House, built about 1720 and later used as a tavern; Ashley House, home of a tory pastor who was locked out of the church by his parishioners; the 1717 Wells-Thorn House, a "split-level" built on a slope.

The basic design of the town, a linear plan with a single main street forming its spine, was common to New England. Most families built their homes within the confines of the village, traveling out each day to their fields. The inconvenience of this system was balanced by the need to band together for protection against the dangers of the wilderness.

And those dangers were real. In 1675 Indian attacks devastated Deerfield. Within ten years it was rebuilt, with stronger fortifications. But when England declared war on France in 1702, vulnerable Deerfield feared the worst from the French in Canada. And before dawn on February 29, 1704, some 300 French and Indian marauders attacked, killing 49 settlers and carrying off 111 prisoners—a night of terror and destruction. Half the populace was gone; much of the town was burned. But Deerfield would not die. By 1750 it was one of New England's most prosperous towns, a market center for wheat and cattle.

Nearly everywhere in New England, the decision to turn inward from the frontier and live together in

BRITISH LION ON GATEPOST, GOVERNOR'S PALACE, WILLIAMSBURG, VIRGINIA
PHOTOMONTAGE BY JAMES L. STANFIELD, NATIONAL GEOGRAPHIC PHOTOGRAPHER

close-knit communities created a strong sense of shared values and corporate identity. Life centered on the village green, a convenient place to transact business and exchange gossip. Nearby were the school, the church-meetinghouse, and, later, the town hall—those three institutions so crucial to the formation of the New England character.

The school functioned chiefly to impart Puritan principles to the young, not to produce intellectuals. But New England was the first region to make a commitment to mass public education. As early as 1647 the general court of Massachusetts Bay Colony directed townships of 50 or more householders to appoint and pay a schoolteacher, since "one chiefe project of that ould deluder, Satan [is] to keepe men from the knowledge of the Scriptures."

Eleven years earlier, the colony had founded a college, named in honor of John Harvard, who bequeathed to it his library and half his property. Deerfield itself boasts one of the country's oldest schools—Deerfield Academy, established in 1797.

In small villages the church-meetinghouse served a dual purpose as the center of spiritual life and as

Grammar school no longer meets here, but the 1695 Wren Building still serves the College of William and Mary in Williamsburg, Virginia. Latin, Greek, and mathematics challenged younger scholars in this room in the 18th century.

DAVID HISER

town hall, but gradually most towns built separate halls. In the 18th century, town meetings—forums for discussion of secular matters and election of town officials—were often dominated by a small group of affluent leaders, but in later years the New England town meeting became an important agency—and national symbol—of democratic government.

Perhaps the most impressive meeting place in New England, both in size and in history, is Boston's Faneuil Hall, built in 1742 and donated to the town by wealthy merchant Peter Faneuil as a market and public meeting hall. Throughout the years visitors walked past meat and cheese stalls on the ground floor to reach the scene of historic orations and debates on the second floor. Today the building—a national historic landmark—houses a museum and library, and is still used as an assembly hall.

Faneuil Hall and its counterparts in other towns played an increasingly large part in community affairs. With the pressures of a growing population and a lively, expanding economy, New Englanders gradually shifted their attention from spiritual concerns toward economic and political affairs. By the time of the Revolution, the citizens of New England, drawing on both their attachment to local self-government and a strong sense of individual rights and privileges, would provide the earliest and most vigorous opposition to British rule.

The colony of New York, though close to New England, displayed quite a different regional character—a diversity of people, religions, and political forms unknown in almost any other part of America. English and Dutch lived alongside French Huguenots, German Palatines, and, later in the 18th century, smaller groups of Scots, Irish, Swedes, Jews, Portuguese, and slaves from Africa. Such ethnic variety occasionally bred hostility. One Anglo-American complained, "Our chiefest unhappyness here is too great a mixture of Nations, and the English the least part."

Religious beliefs varied as much as ethnic origins. At the end of the 17th century, Governor Thomas Dongan noted that in addition to Dutch Calvinists, French Calvinists, Anglicans, Dutch Lutherans, and Quakers, New York contained "Singing Quakers, Ranting Quakers; Sabbatarians; Antisabbatarians;

Hostile Indians menaced the frontier village of Deerfield, Massachusetts, almost from its beginnings in 1671 as a cluster of homes in the wilderness. John Sheldon's nail-studded door, now displayed in Memorial Hall, failed to save his family during a 1704 attack; invaders chopped a hole to shoot through. Sheldon's wife and one child were killed. Proud of its heritage, Deerfield preserves 52 historic buildings. Ashley House (opposite) dates from about 1730.

FARRELL GREHAN

Some Anabaptists; some Independents; some Jews; in short . . . all sorts and opinions. . . ."

Near the New England border and on Long Island there were villages like those of neighboring Connecticut and Massachusetts. Elsewhere in New York community life revolved around the great manors —Livingston, Van Cortlandt, Rensselaerswyck— that encompassed tens of thousands of acres and at first operated as semi-feudal baronies. The township, so important to New England, was in New York often subordinate to the power of the manor lords. But the very extent of these domains made it possible for tenants, yeoman farmers, and even squatters to achieve a measure of autonomy in their lives. The manor lords, try as they might, seldom collected all the taxes and rents due them.

In the 18th century as today, the great bustling port of New York City was, in its economy and its life-styles, worlds removed from the rest of the colony. Beginning as a small village in the early 17th century, it reached a population of 25,000 by the eve of the Revolution. Few buildings from those early years have survived the city's continued growth, but visitors can catch the spirit of the times at the reconstructed Fraunces Tavern. Built originally as a home in 1719, converted to a tavern in 1763, it was the site of George Washington's emotional farewell meeting with his officers in 1783.

Horse-and-buggy days endure for Amish who follow the plain life-style of their 18th-century German immigrant forebears. Today's "Pennsylvania Dutch" also preserve such fine arts as Fraktur, shown in the 1771 baptismal certificate above.

WILLIAM ALBERT ALLARD. ABOVE: THE HENRY FRANCIS DU PONT WINTERTHUR MUSEUM

אנכי י׳
לא יהיה
לא תשא
זכור את
כבד את
לא תרצח
תנאף
לא תגנב
לא תענה
לא תחמד

Taverns multiplied in the colonies, not only as convivial gathering places for residents but also as way stations along the post roads connecting major towns. In the early part of the century, communication between colonies was difficult at best. Roads were rough, few bridges spanned the rivers, ferries were unreliable. In 1704 a Boston woman, Sarah Knight, ventured by horseback to New York, generally following post roads and often in the company of "the post," the mail carrier, himself. Her cheerful journal is a litany of fears, dangers, narrow escapes, uncomfortable lodgings, unsavory meals: "What cabbage I swallowed served me for a cud the whole day after." At most taverns, however, she was "civilly received and courteously entertained."

Taverns were not just rural social centers. At Philadelphia's City Tavern—where still today visitors enjoy colonial-style meals—more resistance against England was formulated than in the Assembly Room of the Pennsylvania legislature.

William Penn's sylvan colony began to acquire a polyglot character soon after its founding in 1682. But most Pennsylvanians, while preserving their Old World heritage, were more successful than their New York neighbors at living in harmony. Penn's success lay in his policies of religious tolerance and equitable land distribution. Unlike New York's manor holdings or New England's villages, Pennsylvania settlements were loose clusters of people with similar backgrounds—the Mennonites, Dunkards, Amish, and Moravians from Germany who settled what has been mislabeled "Pennsylvania Dutch Country." (English neighbors heard the word *deutsch*—"German"—as *Dutch.*) Their towns made a patchwork of different sects.

Philadelphia itself, Penn's "greene Countrie Towne," was laid out in a grid pattern that influenced the design of later American cities. Citizens lined their streets with "shady and wholesome trees" and, initiating a custom that spread from coast to coast, named the streets after local trees.

Fifteen miles west of Philadelphia, at Ridley Creek State Park, the Colonial Pennsylvania Plantation provides a living example of a 1770's farm. Visitors are welcomed to the original farmhouse, a "rambler" begun about 1720. Resident historians, archeologists, folklorists, and craftworkers perform the daily chores—splitting fence logs, making cheese, mending wagons, weeding the kitchen garden, tending stock. Work is done with 18th-century tools and methods. The farm's 112 acres—an average size in those days—are sown with flax, corn, oats, and especially wheat, the "grand article of the province" that enabled Philadelphia to become a booming center of colonial commerce.

Between Pennsylvania and Virginia, historian Henry Adams observed, "every geographical reason argued that the Susquehanna, the Potomac, and the James should support one homogeneous people; yet the intellectual difference between Pennsylvania and Virginia was . . . more sharply marked than that between New England and the Middle States." The reason for this lay not so much in geography as in the social and economic structure of the Chesapeake region—the plantation system.

Plantations spread as the demand for tobacco, rice, cotton, and sugar increased. Vast parcels of land were used for these crops; many workers were needed. By the end of the 17th century, the plantation system was well established in Virginia and was reaching into other Southern colonies.

Stratford Hall, overlooking the Potomac in Virginia's historic Northern Neck, illustrates this mode of life. Famed as the boyhood home of Confederate Gen. Robert E. Lee, Stratford was at its busiest during the days of his forebears. Its 1,400 acres yielded crops of tobacco, wheat, and corn, employing the labor of about 200 slaves and indentured servants. Ships sailed directly from England to load tobacco at Stratford's wharves, an exchange center for other farmers in the area as well.

Tobacco provided a medium of exchange for colonial Virginians and Marylanders. Clergy and soldiers took their pay in leaf. Patrick Henry first gained fame as a lawyer in a case against the crown involving tobacco payments to Anglican clergymen, whose wages were set by law.

Plantations on the scale of Stratford were the exception. The typical holding was 100 to 300 acres,

Touro Synagogue, symbol of religious freedom since 1763, graces Newport, Rhode Island, as the nation's oldest Jewish house of worship. Town meetings and legislature convened here after Revolutionary War battles destroyed public buildings.

JAMES A. SUGAR

cultivated by families who generally aspired to the aristocratic life-style of their richer neighbors. Their hope of success lay in the combination of easily available land and a flexible social order. There were enough examples to feed the hope. Patrick Henry's father arrived in Virginia in 1727 with only a quick mind and acquisitive instincts. By the time Patrick was born in 1736, his father owned more than 13,000 acres and several slaves. Patrick expanded the holdings to some 23,000 acres and 65 slaves.

But this apparently tranquil society rested on a shaky foundation—the slave system, vital to the planters, intolerable to the blacks they enslaved. Runaways, sabotage, and rumors of rebellions kept the region in a constant state of uneasiness. Planter William Byrd II expressed in 1736 the fear that insurrection would "tinge our rivers, as wide as they are, with blood."

In Virginia as in other regions, taverns played an important social role. Patrick Henry, before launching his law career, tended bar and played the fiddle at his father-in-law's Hanover Tavern, now a historic landmark 20 miles north of Richmond. Court days and horse races also offered diversions. Chesapeake society took especially to dancing. Philip Fithian, a young tutor on Robert Carter's plantation, wrote that "Virginians are of genuine Blood—They will dance or die!"

While tavern and plantation house served as principal scenes of social activity, there did exist in the region a few modest towns, such as Annapolis and Williamsburg. Neither counted much as bustling centers of culture or commerce. Virginia's capital came to life at "Publick Times"—twice yearly, when the general assembly convened; for most of the year it remained a quiet little town.

Farther south, Charleston and, later, Savannah ultimately eclipsed the Chesapeake capitals. The Georgia colony developed slowly, inhibited by strict regimentation. But Charleston, which has preserved perhaps more of its 18th-century character than any other large city in America, became truly a magnet for the countryside around it. Such were its attractions—theaters, concerts, dancing societies—that Carolina lowland planters left their plantations much of the year to live in the city.

In the agricultural regions around Charleston, life was much less stable than in the Chesapeake area. From the beginning, unrest plagued "Carolina Colony," a huge proprietary grant deeded in 1663 by Charles II. Its "Fundamental Constitutions," creating classes of feudal seigniors, barons, freeholders, and serfs, never worked. Not until the crown repurchased the grant in 1729 and divided it into two colonies did settlers come in large numbers.

And when settlement began in earnest, a dangerous imbalance grew between freeman and slave. In South Carolina, blacks outnumbered whites two to one. By contrast, the proportion of slaves in most of Virginia rarely exceeded 45 percent.

Moreover, the wealthy and wellborn Chesapeake planters understood the responsibilities of their position. Carolina planters, on the other hand, away pursuing business or pleasure, often left their property in the care of poorly trained overseers. Even the needs of the white farmers were neglected.

As in the other regions, the people of the lowlands developed their own character—distinctive, yet peculiarly American. And just what was an American? An 18th-century French immigrant, J. Hector St. John Crèvecoeur, groped for an answer: "Here individuals of all nations are melted into a new race of men, [who] will one day cause great changes in the world."

Crèvecoeur was certainly correct in predicting "great changes," but the people who caused them were not simply Europeans melted down to form a single cultural stock. The New England Puritans, the Germans tending their Pennsylvania farms, the Virginia and Carolina gentry and the African slaves they exploited—all were part of a social network still in the process of creation. During the Revolution, Americans would come to recognize the common threads that bound them. And in the process of building a new, unified nation, they would also come face to face with the complexity that made up that "new race," the Americans.

Founded by Puritans in 1649, Annapolis became Maryland's capital in 1694 and still retains the town plan of Royal Governor Francis Nicholson. Streets radiate from central State Circle. The State House, oldest in the country in continuous use, served as first capitol of the nation. The United States Naval Academy was founded in this tidewater town in 1845.

VICTOR R. BOSWELL, JR., NATIONAL GEOGRAPHIC PHOTOGRAPHER

Williamsburg

Wandering afoot in Williamsburg, I got lost—lost in the 18th century. The fragrance of woodsmoke and bayberry candles transported me far back into the past. Ponderous oxen pulled a blue cart along the catalpa-shaded Palace Green. At the door of the stately Wythe House, two ladies in farthingaled gowns chatted in the morning sunlight. The rhythmic clang of the blacksmith's hammer, faintly heard, only intensified the peace, the quiet, the serenity....

Suddenly, I caught myself strolling more and more slowly and gracefully, as if I too were wearing a farthingale and thinking about new "ribands" for my bonnet.

But it is also easy to get literally lost in this beautiful "museum city"—a mile long and half a mile wide, with more than a hundred major buildings, more than a hundred gardens. First-time visitors find a helpful orientation film, guidebook, and map at the information center, and shuttle buses circle the restoration. But it still takes a day or so to learn your way around.

"Is this the way to the gunsmith?" "Do we want Merchants Square or Market Square?" "What's an apothecary?" The guides and craftworkers are seldom stumped by questions about 18th-century life in Williamsburg or 20th-century maps of the town. But one innocent query has become local folklore: "Why did you build Williamsburg *here?"*

Why indeed? Jamestown had been the center of the Virginia colony for more than 90 years. It had suffered and barely survived constant setbacks—disease, Indian harassment, disastrous fires. But the town's deathblow finally came in October of 1698 when the fourth new statehouse burned. The following year the general assembly voted to move the capital to the settlement at Middle Plantation and to rename that "healthy and agreeable" site in honor of "our most gratious & glorious King William."

Royal Governor Francis Nicholson began work on an orderly town plan, based on the location of the church and college already built at Middle Plantation. Half-acre lots were laid out, large enough for each homeowner to plant a garden. Laws specified size, pitch, and setback for houses along the main street, and required that each lot be fenced (to protect gardens from stray livestock). The Wren Building of the College of William and Mary—the only building now existing that is older than the town itself—served as temporary home for the governor and meeting place for the general assembly until a suitable residence and a capitol could be raised. Jamestown gradually withered; the new town of Williamsburg flourished.

For 80 years Williamsburg served as the capital of Virginia and was, in the words of historian Rutherfoord Goodwin, the colony's "principal seat of... religion, education, society, commerce, and fashion."

The names of its residents and visitors are well known in American history: George Washington, Thomas Jefferson, Patrick Henry, George Mason. For Williamsburg also became a principal seat of rebellion. Here delegates to the Continental Congress were instructed to initiate a declaration of independence; here Mason's Declaration of Rights was adopted; here the Virginia state constitution was framed, a model for other colonies.

But with the Revolution came the need for a capital less accessible to

Signs of the time welcome 20th-century visitors to Duke of Gloucester Street in 18th-century Williamsburg, Virginia. The restored colonial capital preserves 88 original buildings; dozens more have been meticulously reconstructed. Shops, homes, taverns, church, college, public buildings, and gardens recapture the past; costumed hosts and hostesses and a hundred craftworkers bring it to life.

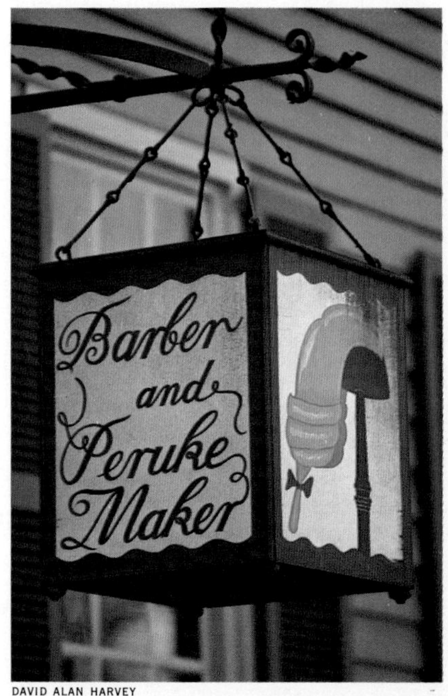

DAVID ALAN HARVEY

invasion. In 1780, as General Cornwallis's redcoats pushed north from the Carolinas, government offices were moved to the "more safe and central" town of Richmond. After the war Williamsburg settled down to the quiet life of a rural county seat and college town.

Nearly 150 years later, in 1926, historian Goodwin, former rector of Bruton Parish Church, shared a dream with John D. Rockefeller, Jr. And so began the great work that has given back to us the colonial capital of Virginia as one of the largest and most important historical restorations in the nation.

April 14, 1740: "I rose about 6 and prepared for my journey to Williamsburg." William Byrd II of Westover plantation, whose diaries record valuable details about 18th-century life, was not the only person planning a journey. Twice each year, in April and October, the cream of Virginia aristocracy left their isolated plantations and came to Williamsburg for the convening of the courts and general assembly. The town's population, normally about 1,800, doubled during these lively "Publick Times." Some planters kept town houses, but most stayed at inns, which soon filled up even though the law allowed three men to a bed. Ladies stayed at the homes of friends.

Publick Times: banquets and balls at the Governor's Palace, fairs and auctions on Market Square, horse races on a track near the Capitol. Miscreants held in the formidable "gaol" came to trial; those condemned to pillory or stocks provided still more entertainment.

Today's visitors to Williamsburg—at peak seasons nearly doubling the town's population—still enjoy the pillory and stocks, by locking each other up in them. Children peer cautiously into grim cells where Blackbeard's pirates once awaited trial. Other rooms held debtors, the insane—and the jailer and his family! The hostess tells us of one jailer, Peter Pelham, who was also the organist at Bruton Parish Church and often took a prisoner with him to pump the organ bellows.

Church and state were one in the colony, just as in England. The rites, services, and charitable work of the Anglican church were a central part of life. In the dark days when a war of revolution seemed inevitable, colonists set aside a special day of prayer at Bruton Parish Church to seek "divine interposition."

Bruton Parish continues to serve, not only as a reminder of the place of religion in the nation's history but also as a thriving modern Episcopal church. Visitors are welcome at regular services and at special candlelight concerts and organ recitals. The rule of 1716 ordering that "the Men sitt on the North side of the Church, and the Women on the left" no longer applies. No Royal governors come now, but their velvet-canopied chair remains.

Visitors tend to linger long at the reconstructed Governor's Palace. Its walled grounds hold not only the magnificent mansion (dubbed a "palace" by the irate colonists, whose taxes paid for its luxuries) but also the numerous "dependencies"—icehouse, laundry, kitchen, scullery, carriage houses, stable—and elegant formal gardens, pleached arbors, a bowling green, canal, fishpond, and

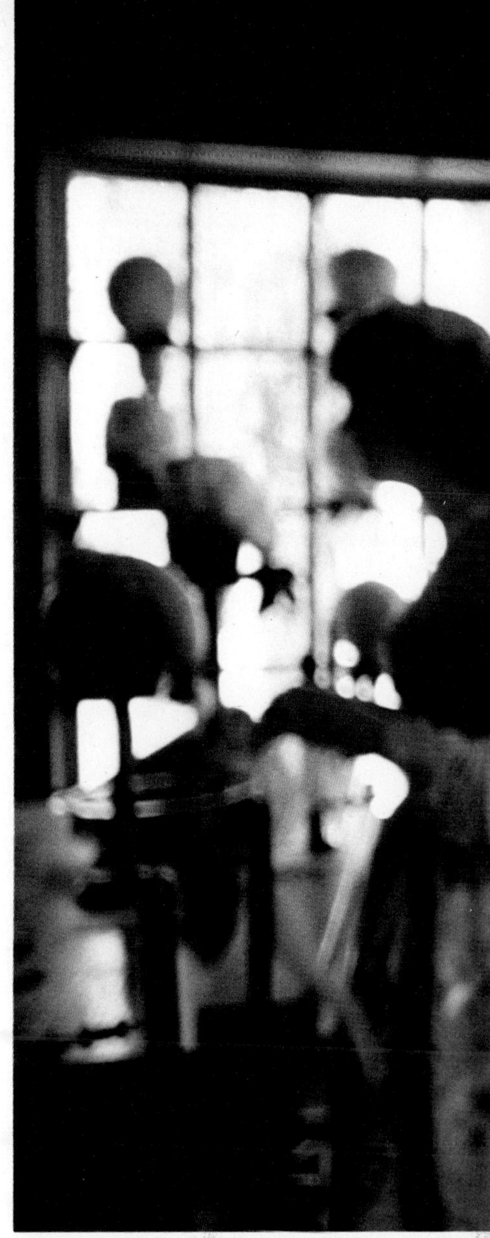

Filling needs from head to foot, some 40 handcrafts served the inhabitants of colonial Williamsburg. Wigs, made in a wide variety of styles, denoted social status; the town once boasted eight wigmakers. The shoemaker provided not only footwear but also leather mugs, buckets, military gear. Crafts thrive here again in an extensive program of masters, journeymen, and apprentices using 18th-century tools and methods.

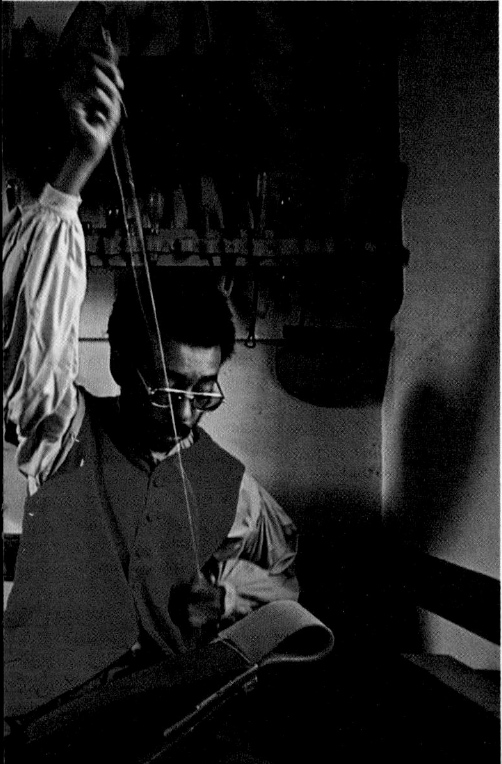

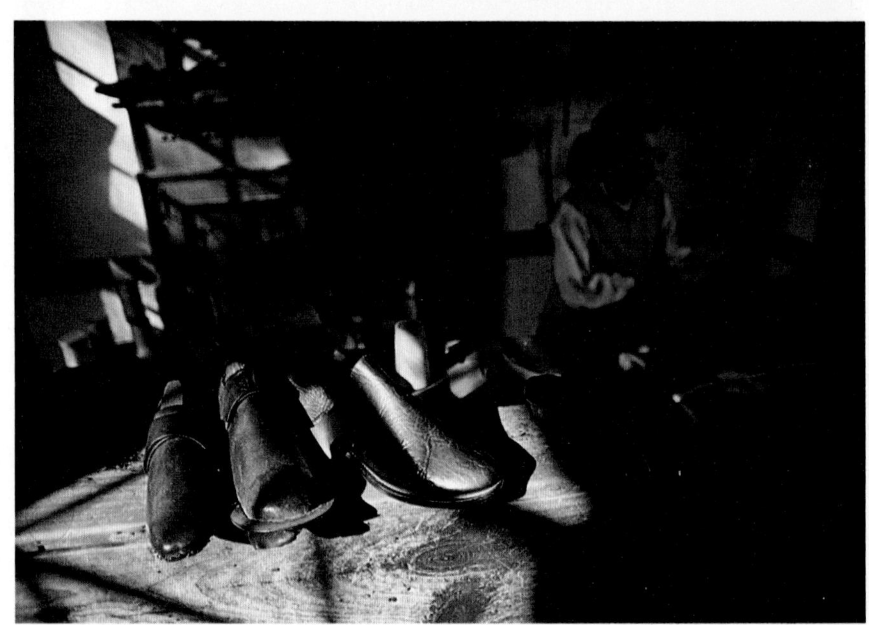

DAVID ALAN HARVEY

To The College and Wren Building

even a complex holly maze, the convolutions of which bewildered me. (The palace guidebook kindly provides directions, but it's easier just to follow small children.)

In the middle of the grounds, a simple cemetery guards the remains of 156 Revolutionary War soldiers. During that war the palace, after serving as a home for Governors Patrick Henry and Thomas Jefferson, became a military headquarters and then a hospital. Barely two months after the conflict ended, the building burned to the ground. In 1930, as excavation began for reconstruction of the palace, workers discovered the unmarked graves.

Furnishings and decorations in the palace fully convey the status and power of the Royal governors. An array of muskets lines the stately entrance hall. Fine mahogany and walnut furniture, rich velvet draperies, Chinese wallpaper, Oriental carpets, glass chandeliers, and silver sconces embellish the parlor, dining room, supper room, ballroom, bedchambers. A rococo silver centerpiece, finely detailed, gleams on the dining table. A row of Chelsea porcelain figurines adorns a marble mantel. Even the hostesses who show us these treasures wear brocades and laces suitable for a palace.

The detailed inventory made in 1770 after the death of Royal Governor Lord Botetourt served as the major guide for the furnishing of the rebuilt palace. (Botetourt was a liberal host; the inventory of the wine cellars lists 3,200 gallons of wines, beers, and spirits.)

All of the restoration's buildings were painstakingly researched, restored, and furnished in careful accordance with original inventories, clues found in letters, diaries, legal documents, paintings of the time, artifacts dug from excavations and old wells. An absorbing exhibit at the James Anderson House describes

1. *Cooper*
2. *Bruton Parish Church*
3. *George Wythe House*
4. *Basketmaker*
5. *Blacksmith, Harness and Saddlemaker*
6. *Governor's Palace*
7. *Wheelwright*
8. *Brush-Everard House*
9. *Candlemaker*
10. *Windmill*
11. *Peyton Randolph House*
12. *James Geddy House and Silversmith Shop*
13. *Spinning and Weaving House*
14. *Boot and Shoemaker Shop*
15. *Courthouse of 1770*
16. *Powder Magazine and Guardhouse*
17. *Chowning's Tavern*
18. *Prentis Store*
19. *Musical Instrument Maker*
20. *Cabinetmaker*
21. *Printer and Bookbinder*
22. *Music Teacher*
23. *James Anderson House*
24. *Tarpley's Store*
25. *Wetherburn's Tavern*
26. *Milliner*
27. *Jeweler and Engraver*
28. *Wigmaker*
29. *Raleigh Tavern and Bakery*
30. *King's Arms Tavern*
31. *Apothecary*
32. *Public Records Office*
33. *Gaol*
34. *Capitol*
35. *Gunsmith*

PAINTING BY PAUL HOGARTH

Outpost of Royalty

Homage was paid to "his Highness William Duke of Gloceter" in the naming of the town's main artery, which stretches for nearly a mile from the Capitol to the Wren Building of the College of William and Mary. Parallel streets, Francis and Nicholson, honor the Royal governor who designed the town. At Bruton Parish Church, a broad green leads to the Governor's Palace.

No automobiles disturb the serenity of the restored area. Visitors stroll the quiet streets and gardens, ride bicycles, catch a shuttle bus, or relax in a horse-drawn coach. The modern section of Williamsburg, the information center, lodgings, and Carter's Grove Plantation are nearby. Restoration of the colonial capital is 85 percent complete. Numbers on the diagram identify houses, craft shops, and other buildings open to the public (admission tickets are required). Visitors also enjoy a full program of tours, recitals, films and lectures, craft demonstrations, and special events in their journey to the 18th century.

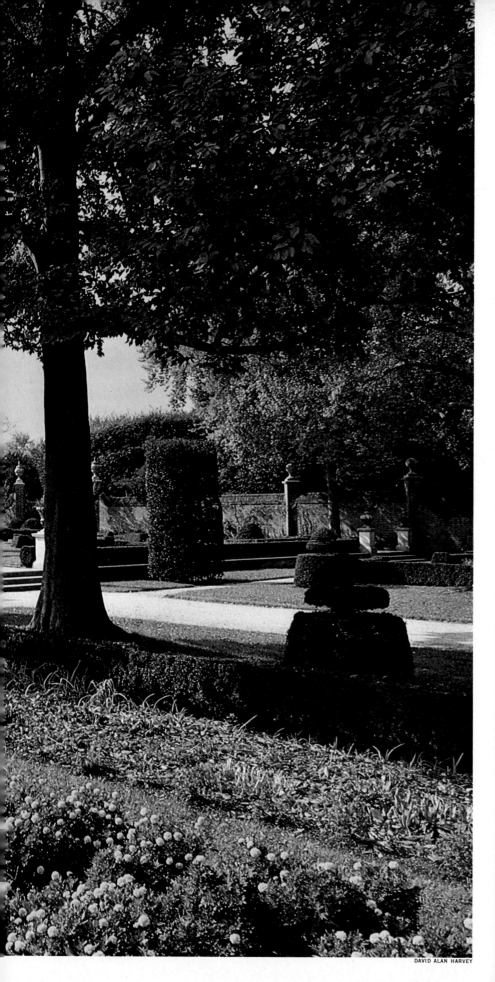

DAVID ALAN HARVEY

the archeological detective work on which the restoration is based and which continues today.

Some original furnishings were available. At the Capitol, the handsome "Speaker's Chair" in the House of Burgesses is the same chair once used by Peyton Randolph, later elected first president of the Continental Congress. Several pieces of original family silver are at home again in the Peyton Randolph House.

At the restored Wetherburn Tavern we walk on floors that George Washington trod, gaze through original wavy windowpanes, admire solid silver serving dishes—Henry Wetherburn catered to the wealthier class. William Byrd dined here almost daily during his Williamsburg visits. On May 2, 1740, he noted: "About 9 went to the capitol and sat till 3, when we dined at Wetherburn's and

The Hanover coat of arms reigns over the ballroom garden of the palace, home of seven Royal—and the first two elected—Virginia governors. In 1776 patriots gathered at the front gate (below) to celebrate the Declaration of Independence.

entertained the Governor.... After dinner we drank arrack punch till 6...." In the Great Room, a punch bowl waits to be filled once more with potent arrack punch; an iron rack stands ready to be hung overnight in the fireplace to dry out the tavern's supply of clay pipes.

Across the street from Wetherburn's, near the Capitol, the popular Raleigh Tavern bustled with activity at Publick Times, hosting dinners, dances, billiard games, long gambling sessions, and heated political debates. It was to the Raleigh that angry burgesses adjourned when Governor Botetourt dissolved the dissident assembly in 1769. And it was here only a few years later that Col. Patrick Henry's officers honored Henry with a farewell dinner.

The Raleigh and Wetherburn's are now exhibition buildings only, but

three other taverns offer hearty colonial-style meals, served in candlelit rooms often enlivened by the serenades of costumed musicians. At Chowning's Tavern, I feasted on Brunswick stew—made today with chicken rather than the more traditional squirrel or rabbit.

Williamsburg's painless history lessons come in many forms—meals and music, carriage rides, "lanthorn" tours. I watched a boy figure out for himself how the ball-and-chain device automatically closes garden gates. At Tarpley's Store another

Venerable art of French sand casting produces delicate objects ranging from buttons to sconces. At the James Geddy Shop, master founder Dan Berg begins work on a candlestick mold; finished molds are filled with molten brass.

DAVID ALAN HARVEY

With muscular authority the printer's apprentice "pulls the devil's tail" to print one copy, then re-inks the type, using leather-covered balls. Type is set by hand from upper and lower cases, origin of our terms for capital and small letters. Williamsburg's Printing Office—which also served as post office—produced books, pamphlets, legal forms, and, from 1736, the weekly Virginia Gazette, *filled with "the freshest Advices, Foreign and Domestick."*

Regarded with suspicion and strictly controlled by the crown, printing was not permitted in Virginia until 1690.

DAVID ALAN HARVEY

child carefully selected a quill pen. Toddlers romping in the oxcart became featured players in everyone else's home movies.

At the Deane Forge, a perspiring apprentice hammered glowing andirons under the watchful eyes of the master smith—and the gaze of a crowd of onlookers. At the Musical Instrument Maker's Shop we were invited to try out a tiny tinny-toned harpsichord. In the backyard of the Wythe House, we watched a workman shape perfect cypress shingles with just five quick strokes of his ax.

These skilled artisans take pleasure in explaining their crafts and answering our questions. We also glean fascinating tidbits about 18th-century life. The music teacher tells us that women did not play wind instruments; tight corsets inhibited deep breathing. At the wigmaker's we are surprised to learn that George Washington apparently never wore a wig; he just powdered his own hair.

But the craft shops and exhibition buildings empty quickly when fifes and drums are heard and the militia muster begins late in the afternoon. Crowds ring Market Square to cheer the parade, applaud the drills, flinch at the roar of muskets and cannon, and thrill to the music of "Yankee Doodle" and "The World Turned Upside Down"—the tune, tradition says, played by the British as they surrendered at Yorktown.

Quieter than fifes and drums, but no less enthralling, is the recital and demonstration of an 18th-century organ in Wren Chapel at the College of William and Mary. The Wren Building, begun in 1695, is the oldest academic building in continuous use in English-speaking America.

Jamestown was still the capital when the colony, in 1693, obtained a Royal charter for a college, "that the Church of Virginia may be furnish'd with a Seminary of Ministers of the Gospel, and that the Youth may be piously educated ... that the Christian Faith may be propagated amongst the Western Indians...." The Indian school had only small success, but the college filled a need as fathers grew more and more reluctant to send their sons to England for higher education. During the 18th century, enrollment averaged less than 100, but those students included Thomas Jefferson, Benjamin Harrison, James Monroe, and Peyton Randolph. It is appropriate that the Wren Building, at one end of Duke of Gloucester Street, stands

Meeting place of the nation's oldest representative assembly, the Capitol's Hall of the House of Burgesses reflects conflicting political loyalties: portraits of King William and Queen Mary; a copy of Patrick Henry's rebellious Stamp Act Resolves, passed by the House in 1765.

DAVID ALAN HARVEY. RIGHT: GEORGE F. MOBLEY, NATIONAL GEOGRAPHIC PHOTOGRAPHER

facing the Capitol at the other end. Behind the Wren Building today sprawls a campus of some 40 more buildings serving an average enrollment of 6,000 students.

The college also boasted America's first law professor, George Wythe, whom Thomas Jefferson called his "faithful and beloved Mentor." One of the most influential men in the colony, Wythe served as a member of the House of Burgesses, chancery court judge, and mayor of Williamsburg. His home in the town is a "plantation in miniature," complete with herb and vegetable gardens, stable, chicken house, smokehouse, kitchen (many colonial kitchens were separate from the house, chiefly because kitchens often caught fire). The laundry building contains slave quarters. Wythe owned as many as 18 slaves, most of whom he eventually freed.

The imposing main house features a "student's room" with a collection of 18th-century scientific books and

"All who please to favour me with their Custom may depend upon the best" in colonial-style meals and entertainment at Josiah Chowning's (right) and two other Williamsburg taverns, the King's Arms and Christiana Campbell's.

DAVID ALAN HARVEY

instruments: telescope, orrery, various globes, microscope, an air pump.

But Wythe was more than a mild and benevolent scholar, teacher, lawyer, and statesman. He hastened to join the Williamsburg militia in 1775—and was gently turned down, because of his age (48). A few years later, however, he and two hunting companions gleefully helped the militia fend off a British invasion from the James River. And Wythe was the first Virginia delegate to sign the Declaration of Independence.

Why, then, in 1765, had he opposed Patrick Henry's defiant Stamp Act Resolves? Perhaps Wythe remembered Henry as the ungainly, ill-prepared candidate for the bar who had appeared before him five years earlier. Wythe, however, was not alone in protesting hasty rebellion; Henry's fiery oratory appalled many. But the resolves were passed, and Royal Governor Francis Fauquier wrote that "The Flame is spread thru' all the Continent, and one Colony supports another in their Disobedience to superior powers."

A British flag tops the tower of the Capitol. Looking at it, I suddenly saw that the building has no chimneys. The burgesses had remembered the fiery fate of several Jamestown statehouses and forbade fires, candles, and smoking in the new building. But in vain. These impractical prohibitions were soon revoked, chimneys were added, and in 1747 the Capitol burned down.

A new one replaced it, but in the restoration of Williamsburg it was decided to follow the plan of the first Capitol. As with other rebuilt structures, its bricks were made by hand in Williamsburg from local clay in order to match the unique rich color of the original bricks.

More than any other Williamsburg building, the Capitol evokes a quiet and solemn response in its visitors. We stand musing in the austere Hall of the House of Burgesses, the plush Council Chamber, the richly-paneled Courtroom. We take the time to read carefully the contemporary copy of the Stamp Act Resolves. Studying the portraits, we meet the eyes of George Washington, Patrick Henry, and Thomas Jefferson, aware of our debt to them and of our own responsibility for upholding the ideals they cherished.

GEORGE F. MOBLEY, NATIONAL GEOGRAPHIC PHOTOGRAPHER

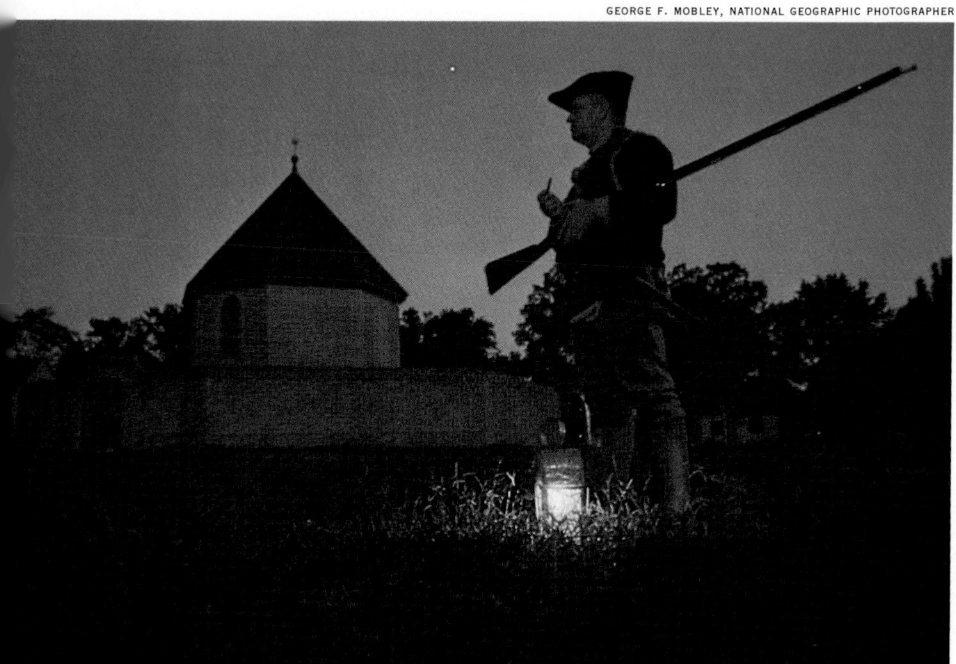

Built in 1715, the Powder Magazine stored an arsenal to protect the colony. But it became the ramrod of revolution in Williamsburg when a nervous Royal governor, Lord Dunmore, ordered British marines to spirit away a supply of the colony's gunpowder on the night of April 20, 1775. Someone spotted them; alarm drums roused the townsfolk from their beds. Patrick Henry raised a volunteer force in Hanover County. Calm prevailed after the receiver-general paid for the powder, but the fuse was lit. A few weeks later, Dunmore fled under cover of darkness.

The Williamsburg militia assembles again on Market Square in regular musters that rouse the town with musket crackle and cannon thunder and the stirring music of fifes and drums.

I rose about 6 one morning, following William Byrd's example, and went to sit under a maple on Market Square to watch Williamsburg wake up. To the casual eye, nothing of the 20th century was visible. A mockingbird serenaded the day from the Guardhouse roof. A young man jogged by, and I recalled reading that Tom Jefferson exercised that way during his student days here.

I strolled along the quiet street, pausing to study the notices in the Printing Office window, the finery displayed at the Milliner's. Smoke began to rise from the chimney of the Raleigh Tavern Bakery.

Around a bend came other visitors—not William Byrd in a coach but a family riding bicycles, a pleasant way to tour the town. The two little girls wore denims, T-shirts, and lace caps—an odd combination at first glance but, on second thought, quite appropriate. In Williamsburg the past, present, and future merge, a living history lesson to prepare us for history yet to be made.

SHIRLEY SCOTT

Candlelight still glows in the quiet sanctuary of Bruton Parish Church, built in 1715. A brass baptismal ewer (opposite) honors the memory of the infant son of the Reverend Dr. Rutherfoord Goodwin, co-founder of the Williamsburg restoration project. The stone font, according to tradition, was brought here from the church at Jamestown. Bruton Parish's earlier church at this site, quickly outgrown when Middle Plantation became the new capital city of Williamsburg, was replaced by the present larger structure. Royal Governor Alexander Spotswood designed its symmetrical cruciform plan.

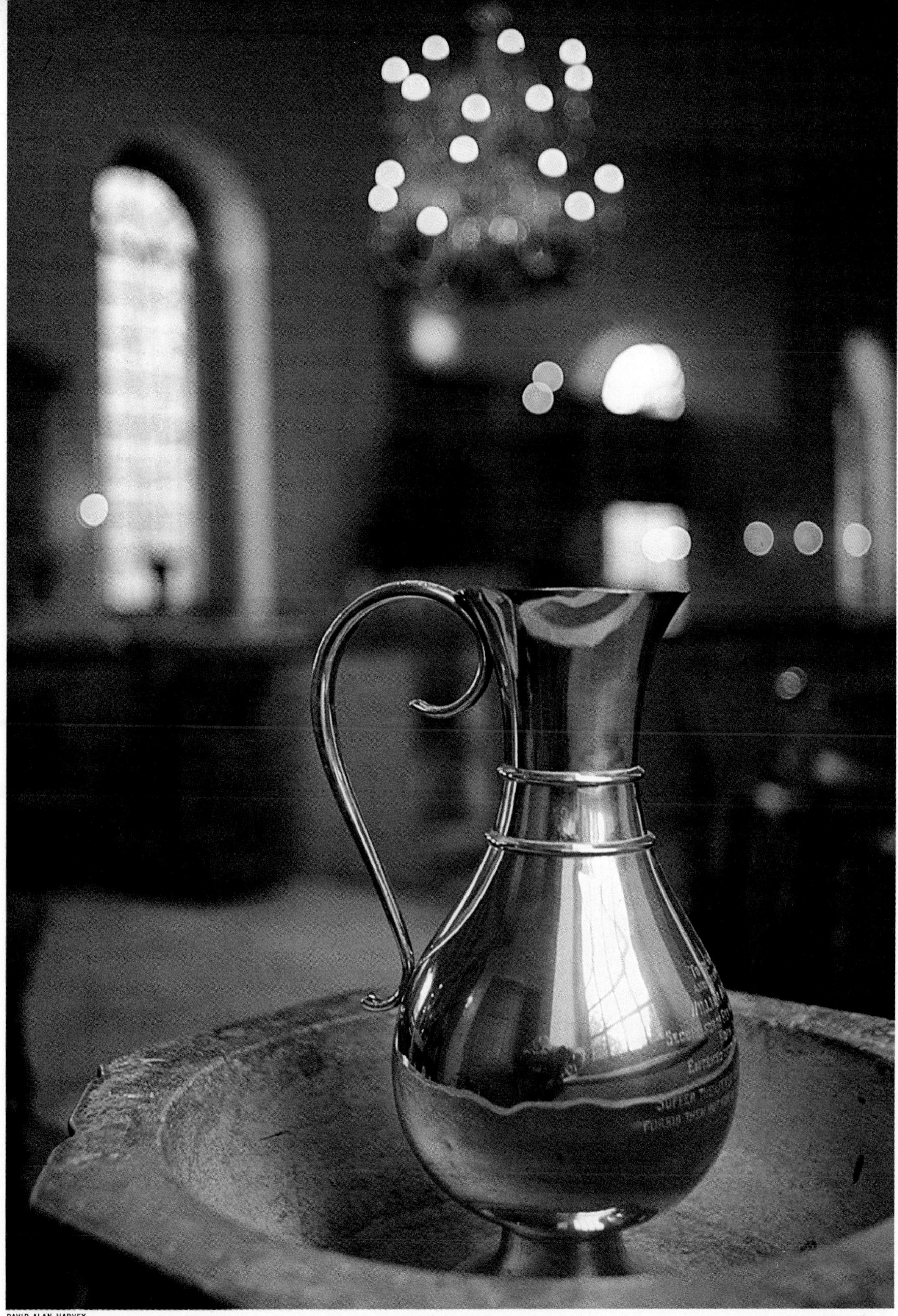

DAVID ALAN HARVEY

Tidewater Plantations

From Jamestown and Williamsburg, the modern highway winds westward along Virginia's James River through some of the loveliest country in all the Chesapeake Bay tidewater. Here, in early summer, piney woods and green hay perfume the air, bees hum in fragrant honeysuckle blossoms, and mockingbirds sing in the magnolias.

Many times I have traveled this road, grateful for the natural beauty of the land but bent primarily on voyaging back into what was, for the white planter, a golden era of American history. At a time when few roads pierced the wilderness, tidewater manors rose along navigable waterways. Here beside the James River were the richest of the great plantations that flourished in Maryland, Delaware, and Virginia.

Westover is Virginia's finest example of Georgian grandeur. The lawn sweeps 150 feet to the James. William Byrd II, who feared Indian attack, built an escape tunnel from the garden to the river.

The house itself is a private home, but visitors are welcomed to the gardens. Byrd is buried there, where he was fond of strolling in the evening, dreaming of England, no doubt. His father, born in London, was a prosperous trader near the falls of the James. To ensure his son's safety, he sent him "home" during Bacon's Rebellion. There the boy was later educated. He learned to love the

Aged tulip poplars frame Westover's mellow red bricks, made locally in the 1730's. Builder William Byrd II's designer copied English Georgian manors with steep roofs and hipped dormers.

FARRELL GREHAN

masked balls, the theater, the genteel life of the aristocracy.

When Byrd wasn't visiting across the Atlantic, he worked hard to transform his thousands of acres of frontier Virginia into a piece of home. He collected some 3,600 books, the largest private library in the colony. He rose early, said his prayers, read the Bible (in Hebrew) and Homer (in Greek), ate breakfast, and "talked with my people"—his hundreds of slaves. He saw himself as a kind of Biblical patriarch: "I have my Flocks and my Herds, my Bond-men and Bond-women. . . ."

They talk of ghosts at Westover. The most compelling is Byrd's oldest daughter, Evelyn. A dark-haired beauty, she was presented at court at 16, caught the eye of the nobility, then fell in love with a man her father disapproved of. Byrd brought her home, and at Westover she pined away the years and died unmarried at the age of 30.

Of the more northerly plantations, Stratford Hall, on the Potomac, was one of the richest, with its four wings and an array of outbuildings, formal gardens, and orchard. Begun by Thomas Lee in 1725, it took five years to build and stayed in the family until 1822. An austere, masculine house, Stratford Hall has massive chimney clusters, where lookouts climbed to scan the Potomac River for roving bands of pirates.

In the Great Hall, an imposing 30 feet square, carved pilasters, gilt mirrors, and family portraits adorn the paneled walls. Here the Lees held parties and country dances, stepping to the rhythms of a traditional Virginia reel.

At Stratford Hall were born two signers of the Declaration of Independence, Richard Henry Lee and Francis Lightfoot Lee.

Stately Carter's Grove stands on an estate once owned by Robert "King" Carter. His grandson Carter Burwell began the main house in 1750. I came to it the first time by water, the old way. Oceangoing ships once sailed up the James to unload at plantation wharves.

A 12-foot-wide fireplace in Stratford Hall's kitchen (left) could roast a whole ox. Beside the white sugar loaf stand copper vessels joined by tubing—a still that made corn whiskey and brandy. A costumed guide cleans a sieve. The manor's canopied cradle rocked four generations of the Lee family, including Confederate Gen. Robert E. Lee.

JAMES L. STANFIELD, NATIONAL GEOGRAPHIC PHOTOGRAPHER

MARYLAND
MONTPELIER
Laurel
SULLY
Chantilly
BERKELEY
Charles City
SCOTCHTOWN
Ashland
ST. LUKE'S CHURCH
Smithfield
SHIRLEY
Charles City
EVELYNTON
Charles City
MARYLAND
VIRGINIA
Baltimore
Laurel
Annapolis
Chantilly
Washington
Galesville
MOUNT
VERNON
GUNSTON HALL
Patuxent
SOTTERLEY
WAKEFIELD
STRATFORD
HALL
St. Marys City
Potomac
Chesapeake
Bay
Rappahannock
Ashland
Richmond
Charles City
WESTOVER
Williamsburg
York
Petersburg
James
Jamestown
Surry
Smithfield
Norfolk
Virginia
Beach

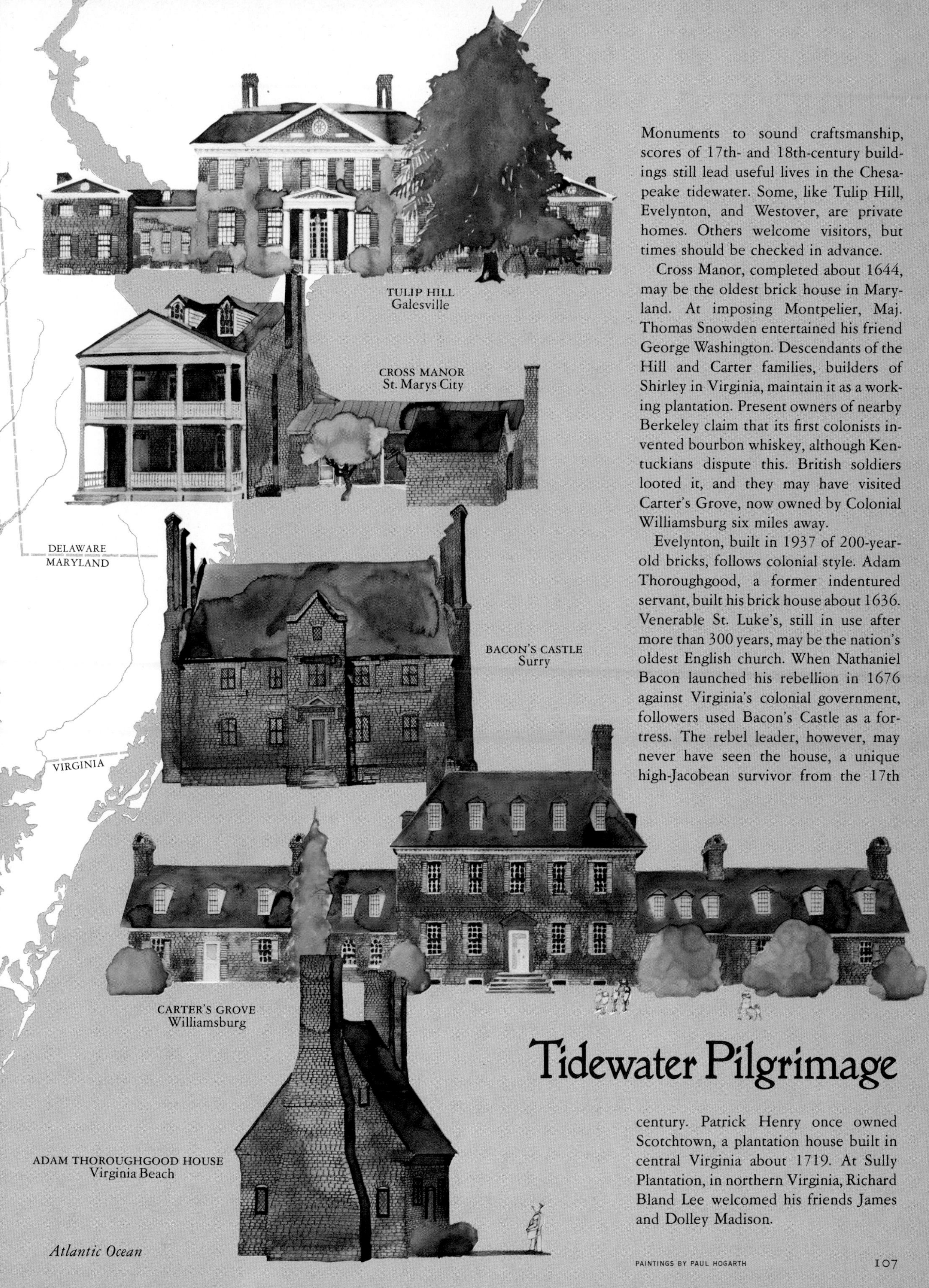

TULIP HILL
Galesville

CROSS MANOR
St. Marys City

BACON'S CASTLE
Surry

CARTER'S GROVE
Williamsburg

ADAM THOROUGHGOOD HOUSE
Virginia Beach

Monuments to sound craftsmanship, scores of 17th- and 18th-century buildings still lead useful lives in the Chesapeake tidewater. Some, like Tulip Hill, Evelynton, and Westover, are private homes. Others welcome visitors, but times should be checked in advance.

Cross Manor, completed about 1644, may be the oldest brick house in Maryland. At imposing Montpelier, Maj. Thomas Snowden entertained his friend George Washington. Descendants of the Hill and Carter families, builders of Shirley in Virginia, maintain it as a working plantation. Present owners of nearby Berkeley claim that its first colonists invented bourbon whiskey, although Kentuckians dispute this. British soldiers looted it, and they may have visited Carter's Grove, now owned by Colonial Williamsburg six miles away.

Evelynton, built in 1937 of 200-year-old bricks, follows colonial style. Adam Thoroughgood, a former indentured servant, built his brick house about 1636. Venerable St. Luke's, still in use after more than 300 years, may be the nation's oldest English church. When Nathaniel Bacon launched his rebellion in 1676 against Virginia's colonial government, followers used Bacon's Castle as a fortress. The rebel leader, however, may never have seen the house, a unique high-Jacobean survivor from the 17th century. Patrick Henry once owned Scotchtown, a plantation house built in central Virginia about 1719. At Sully Plantation, in northern Virginia, Richard Bland Lee welcomed his friends James and Dolley Madison.

Tidewater Pilgrimage

PAINTINGS BY PAUL HOGARTH

There is no wharf now at Carter's Grove. I beached my small sailboat and walked to the mansion along the route of the plantation's road to the river. Down this lane, now bordered by a ravine choked with trees and underbrush, moved the farm products—probably wheat and corn—that the Carters shipped to England. Back up came the books, silver, porcelain, and fine furniture the English ships brought in return.

The most important export that rumbled down such "rolling roads" was tobacco in huge hogsheads. "Sotweed," as the English came to call it, even served as currency in 18th-century Maryland and Virginia.

From the outside, the big house at Carter's Grove resembles Westover. Typical of houses of the period, it was built without benefit of an architect and constructed instead by master masons, joiners, and carvers working from English books. The place has its legends. According to one colorful yarn, the swashbuckling British dragoon, Col. Banastre Tarleton, rode his horse up the main staircase, slashing the carved walnut banister with his saber. The marks are plainly visible.

Tarleton overlooked another fine target a day's ride upriver from Carter's Grove. This was Berkeley, estate of the Harrison family, which would produce a signer of the Declaration of Independence and two United States Presidents.

Its history reads like a novel. The first Thanksgiving Day in the New World was observed here by the estate's original settlers on December 4, 1619, nearly a year before the Pilgrims set foot in New England. Three years after the pioneers came,

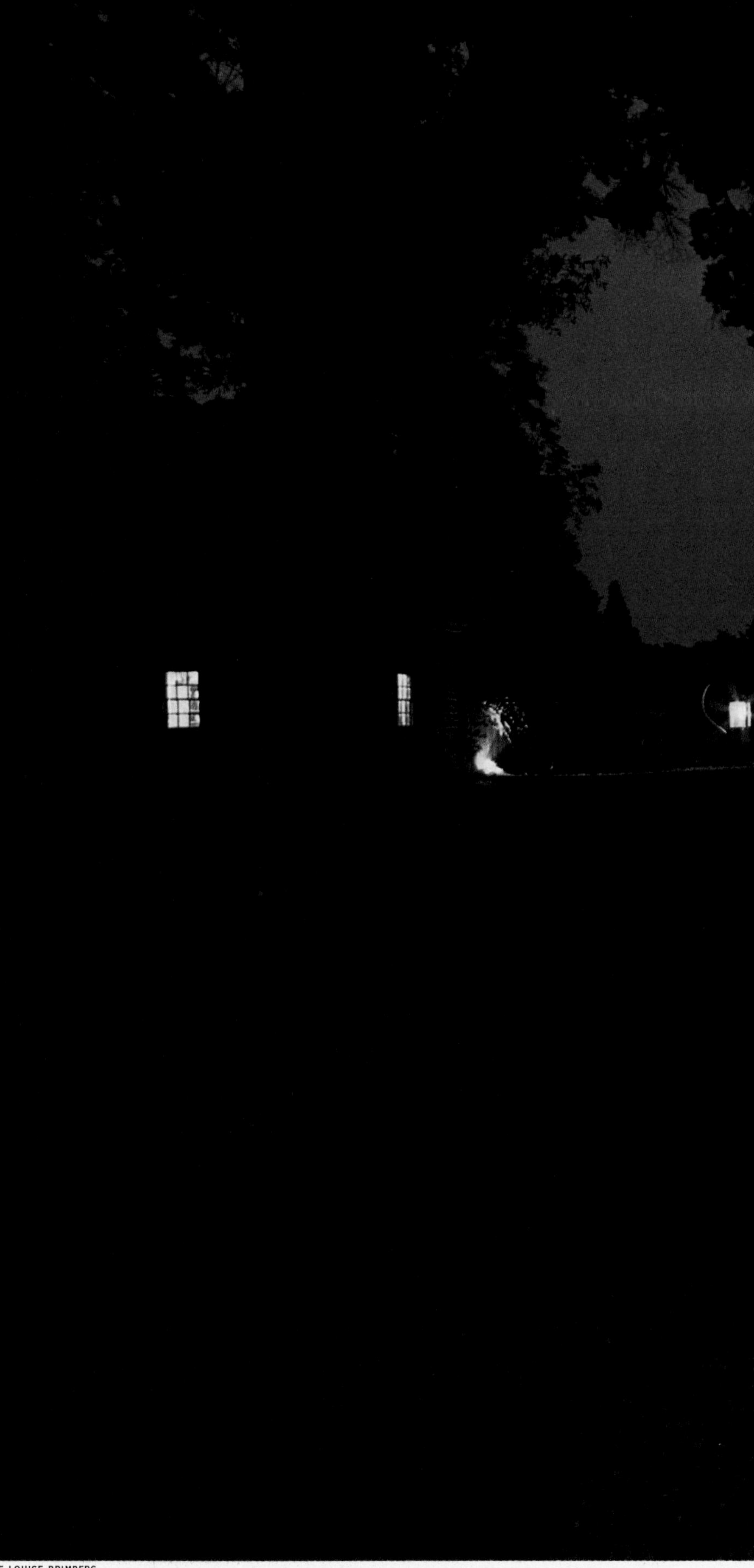

In graceful Gunston Hall near Mount Vernon, seat of George Mason's 5,000-acre plantation, the "pen of the American Revolution" labored for liberty.

MARIE-LOUISE BRIMBERG

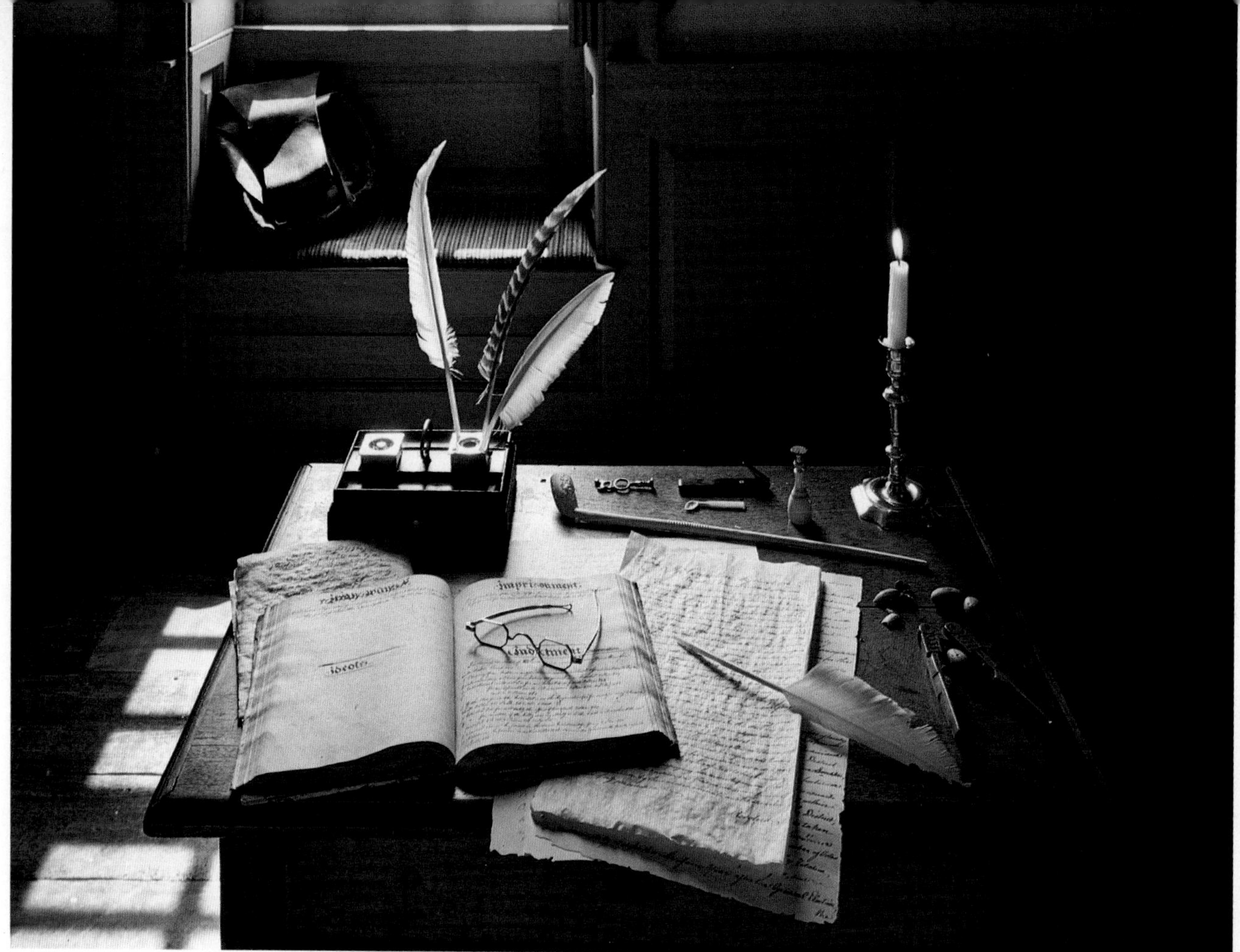

Paraphernalia of a thoughtful man litters the study table of George Mason at Gunston Hall. His elegant drawing room (opposite) displays wood wall carvings of Palladian design adapted by the young carpenter William Buckland.

the settlement was nearly wiped out by Indians taking part in the colony-wide uprising of 1622.

In 1781, British troops under Benedict Arnold plundered the plantation. But the solid three-story brick house built by Benjamin Harrison in 1726 survived the attack. It also withstood occupation by federal troops in the Civil War and almost a century's abandonment to squatters and vandals, a fate shared by many another tidewater mansion. Berkeley is now completely restored, with authentic period furniture, some of it originally from nearby Westover.

Given a fair wind or strong slaves at the oars, the Lees of Stratford could travel by water to the upriver Potomac estate of their friends, the Masons, at Gunston Hall. By stretching the voyage only an hour or so, they could call on the George Washingtons at Mount Vernon.

George Mason, who built Gunston Hall, played an important role in our nation's early days. Best remembered for his authorship of the Virginia Declaration of Rights, the basis of the federal Bill of Rights, he was never a lawyer, yet he was well-versed in law; he had studied law books in his guardian's library.

Mason harbored a fierce love of liberty. He helped draft resolutions against the Townshend Acts, and in 1774 wrote the Fairfax Resolves, which confronted the crown with the constitutional position of the colonies. Bitterly disappointed when the new republic failed to abolish the slave trade, he called slavery "diabolical in itself and disgraceful to mankind." And yet Mason was the second largest slave owner in the county—a puzzling contradiction in this man of strong conviction.

More than any other tidewater manor I know, Gunston Hall gives its visitors the eerie feeling that its distinguished owner might walk in any minute. Poignant reminders of his humanity fill the study: crutches, cane, and a chair with an elevated footrest, for Mason suffered from gout most of his adult life. From the river porch, visitors gaze through an avenue of mammoth boxwood hedges, taller than a man, toward the Potomac River beyond. Flanking the hedges, which Mason planted, formal gardens display typical 18th-century flowers and shrubs.

Gunston Hall had an unusually cumbersome route to its landing. A rolling road led to a canal, on which barges carried goods to ships waiting in Gunston Cove.

North and east of the Potomac, dividing line between the colonies, Maryland planters lived similar lives, though usually in manor houses more simply built. Sotterley, on the

MARIE-LOUISE BRIMBERG

Patuxent, was the seat of the distinguished Platers, one of whom was governor of Maryland. The manor has the usual tobacco shed, smokehouse, slave cabins, and gatehouses. But the low, rambling house is frame rather than the more expensive brick. Its massive joists, held together with wooden pegs and handmade nails, are as sound today as when construction began in 1710.

The upstairs bedrooms are much like those of a simple farmhouse. But the richness of the first floor bespeaks the wealth that came to later generations of one of Maryland's eminent families.

Tobacco planters had their troubles even before the Revolution closed the essential English market. Navigation laws forbade Marylanders and Virginians to ship the leaf anywhere but to England. The result was a periodic glut on the market and drop in prices.

The Revolution brought a kind of false prosperity because of inflation. After the war, the demand for goods declined, and everyone felt the pinch—even George Washington, who had to borrow money so he could journey to New York for his inauguration ceremonies.

The War of 1812 came as a second economic blow. There were others. New cities took over the profitable business of handling tobacco for the smallholders, formerly a source of income for large planters. Moreover, the land wore out fast under the harsh demands of the tobacco plant. George Washington had started rotating crops as early as 1766.

The Civil War was the ultimate disaster. As the black workers who performed most of the plantation labor laid down their hoes, wild broom sedge took over the fields and the fiddles sang no more in the gilded ballrooms. The white planter's golden era had ended.

NATHANIEL T. KENNEY

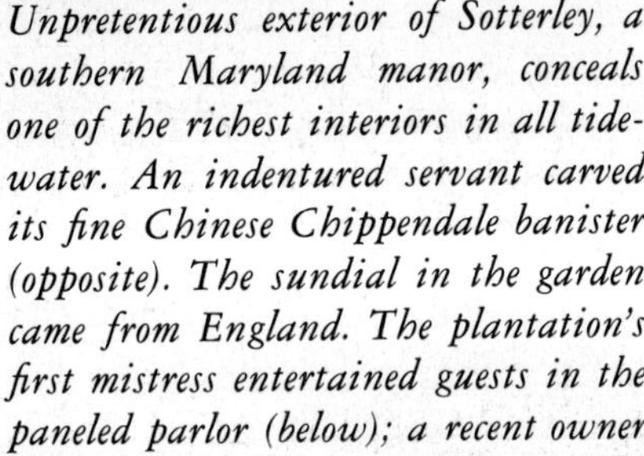

Unpretentious exterior of Sotterley, a southern Maryland manor, conceals one of the richest interiors in all tidewater. An indentured servant carved its fine Chinese Chippendale banister (opposite). The sundial in the garden came from England. The plantation's first mistress entertained guests in the paneled parlor (below); a recent owner painted the walls red. From this room, a secret stairway, its original purpose a mystery, ascends to a second-story bedroom. Sotterley is rich in legends. One claims that two pirates, slain in an unsuccessful raid, lie buried somewhere on the estate. George Plater V, the owner in 1808, gave up the plantation to settle his gambling debts.

MARIE-LOUISE BRIMBERG

The Colonial Southland

In the "fair and spacious Province" of Carolina, the aristocrats were given to high living—in the opinion of some, to downright sin. "Cards, dice, the bottle and horses" absorbed the Charleston gentry. Many a gentleman was rarely at home, but often at the theater, a musical entertainment, or one of his clubs: the Whisk Club, the Laughing Club, the Smoaking Club. Henry Laurens, a hard-working merchant, grumbled that the assembly adjourned so that its members could attend a ball.

This affluent colony boasted coastal settlements from Albemarle Sound in North Carolina to Savannah, Georgia, by the 1730's. But Charleston, the only metropolis south of Philadelphia, shone like a star—a social and commercial center of the British colonies.

On outlying estates, planters prospered by the sweat of slaves who labored in indigo fields and steaming, mosquito-ridden rice swamps. Leaving spacious country seats to summer in Charleston, these tidewater planters and merchants built "excessive grand" town houses with lacy iron gateways and small slave quarters placed conveniently in backyards. Josiah Quincy of Boston visited in 1773 and described a house that still stands—the Georgian mansion of Miles Brewton, slave trader: "The grandest hall I ever beheld, azure blue satin window curtains, rich blue paper with gilt, mashee borders, most elegant pictures."

Hub of the Carolina low country, Charleston rose on a finger of land between the Ashley and Cooper rivers. Rice fleets sailing from the busy harbor returned with rum, sugar, and slaves.

J. BRUCE BAUMANN

Dock Street
Theatre
76

WILLIAM S. WEEMS. ABOVE: J. BRUCE BAUMANN

By importing some 3,500 blacks a year, Brewton and others in the "Guinea business" made fortunes. The captives were auctioned in the "public Negro yard" or even at the racecourse between heats. Today's visitor will find only the Old Slave Mart, a 19th-century auction house for general goods, now a museum of black history and handicrafts.

Charlestonians lived with the threat of violence—a slave revolt or a pirate attack. In 1718 the town witnessed the execution of buccaneer Stede Bonnet, a major in the king's army who had turned to piracy, some said to escape a nagging wife. At White Point Gardens, today a favorite promenade, pirate and crew twisted slowly in the wind.

In 1740 a great fire leveled half the city, and 12 years later a major hurricane struck. "The flood came in like a bore.... many of the people... being up to their necks in water." Despite such disasters, Charleston's historic section still has an 18th-century ambience enjoyed by a torrent of visitors every spring, when many of the old houses open.

From the city, a winding road lined with moss-laden oaks leads to the Ashley River plantations. They say the wealthy owner of Middleton Place raised and supported an entire regiment for the Revolution. His

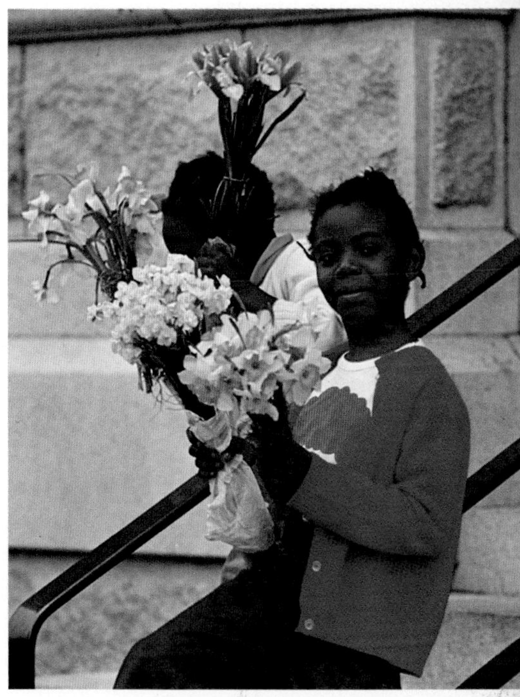

As in colonial days, street vendors try for a sale in historic Charleston, a city abloom while the North still shivers in winter's grip. Down byways fragrant with jasmine and tea olive, sightseers peek into the walled gardens of "Charleston houses," cooled by tiered piazzas. Colorful flags evoke heroic rebellion in 1776; by then, opulent colonials had already built the first Dock Street Theatre on this site and, with taxes levied on rum and slaves, St. Philip's Church—rebuilt in 1835.

gardens and nearby Magnolia Gardens display a wonderland of magnolias, camellias, and azaleas.

To the north, in the other Carolina, there were fewer plantations and no glittering urban centers. Migrants, many from neighboring states, poured into the backcountry. Bath, North Carolina's first town, is haunted by Indian and pirate raids. New Bern became the Royal capital and site of Governor William Tryon's famous "Pallace."

When Gen. James Oglethorpe settled Georgia in 1733, neighboring South Carolina hailed the new colony as a buffer against the Spanish in Florida. Oglethorpe hoped to resettle imprisoned debtors, but few came. From his damask-lined tent, the general saw to it that Savannah was laid out in squares by the river. The settlers were to grow silkworms and grapes in a planned utopia that limited holdings and banned liquor and slaves. But regimentation nearly killed the colony, and many changes would come before slave-tilled cotton enriched the state.

Fire swept Savannah in 1796. Rebuilt, the graceful city stands as the legacy of Oglethorpe's dream.

MARY SWAIN HOOVER

Middleton Place plantation dreams by the Ashley River near Charleston. No longer do hundreds of blacks toil in the flooded rice fields. Gone is the stately mansion house, burned by General Sherman's troops in 1865. Only a restored guest wing and serene 18th-century gardens remain, a haven for deer, peacocks—and visitors. Azaleas ramble by the pond that once powered the rice mill, and nearby, camellias planted two centuries ago still bloom.

J. BRUCE BAUMANN

But for the wiles of a "very ingenious Indian," Carolina's capital might have been Beaufort instead of Charleston. When English settlers dropped anchor in Port Royal Sound in 1670, an Indian chief persuaded the newcomers to settle in his country—farther up the coast on the banks of the Ashley River. The chief was hoping for English allies against a rival tribe. Since Port Royal Island lay in "the very chops of the Spaniards," the English agreed to the Ashley site, preserved today at Charles Towne Landing. By 1680 they had moved across the river to present-day Charleston.

Touring the Low Country

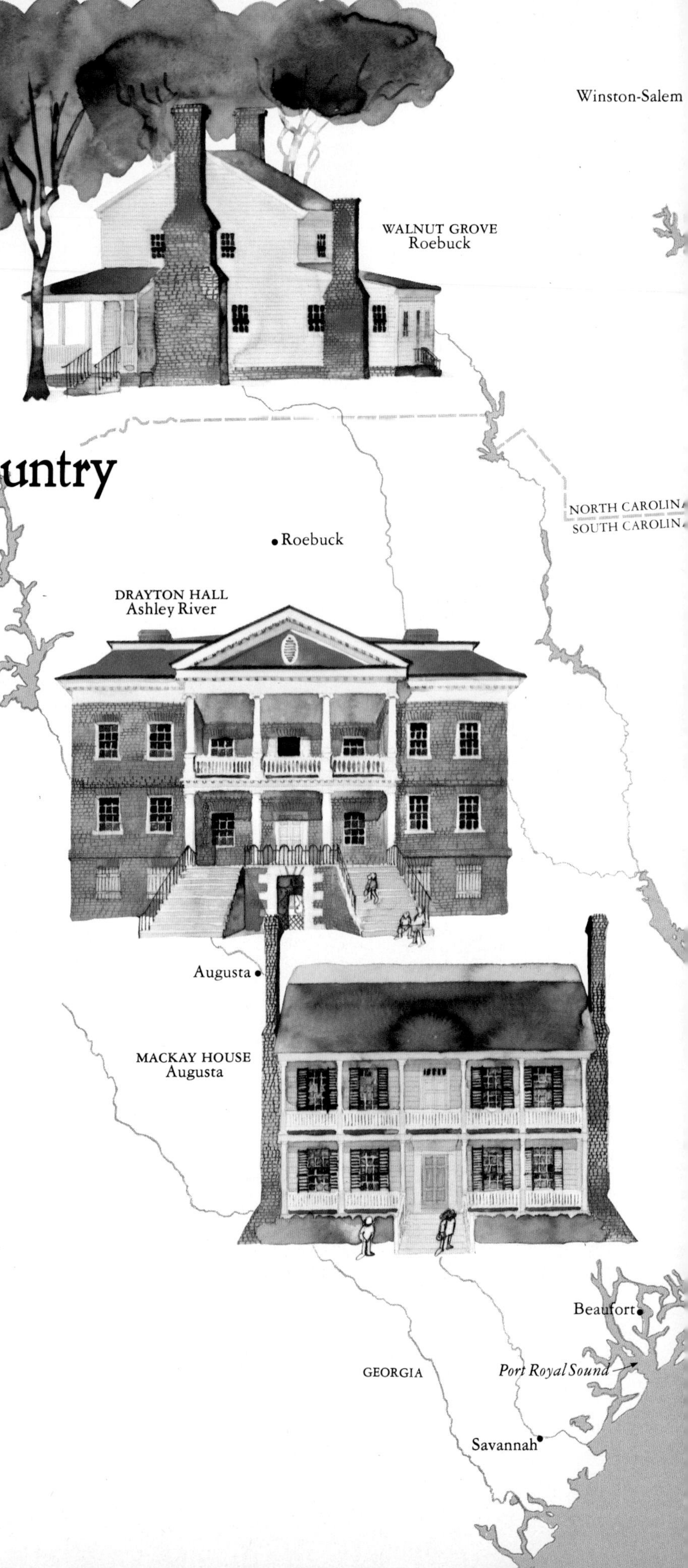

In Beaufort, now a sleepy waterfront town, victims of a violent past—from Indian raids to the Civil War—rest in St. Helena's churchyard. John Verdier, a prosperous merchant, built a house by the river where his own ships loaded indigo—a money crop pioneered in Carolina by a teen-ager, Eliza Lucas, who managed her father's estates.

A few South Carolina plantations open their doors to visitors. Hopsewee, on the Santee, has changed little in some 235 years. At Drayton Hall—an Ashley River manor bypassed by the Yankees in 1865 when they heard it was a smallpox hospital—the gentry sipped Madeira and dined on she-crab soup and yam pudding, their every want supplied by slaves. "These people," wrote a tutor to the Draytons, "were always attended by their negroes to fan them with a peacock's feather." Visitors see original slave cabins at Boone Hall, near Charleston; the manor house was rebuilt in 1935.

North Carolina, too far away to be governed from Charleston, gradually split off. Tryon Palace, the governor's house in New Bern, was said by George Washington to be "hastening to Ruins." Today it mirrors aristocratic colonial life. Memories of revolution cling to the Burgwin-Wright House, occupied by Lord Cornwallis; Walnut Grove in the South Carolina piedmont, home of Kate Barry, a patriot courier; and Augusta's MacKay House, restored as a memorial to 13 patriots hanged by the British.

PAINTINGS BY PAUL HOGARTH

Edenton
Albemarle Sound
NORTH CAROLINA
Raleigh
Bath
New Bern
TRYON PALACE
New Bern
ST. HELENA'S CHURCH
Beaufort
Wilmington
BURGWIN-WRIGHT HOUSE
Wilmington
SOUTH CAROLINA
Georgetown
Santee
HOPSEWEE
Cooper
Ashley River
IDDLETON PLACE
MAGNOLIA GARDENS
DRAYTON HALL
arleston
Mount
Pleasant
HOPSEWEE
Santee River
JOHN MARK VERDIER HOUSE
Beaufort
BOONE HALL
Mount Pleasant

Old Salem

At 8:30 sharp the bells of the Home Moravian Church toll, and the brass band bursts forth with "America." Around the village square, still glistening with morning dew, cluster the men, women, and children of Old Salem. Among them stand a number of visitors, here this Fourth of July for a glimpse of our 18th-century past.

Voices join, crescendoing into a fervent chorus that fills the air with music, song, and an unmistakable spirit of brotherhood.

Spirits of yesteryear abide in the half-timbered houses and tidy shops of this restored Moravian congregation town, nestled in the heart of Winston-Salem, North Carolina. A tribute to the persistent efforts of concerned citizens, the historic old town was rescued from the doom of urban blight in the 1950's. Now private homes, restored by present-day Moravians and others interested in preservation, stand alongside buildings open to the public, making Old Salem a "living restoration."

Guides in colonial dress welcome you to the Wachovia Museum, and show you through such places as the Winkler Bakery and the home of craftsman John Vogler. Cooper, potter, and gunsmith demonstrate the 18th-century intricacies of their crafts. And the music, so ingrained in Moravian life and worship, still stirs a visitor's soul.

Devout Germanic people, Moravians trace their origins to Czech martyr John Hus, burned at the stake in 1415. In 1457, half a century

Festive strains of "Joy to the World" warm the wintry North Carolina night as Old Salem greets the Nativity season. Music has been part of the Moravian tradition here since the 18th century.

ROBERT W. MADDEN, NATIONAL GEOGRAPHIC PHOTOGRAPHER

before Martin Luther, followers of Hus broke away from the Catholic church, declaring a new *Unitas Fratrum* (Unity of Brethren). For some 300 years the sect survived despite persecution. In 1722 a small group escaped from Moravia, a province in today's Czechoslovakia, and took refuge in what is now Germany. From their haven, the "Moravians" began sending missionaries to other parts of the world, even to the wilds of North America.

In Pennsylvania, the Moravian Brethren proved to be such responsible colonists that Lord Granville, a Royal proprietor of Carolina, invited them in the early 1750's to help settle that vast property.

"The land on which we are now encamped seems to me to have been reserved by the Lord for the Brethren [with] countless springs, and numerous fine creeks" and "much beautiful meadow land." Thus recorded Bishop August Gottlieb Spangenberg, leader of the scouting party sent in the winter of 1753 to stake out a site for a new settlement.

Before the year ended, the first pioneers arrived. For more than a decade they worked at transforming the backcountry into productive farmland. That accomplished, they began their central town in 1766. Salem was carefully designed to serve as the hub of a prosperous commercial life, a town of craftsmen and merchants.

Wandering through Old Salem today, you see how well the Brethren succeeded. Clever, finely detailed devices surprise you at every step. A rotisserie whose iron spit was turned by weights and chains. A washing machine with a cylindrical wooden clothes beater cranked by hand. A brick oven, with three deep wells on top that held large cast iron pots which cooked stews and vegetables for 60 people at a time. The Brethren fashioned "rat-tail" cupboard hinges and smooth-working locks and handles for doors. They even imported a coin-operated tobacco dispenser dubbed the "honesty box"—a man was on his honor to take just one pipeful.

Salem homes and shops were among the first in the colonies to boast the new ceramic-tile heating stoves. By combining hollow logs and the law of gravity, the Brethren engineered one of America's earliest systems of piped water. And after fire devastated the first tavern in 1785, Salem imported strange contraptions from Europe: two hand-pumped fire "engines," first of their kind in North Carolina.

The Moravian church served as benevolent overseer of all activities, material as well as spiritual. It owned all the land, leasing lots to individual Brethren.

Important questions, from business propositions to selection of a mate, merited divine intervention through a practice known as the lot. Three hollow reeds were placed in a wooden bowl. One contained a paper marked *"ja,"* the second *"nein."* The third was blank, indicating that the question was premature or needed rephrasing. After deliberation and prayer, one reed was drawn; its message was deemed the Lord's will.

Within the half-timbered Single Brothers House, where young men of Salem once lived communally and plied their trades, you browse

ROBERT W. MADDEN, NATIONAL GEOGRAPHIC PHOTOGRAPHER. OPPOSITE: NICK KELSH

The Home Moravian Church, once focal point of a church-run town, today ministers to spiritual needs of a 2,000-member congregation. Moravians scour headstones in God's Acre in preparation for Easter sunrise service.

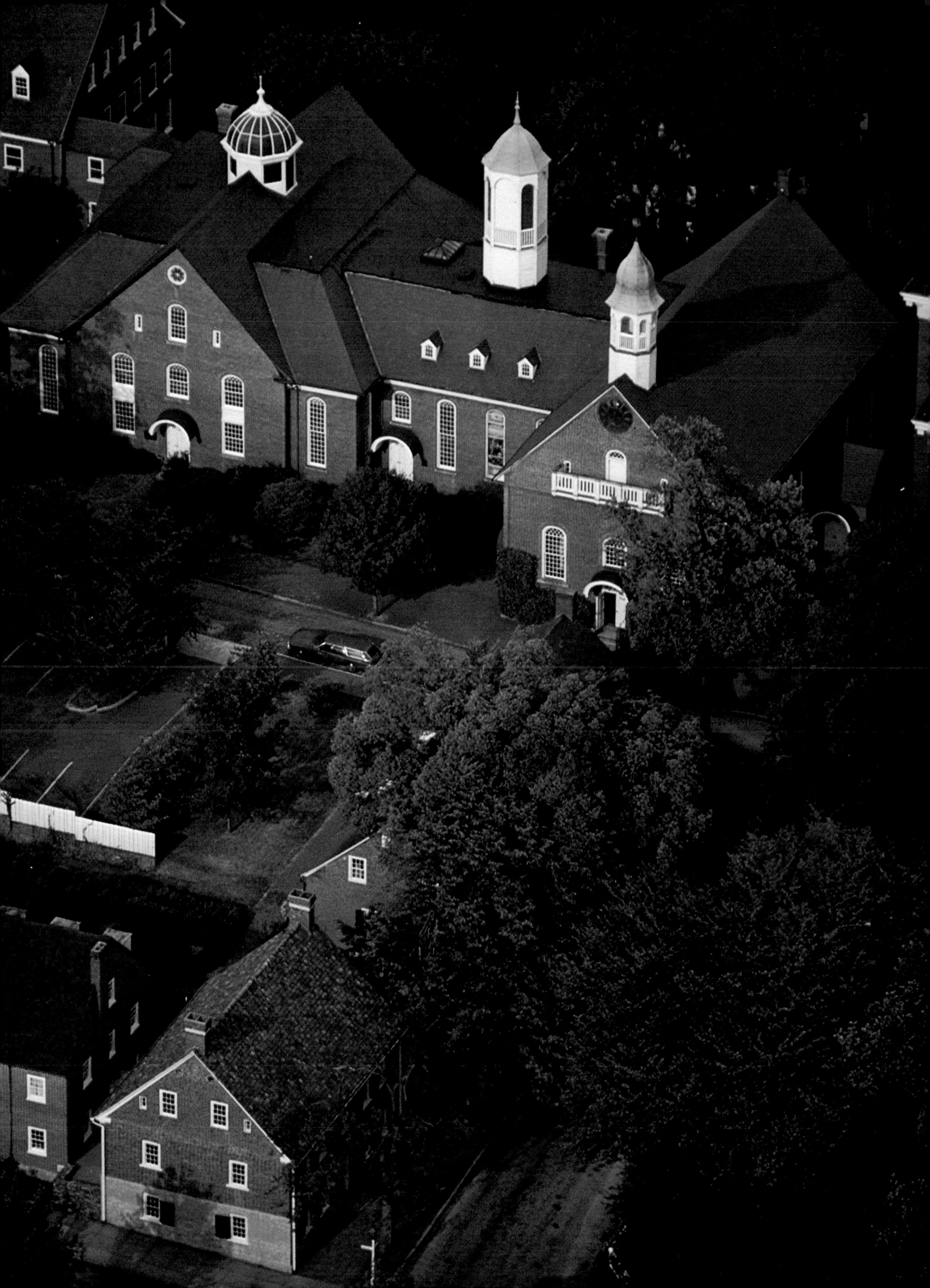

through the restored workshops of craftsmen, just as visitors did in the 1700's. A shoemaker tells you that women had to send foot measurements by messenger, for only men were admitted to the Brothers House. Shoes were polished with lampblack, and waterproofed with pitch and tallow. The same form was used to fit both left and right foot. A tailor invites you to pick up his 20-pound iron. The gunsmith explains that pacifist Moravians made only hunting rifles. A tinsmith shows off unusual cookie molds—a fiddle, hands, a woman's profile.

Church congregation boards set stern guidelines for craftsmen. Only one master per craft was generally permitted, and he was told just what "fair price" to charge for his goods.

Though strict by today's standards, life in early Salem made room for laughter and music. Most Moravians played at least one instrument, for the Brethren celebrated virtually every occasion with song. Strains of Bach and Handel, Mozart and Haydn filled the wilderness air. Formal concerts and choral presentations were regular fare. The six string quintets composed by Minister John Frederick Peter in the 1780's are believed to be America's first chamber music.

Education was held in high regard. Salem boasted excellent schools that drilled classical and practical subjects—and good character as well—into youngsters.

Nor was education limited to boys. Back in the 17th century, Moravian Bishop John Comenius had written: "No reason can be shown why the female sex . . . should be kept from a knowledge of language and wisdom. For they are also human beings, an image of God. . . ." Heeding the bishop's logic, Moravians schooled their daughters soundly in the three "R's" and science, music, and art.

The Miksch Tobacco Shop, built in 1771, is reputed to be the oldest still standing in the nation. The manufactory out back contains reproductions of early tobacco-making implements: a roller by which tobacco leaves were formed into ropes and the press which molded long ropes into coils. Visitors examine an array of 18th-century tobacco products and learn that sales of Matthew Miksch's snuff were boosted by the belief of some that sneezes

German tiles, imported in 1797, roof the Christoph Vogler House. Half-timbered styling marks Old Salem's first dwellings. Townsfolk preserve exterior details of historic homes, adapting interiors to 20th-century needs.

NICK KELSH

With simple tools and time-proven ways, Old Salem's craftsmen carry on a proud legacy. A cobbler drives wooden pegs by the flickering light of a "shoemaker's window"—one candle magnified through four water-filled globes.

Heart-shaped cookies (above) will rise to tasty perfection in the Winkler Bakery's huge oak- and hickory-fed oven. Tantalizing whiffs of fresh-baked Moravian treats have lured customers to its doors since 1800.

Old Salem's dyers dip into nature's palette. To tint flax and wool they simmer roots, flowers, barks, berries, and even insects. A brew of onion skins (below) will yield a sunny yellow.

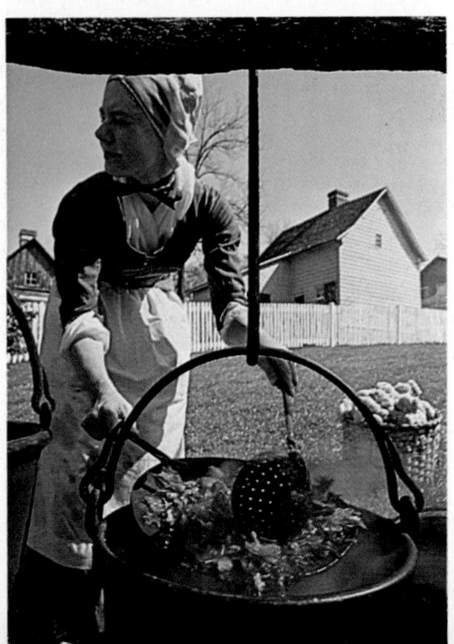

induced by sniffing snuff cleared out a gentleman's head and resulted in better thinking!

Farther down the street stands Salem Tavern, where for the equivalent of about 35 cents in today's currency, an 18th-century traveler could find a bed, a meal, and a warm welcome. This 1784 brick building, now a museum, evokes vivid images of days gone by . . . of boisterous laughter in the public dining room where guests were invited to try their hand at chess, checkers, or dominoes, sanctioned by the church as games of skill . . . of well-to-do merchants closing business deals in the Gentlemen's Room across the hall, enjoying better service for an added cost.

Throughout the common sleeping quarters upstairs, you almost see weary travelers piled two and three in lumpy beds. And in the best Gentleman's Bedroom lingers the ghost of George Washington, who slept here during a 1791 state visit.

In the cheerful, yellow-frame annex, built in 1816 to house overflow customers, young people in colonial dress still dish up hospitality. In a convivial din, by tin-lantern candlelight, diners savor the hearty pumpkin soup and hefty cuts of fish, fowl, and meat that won the tavern its earlier fame.

Perhaps the Moravian love feast best sums up the spirit of Old Salem. Its outward signs are simple—a sweet bun and mug of steaming coffee. Brethren gather for this traditional service in the Home Moravian Church, pray together, and sing the glory of their Lord, then share the symbolic "meal" as a sign of their continued unity.

The church relinquished economic control of Old Salem in the mid-19th century. But its spiritual influence remains strong, and the rich culture it shaped endures.

MAUREEN PALMEDO

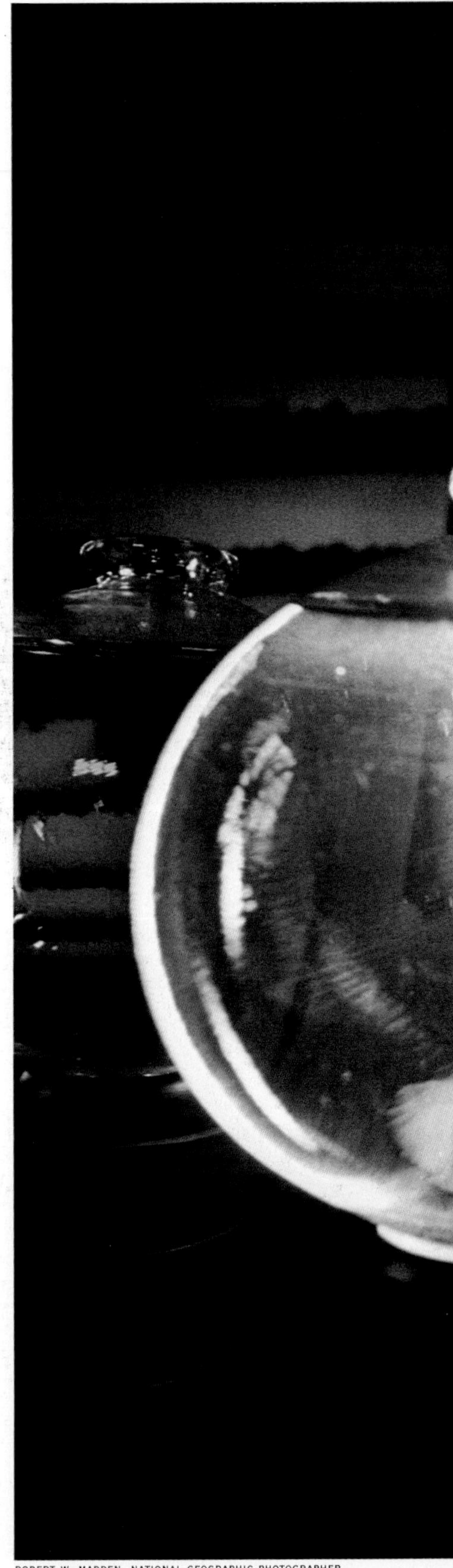

ROBERT W. MADDEN, NATIONAL GEOGRAPHIC PHOTOGRAPHER

In Pursuit of Liberty

The rift began as an argument between England and her disenchanted colonies about political rights, grew into a battle over liberty and power, and ended in a people's war for national liberation—the American Revolution. In a six-year struggle for independence, an "experiment in democracy" was born.

JAMES MORTON SMITH

For seven years Britain and France fought for possession of North America. Britain won and in February 1763 signed the Treaty of Paris, ending the French and Indian War. But Britain faced a new problem. Land-hungry colonists moved across the Alleghenies in growing numbers. The Indians resisted. Land frauds stirred unrest. In October King George III signed the Proclamation of 1763, strictly limiting westward migration and Indian trade.

The British stationed troops along the Proclamation Line and, to help defray the expense, Parliament for the first time levied direct taxes on the colonies—the Sugar Act in 1764 and the Stamp Act in 1765.

Outrage flared immediately. The colonists, angered by the Proclamation itself, were almost unanimous in refusing to pay the taxes. A young member of the Virginia House of Burgesses, George Washington, expressed the view of many when he wrote that Parliament "hath no more right to put their hands into my pockets without my consent, than I have to put my hands into yours for money."

Fellow burgess Patrick Henry warned the king: "Tarquin and Caesar had each his Brutus, Charles the First his Cromwell, and George the Third..."

"Treason!" cried the Speaker.

"...may profit by their example. If this be treason, make the most of it."

James Otis of the Massachusetts assembly said that Parliament's action "set people a-thinking, in six months, more than they had done in their whole lives before." But reaction was not limited to thought and words. Sons of Liberty rioted; burning and looting, they hanged the crown's tax agents in effigy. In Boston they forced Andrew Oliver to make a "public Resignation" under the Liberty Tree where his stuffed image had swung from a rope. The New York *Gazette* envisioned the country "utterly crushed by the cruel rod of power."

Taking the first step toward union, delegates from nine colonies convened in New York in October 1765. Dubbed the Stamp Act Congress, they said taxation with representation was "essential to the Freedom of a People, and the undoubted right of Englishmen." But the colonists were not represented in the House of Commons. Thus, the Stamp Act had "a manifest Tendency to subvert... Rights and Liberties" and should be repealed.

British merchants petitioned the government for relief when Americans refused to buy their goods. In Parliament William Pitt, reminding his peers that "Americans are the sons, not the bastards of England," demanded "that the Stamp Act be REPEALED ABSOLUTELY, TOTALLY, and IMMEDIATELY." It was, only to be replaced by the Declaratory Act, which asserted that Parliament had "full power and authority to make laws...to bind the colonies and the people of America in all cases whatsoever."

In 1767 Parliament exercised that power. It levied

HOUDON BUST OF GEORGE WASHINGTON, MOUNT VERNON LADIES ASSOCIATION; DETAIL OF A PAINTING OF THE BATTLE OF PRINCETON BY JOHN TRUMBULL, YALE UNIVERSITY ART GALLERY; PHOTOMONTAGE BY JAMES L. STANFIELD, NATIONAL GEOGRAPHIC PHOTOGRAPHER

shipping duties on glass, paint, lead, paper, and tea. The switch from internal stamp taxes to import taxes triggered new protests, and the colonies resorted to nonimportation of British goods.

The burden of quartering British troops increased tension. In New York "Liberty Boys" brawled in the streets with Gen. Thomas Gage's redcoats. In Boston violence flared on the wharf. Merchant John Hancock prevented customs commissioners from inspecting his ship *Liberty,* laden with taxable wines. General Gage was outraged. "Quash this Spirit at a Blow," he urged.

British warships entered Boston Harbor in late September 1768. On October 1, George III's troops, "Drums beating, Fifes playing and Colours flying," paraded up King Street. Denied housing, they camped on the Common and in public buildings until General Gage arrived and demanded permanent quarters. The Boston town meeting came to regard the standing army in their midst as a threat to their "Liberties, Privileges, and Immunities." The presence of British soldiers, observed patriot writer Mercy Otis Warren, "introduces a revolution in manners, corrupts the morals, propagates... vice, and degrades the human character."

Pent-up animosity erupted on March 5, 1770. A mob of dockside toughs, shouting insults and hurling snowballs, goaded soldiers into firing. When the smoke cleared, five Americans lay dead or dying.

On the same day as the so-called Boston Massacre, Lord North, the new prime minister, proposed repeal of the import duties. However, the tax on tea would be retained as a "peppercorn" to symbolize Parliament's authority over the colonies.

A mood of reconciliation, coupled with three years of prosperity, followed repeal. But in 1773 the colonists were again compelled to resist imperial taxation. In May Parliament passed the Tea Act to rescue the East India Company from financial disaster. The act eliminated English export duties, thus making the East Indian tea cheaper than smuggled Dutch tea. But the import tax was retained. Americans regarded the act as a bribe. The tea was cheap, but in buying it they would be acknowledging the right of Parliament to levy the tax.

From Charleston to Boston, tea agents were forced to resign by threats and harassment. Captains of tea ships were persuaded to return to London with the cargo still below decks. And in Boston a band of men "cloath'd in Blankets with heads muffled, and copper color'd countenances" dumped chests of tea into the harbor.

The Boston Tea Party electrified John Adams: "This Destruction of the Tea is so bold, so daring, so firm, intrepid and inflexible, and it must have... important Consequences...." They were not long in coming. Lord North persuaded Parliament to adopt a policy to isolate Boston and subdue Massachusetts. The Intolerable Acts closed Boston to shipping until the town paid for the tea, moved the capital to Salem, and abolished the elected council. Town meetings—"hotbeds of seditions," George III labeled them—were forbidden, except during the annual election of town officials.

The effect of the repressive legislation was to unite the colonies as never before. In September 1774 the First Continental Congress convened in Philadelphia and resolved that Parliament, rather than having all power in all cases whatsoever, had no power. Although the delegates pledged allegiance to the king, they predicted that if Great Britain should attempt to execute the Intolerable Acts by force in Massachusetts, "all America ought to support [the New Englanders] in their opposition."

George III declared that "the die is now cast, the colonists must submit or triumph." Since New England was in a state of rebellion, "blows must decide whether they are to be subject to this Country or independent." Gage, instructed to take a "more active and determined part," should arrest the "principal actors" in the Massachusetts provincial congress, even if it precipitated hostilities. "It will surely be better," Lord Dartmouth wrote from England, "that the conflict should be brought on upon such ground than in a riper state of Rebellion."

Beaver II, *replica of one of three tea-party ships, heads for a permanent berth in Boston Harbor. Patriot protest began in 1765, when Parliament taxed the colonies by requiring a stamp (above) on newspapers, licenses, even playing cards.*

GEORGE F. MOBLEY, NATIONAL GEOGRAPHIC PHOTOGRAPHER
ABOVE: MASSACHUSETTS HISTORICAL SOCIETY

Boston to Bunker Hill

Snow paved the streets and chilled the night on March 5, 1770, but the heart of Boston burned with hate and fear. In King Street, just down from the Town House, a howling, cudgel-wielding mob 300 to 400 strong, triggered by some forgotten insult, shoved against a corporal's guard of eight redcoats.

Soldiers and civilians had clashed before. The 600 redcoats sent to keep the peace in Boston could neither find it nor keep it. Convenient targets of abuse by radical Sons of Liberty, the soldiers endured a fragile co-existence with 16,000 citizens backed up by 30,000 farmers and minutemen in the countryside —"Yankee doodles," clowns, the British called them.

This bitter Monday night particular mischief was afoot. Church bells tolled, gangs of youths charged through narrow lanes banging brickbats against houses, and men cried "Fire!" when there was no fire.

Now, in King Street, 6-foot Crispus Attucks, part Indian, part Negro, pushed with club in hand to the front of the mob. A hurled stick knocked one soldier down. He came up firing. A volley followed. Rowdies and bystanders alike went down; Attucks took two musket balls in the chest. The angry crowd melted away, carrying the dead and dying, leaving bloodstains in the snow.

The Boston "massacre" was over. Some regarded it only as another street brawl in a tar-tough port town where fights between North End and South End gangs had become ritualized. John Adams, a lawyer and a future President of the United States, even won acquittal for five of the soldiers. But the incident lit a fuse that would sputter to Lexington, Concord, and Bunker Hill.

Today the Freedom Trail, marked by a red strip on the sidewalk, zigzags through downtown Boston past sites that reveal the temper of the times. The sites help explain why the Revolutionary War began in and around Boston, where, fumed the British, even the "pulpits were converted into Gutters of Sedition."

Men in blue, not red, are now the symbols of authority, but Boston's finest come armed with a whimsical sense of humor. Wandering outside the Town House, now the Old State House, I asked a patrolman to point out the massacre site. He motioned to a ring of cobblestones in the street. Then he noticed my camera and said with a grin, "Lay down over there. I'll take your picture."

The centuries have a way of leavening tragedy. Yet I knew, looking up at the Old State House, that for the patriots who stoked the fires of rebellion, freedom was serious business. There, in 1761, razor-tongued James Otis, legal counsel for Boston merchants, argued against writs of assistance, special warrants that permitted Royal customs officials to search, without obvious cause, "any Vaults, Cellars, Warehouses, shops or other Places" for taxable goods. Protection against "unreasonable searches and seizures" would later be written into the Bill of Rights.

John Adams, present during the plea, recalled that Otis cried, "Taxation without representation is tyranny!"—an argument that did not bear directly on the issue. Yet for Adams, American independence "was then and there born."

North on Congress Street beside Faneuil Hall, that bastion of the tumultuous town meeting, stands Sam Adams in bronze. Unkempt, watery-eyed, shaking with palsy,

The midnight ride of Paul Revere never ends for the bronze hero in Boston's Revere Mall. From the top of Old North Church behind him, lanterns signaled the British route to Lexington and Concord. Copies hang from the steeple on Patriots' Day in April; the Antiquarian Museum in Concord preserves one of the originals (below). Near the church stands the Paul Revere House (above), which the artisan owned from 1770 until 1800. He fathered 16 children, 8 by each of two wives.

IRA BLOCK

Arnold: "There wa'n't no waste timber in him." On October 17, Burgoyne surrendered.

A visitor to Saratoga National Historical Park can stand on Bemis Heights, overlooking the Hudson, and imagine Burgoyne's dilemma. There, Americans, behind breastworks laid out by Polish volunteer Thaddeus Kościuszko, commanded the floodplain and the river. Scene of the Revolution's turning point, Saratoga paved the way for France's entry into the war in 1778; it also changed British thinking. General Clinton, Howe's successor, was to evacuate Philadelphia and return to New York. Washington dogged him across New Jersey and fought him to a draw at Monmouth Courthouse.

While armies maneuvered in the East, men in buckskin armed with butcher knives pushed west. Led by George Rogers Clark, a captain of Virginia militia, the "Big Knives" seized the British post of Kaskaskia on the Mississippi. In 1779 they slogged through "Drownded Cuntrey in the Debth of Wintor" and attacked the stockade at Vincennes. The British surrendered.

Looking south for loyalist support, the British swept through Georgia and in May 1780 took Charleston, South Carolina. Cornwallis moved confidently into North Carolina, but the campaign was costly. At Kings Mountain a band of "over mountain men" armed with hunting rifles defeated the hated loyalists. At Cowpens, South Carolina, in January 1781, Gen. Dan Morgan whipped a larger British force led by Col. Banastre Tarleton. Cornwallis won at Guilford Courthouse, North Carolina, but not without a struggle. Gen. Nathanael Greene reported, "We fight, get beat, rise, and fight again." These three battlefields are now national parks.

Battered and crippled, Cornwallis marched north into Virginia. At Yorktown he built fortifications and waited for Clinton to send reinforcements. Clinton sent a message instead: "It would seem that Mr. Washington is moving an army to the southward [and] expects... a considerable French armament." Clinton's information was accurate.

In August of 1781 French Admiral de Grasse's fleet sailed into Chesapeake Bay, bringing 3,000 soldiers and cutting off aid to Cornwallis. Washington and Comte de Rochambeau besieged Yorktown, pounding the British around the clock. Cannonballs embedded in walls, like those of the Nelson House, bear witness today of the awesome bombardment.

On October 17, Cornwallis called for "a cessation of hostilities" and proposed that emissaries from both sides "meet at Mr. Moore's house, to settle terms for the surrender...." There in the battered frame dwelling, now handsomely restored, negotiators hammered out terms. At British Redoubt No. 10, taken by 400 Americans in a savage bayonet attack led by Col. Alexander Hamilton—and since occupied by legions of visitors—Washington signed the articles. He added a line: "Done in the trenches before York Town in Virginia Oct 19, 1781." At 2 p.m. the British marched out and grounded arms while their band played "The World Turned Upside Down." Sightseers retrace their steps along Surrender Road, surveying rebuilt earthworks.

When Lord North heard the news from Yorktown, he gasped: "Oh God! It is all over." But for America, it was the dawning of a new age.

Weaponry of war—a French mortar and an armed redoubt—helped turn the Yorktown battlefield into a grim trap for Cornwallis, who lost 552 men to furious patriot onslaughts and the "aweful music" of bombardment. Defeated British soldiers wept with "unfeigned sorrow." Cornwallis sent his sword to the surrender ceremonies but did not attend.

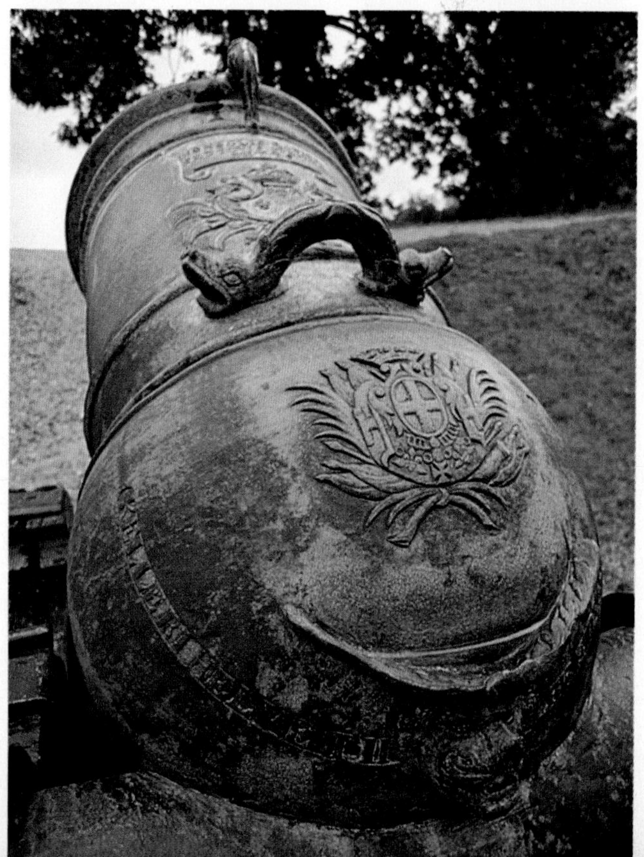

FARRELL GREHAN

Room of the State House in Philadelphia: "Resolved, that these United Colonies are, and of right ought to be, free and independent States, that they are absolved from all allegiance to the British Crown, and that all political connection between them and the State of Great Britain is . . . totally dissolved."

Thomas Jefferson, listening while others debated, noted that "the question was not whether, by a declaration of independence, we should make ourselves what we are not; but whether we should declare a fact which already exists." Within a month he laid before the delegates an 1,800-word draft, which they trimmed. On July 4, 1776, the chairman announced "that the committee of the whole Congress have agreed to a Declaration," which he then read.

On July 9, General Washington, who had moved his headquarters to New York City, had the Declaration of Independence read before the assembled army. He emphasized to "every officer and soldier . . . that now the peace and safety of our country depend, under God, solely on the success of our arms." Washington paid dearly to defend New York, "the place that we must keep from the British." His green militia melted before General Howe's Hessians and Highlanders slashing across Long Island. Washington's soldiers huddled in boats and crossed to Manhattan. Howe pursued at Kip's Bay, panicking militia who, Washington moaned, "ran away without firing a shot." But at Harlem Heights they held their ground.

Thanks to "Providence, or some good . . . fellow," Washington regrouped while a fire gutted New York City. Smelling arson, the British were furious. Their rage may account for the summary execution of Nathan Hale, caught spying on Long Island. Declared the condemned patriot: "I only regret that I have but one life to lose for my country."

Hitting and running, Washington fell back to White Plains, retreated across New Jersey, and crossed the Delaware into Pennsylvania. Congress abandoned Philadelphia and fled to Baltimore. "The Heart of the Rebellion is now nearly broken," wrote a British officer. Washington himself thought "the game will be pretty well up" without more men.

Having written Congress that "desperate diseases require desperate remedies," Washington recrossed the stormy Delaware on Christmas night, launched a surprise raid on the British force at Trenton, and captured 900 Hessians without the loss of a man. When Washington crossed into New Jersey again, Cornwallis boasted that he would "bag the fox" by bottling up the American army. But Washington outsmarted him, stealing a night march around his flank to attack Princeton. Buoyed by victory, he headed for winter quarters in Morristown. In March Congress reconvened in Philadelphia. Six months later the members would again be forced to leave—for Lancaster, then York—but first they would welcome volunteers recruited in France. Among them was the 19-year-old Marquis de Lafayette.

British strategy in 1777 called for General Burgoyne to lead an invasion from Canada to Albany, General Howe to campaign against Philadelphia, and General Clinton to hold New York.

In September, Washington, moving south to block Howe's advance, clashed with the British at Chadds Ford on Brandywine Creek. Young Lafayette, rallying troops, was wounded by a musket ball. Outflanked by Cornwallis, Washington withdrew to Chester. His attack on Germantown foundered in thick fog. He led his whipped army, "barefoot and otherwise naked," toward a wooded ridge misnamed Valley Forge. There, in raw winter, former Prussian officer Friedrich von Steuben drilled discipline into demoralized troops. None was more dispirited than Albigence Waldo of Connecticut. One entry in his diary: "It snows—I'm sick—eat nothing—no whiskey—no forage—Lord—Lord—Lord."

Burgoyne's invasion from Canada went smoothly at first. Fort Ticonderoga fell easily. But Col. Barry St. Leger's drive from the west sputtered, and German troops foraging near Bennington ran afoul of Gen. John Stark's brigade of farmers. "We'll beat them before night," he promised, "or Molly Stark will be a widow." Twice Burgoyne tried to break past entrenched Americans at Saratoga; twice General Arnold, with Dan Morgan's Virginia riflemen, stopped him cold. Said an admiring soldier of

"Now is the seedtime of continental union. . . ." Thomas Paine's stirring pamphlet Common Sense, *published in January 1776, convinced thousands that reconciliation with Britain was impossible, independence inevitable. Paine's cottage at New Rochelle, New York, displays copies of the tract.*

GEORGE F. MOBLEY, NATIONAL GEOGRAPHIC PHOTOGRAPHER

COMMON SENSE;
INHABITANTS
OF
COMMON
SENSE

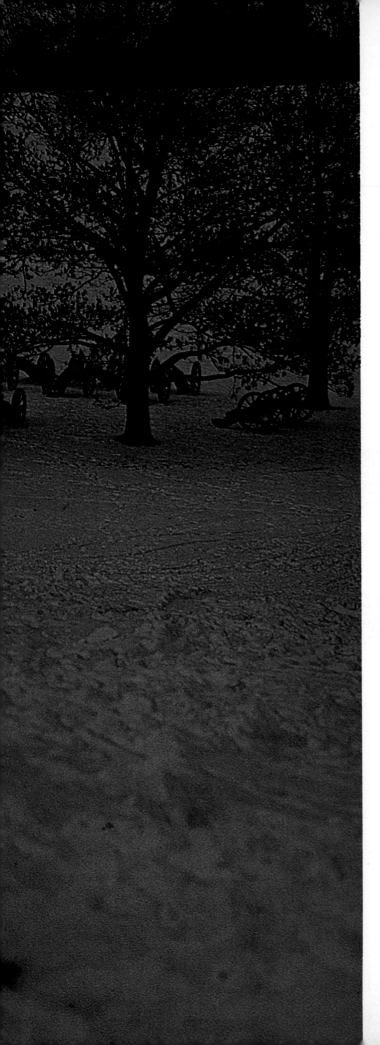

British stronghold and its artillery "in the name of the Great Jehovah and the Continental Congress."

On that day of triumph, the Second Continental Congress assembled at the State House in Philadelphia. The Congress resolved that "these colonies be immediately put into a state of defense" and on June 15 unanimously elected 43-year-old George Washington "to command all the continental forces . . . for the defense of American Liberty."

General Washington took charge of the Continental army outside Boston on July 3. Abigail Adams observed that "the gentleman and the soldier look agreeably blended in him." Although short of men, muskets, and almost everything else an army required, by autumn Washington could write that "we mend everyday, and I flatter myself that in a little time, we shall work up these raw materials into good stuff." He sent Henry Knox after the heavy ordnance captured at Fort Ticonderoga. Knox dismantled the cannons, floated them across Lake George, then dragged them on sleds 300 miles over ice and snow. With "this noble train of artillery," Washington seized Dorchester Heights, forcing Howe to withdraw from Boston.

The contagion of war had spread north and south by the spring of 1776. From Fort Ticonderoga, Gen. Richard Montgomery moved up Lake Champlain to capture Montreal. He was killed attacking Quebec. American forces laid siege to the town until British reinforcements arrived to force a retreat. Benedict Arnold, wounded in the leg, wanted to quit the Canadian diversion "and Secure our own Country before it is too late."

Seeking a foothold in the South, the British navy aimed a thrust at Charleston. But Col. William Moultrie's garrison on Sullivan's Island stood firm. A "Smart Cannonade . . . return'd with Coolness and deliberation" drove the ships off.

While guns boomed in Charleston Harbor, the words of Richard Henry Lee shook the Assembly

Fire of freedom burned low in the hearts of 10,000 men camped at Valley Forge in the winter of 1777-78. Each soldier celebrated Thanksgiving with "half a gill of rice and a tablespoonful of vinegar." Today a national park honors the 3,000 patriots who died here of disease and privation.

NATHAN BENN

Gage dispatched a large force to seize military supplies at Concord, 20 miles west of Boston. Such "principal actors" as Sam Adams and John Hancock might be taken also. It was a fateful move, one that stirred armed insurrection on April 19, 1775: token defiance by a small band of militiamen at Lexington, massive resistance by colonials at Concord, a gauntlet of enraged farmers along the road back who converted a British retreat into a rout.

After Lexington and Concord, citizen soldiers poured in; nearly 15,000 bottled up the British in Boston. When British reinforcements arrived—including Generals Burgoyne, Clinton, and William Howe—the stage was set for bloody prelude to all-out war, the Battle of Bunker Hill.

The battle would take its name from where the colonials camped, not from nearby Breed's Hill, where most of the fighting took place. There, on June 17, British troops suffered nearly 50 percent casualties before overrunning the entrenched Americans. Howe, who would soon succeed Gage as commander in chief, confessed that "the success is too dearly bought." Another such victory, reflected Clinton, "would have ruined us."

Adding insult to injury was news of the daring predawn raid on Fort Ticonderoga, New York, now restored as a museum for besieging visitors. They relive those tense moments of May 10, 1775, when Ethan Allen and his Green Mountain Boys, aided by Benedict Arnold's militia company, captured the

Founded in 1802, the United States Military Academy at West Point surveys the Hudson River. Patriots built fortifications on the strategic heights and stretched a great chain, each link weighing 100 pounds, across the river, blocking British warships. A few links are preserved at the academy.

ROBERT W. MADDEN, NATIONAL GEOGRAPHIC PHOTOGRAPHER

Samuel Adams seemed an unlikely fomenter of revolution. But he was, in fact, a superb politician and manipulator of men. The real ruler of Boston, he controlled the Sons of Liberty, who controlled the mob, which controlled the town. Because it was rumored—falsely—that native-born Massachusetts Chief Justice Thomas Hutchinson favored the Stamp Act, the mob in 1765 sacked his brick mansion, even "open'd his Beds and let all the Feathers out" and "cut the Balcony off the Top of his House." The damage came to more than 2,000 pounds.

At the Old South Meeting House, to which assemblies often adjourned when they overflowed Faneuil Hall, Sam Adams made the Royal lion roar. On the night of December 16, 1773, with the church filled with patriots determined to act against Parliament's tax on tea, he gave the signal for the Boston Tea Party. Disguised as Indians, 150 Sons of Liberty raced to the wharf, swarmed over three ships, and dumped their chests of tea into the harbor.

A replica of one ship, the brig *Beaver II,* lies moored at the Congress Street Bridge. For a fee, you can relive history by tossing a tethered case over the side.

Old South Meeting House, restored to its colonial crispness, bears unseen scars of that brutal time. In 1775, redcoats besieged in Boston ripped out the pulpit and pews, hauled in dirt for the floor, put up a jumping bar for horses, and turned the nave into a riding school for the Queen's Light Dragoons.

Cross under the Fitzgerald Expressway to the Italian North End. Historically, one area belongs to that famous son of a Huguenot immigrant, Paul Revere, silversmith, engraver, and dispatch rider for the Committee of Correspondence. In the Paul Revere House, little remains of his possessions—a bedpost, a

Bunting-draped Faneuil Hall dwarfs the figure of firebrand Sam Adams, whose eloquent orations inside helped make it the "Cradle of Liberty." At town meetings the former tax collector swayed patriots against Royal taxes. In 1805 architect Charles Bulfinch raised the roof by adding a third story. Nearby, the Old State House (above) witnessed the "Boston Massacre" in 1770 when redcoats fired into a heckling mob. Engraved by Paul Revere, the scene fueled patriot fury.

AMERICAN ANTIQUARIAN SOCIETY (ABOVE) AND IRA BLOCK

brace of pistols, an iron stake to which he tied his cow on the Common. Yet it was from this house in 1775 that he left to make the ride immortalized in Longfellow's poem.

Who doesn't know that Revere, "booted and spurred," spread "his cry of alarm to every Middlesex village and farm" that the British were coming? But here you learn that when he was rowed across the Charles River to Charlestown the oars were muffled by a petticoat "yet warm from the body of a fair daughter of Liberty," and that he borrowed a horse from Deacon Larkin, who never got it back—a British patrol "commandeered" it when Revere was captured near Concord.

Before he left Boston, Revere arranged for signals to reveal the supposedly secret British route in their raid of patriot military stores in Concord. Lanterns would be hung from the steeple of Old North Church, "one, if by land" (across Boston Neck), "two, if by sea" (by boat across the Back Bay).

Patriots and loyalists worshiped side by side in Old North Church. Radical Robert Newman, who hung the lanterns, and British General Gage owned box pews on the same aisle. Look for the chancel niche that holds a bust of George Washington. It was once a window. After hanging the lanterns, legend says, Newman slipped out that window to avoid redcoats in the streets. Then he had to steal back through his bedroom window because redcoats were quartered in his house.

Basement crypts in Old North Church hold 1,000 bodies, including that of Maj. John Pitcairn. One of the

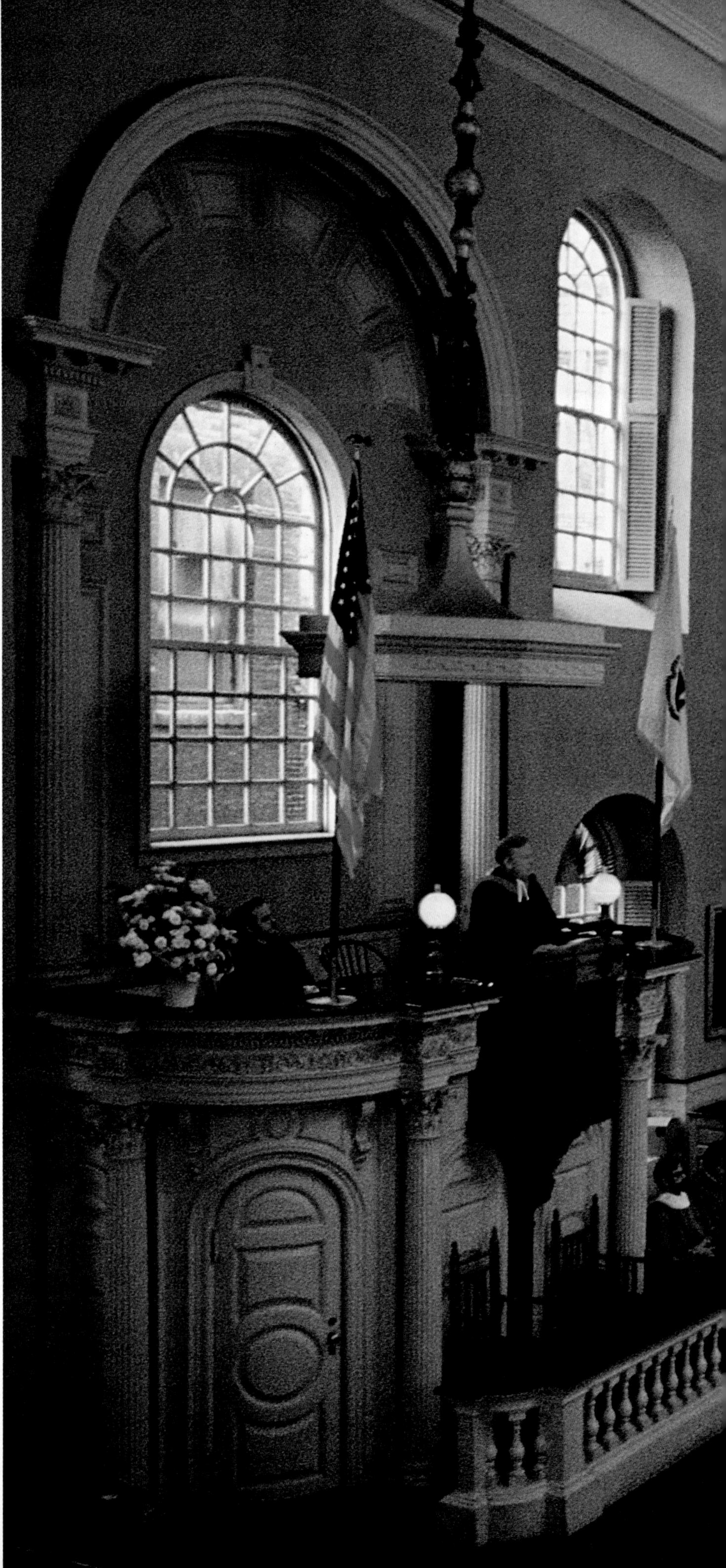

Boston's Old South Meeting House echoes to the annual Forefathers Day service. From this church Sam Adams launched the patriot raid that mixed a mighty brew—the Boston Tea Party.

GEORGE F. MOBLEY, NATIONAL GEOGRAPHIC PHOTOGRAPHER

EXIT

officers who led the redcoats to Lexington, he survived the bloody retreat from Concord, only to fall at Bunker Hill. Years later, it is said, Westminster Abbey requested his remains. But the wrong body was sent; Pitcairn still rests in Boston.

Lexington—six miles east of Concord and first crucible of war. There a small group of armed colonials, foolishly brave, dared to defy His Majesty's military might. To capture the mood of that historic dawn, get there any cool misty morning with a scarlet sun backlighting the trees around the village green. But aim for Patriots' Day, the Monday nearest April 19. Then pomp and tragedy are re-enacted, militiamen and redcoats re-incarnated—some by descendants of Lexingtonians and British regulars.

In 1775 it was 5 a.m. when the British column of 700 men swung into view. Capt. John Parker and some 70 colonials, alerted first at midnight by Revere, reassembled in two ranks across the green. Parker's apocryphal words to his citizen-soldiers are etched on a stone at the spot: "Stand your ground. Don't fire unless fired upon. But if they mean to have a war let it begin here." Pitcairn, at the head of the troops, shouted, "Lay down your arms, you damned rebels, and disperse!"

Parker ordered his men to march away. Then a shot rang out, and the roar of a British volley. Redcoats charged with bayonets. The rebels withered. Some fell, others fled, some stood and fought. But it was all over in minutes. The British reformed and tootled off toward Concord, leaving eight Americans dead.

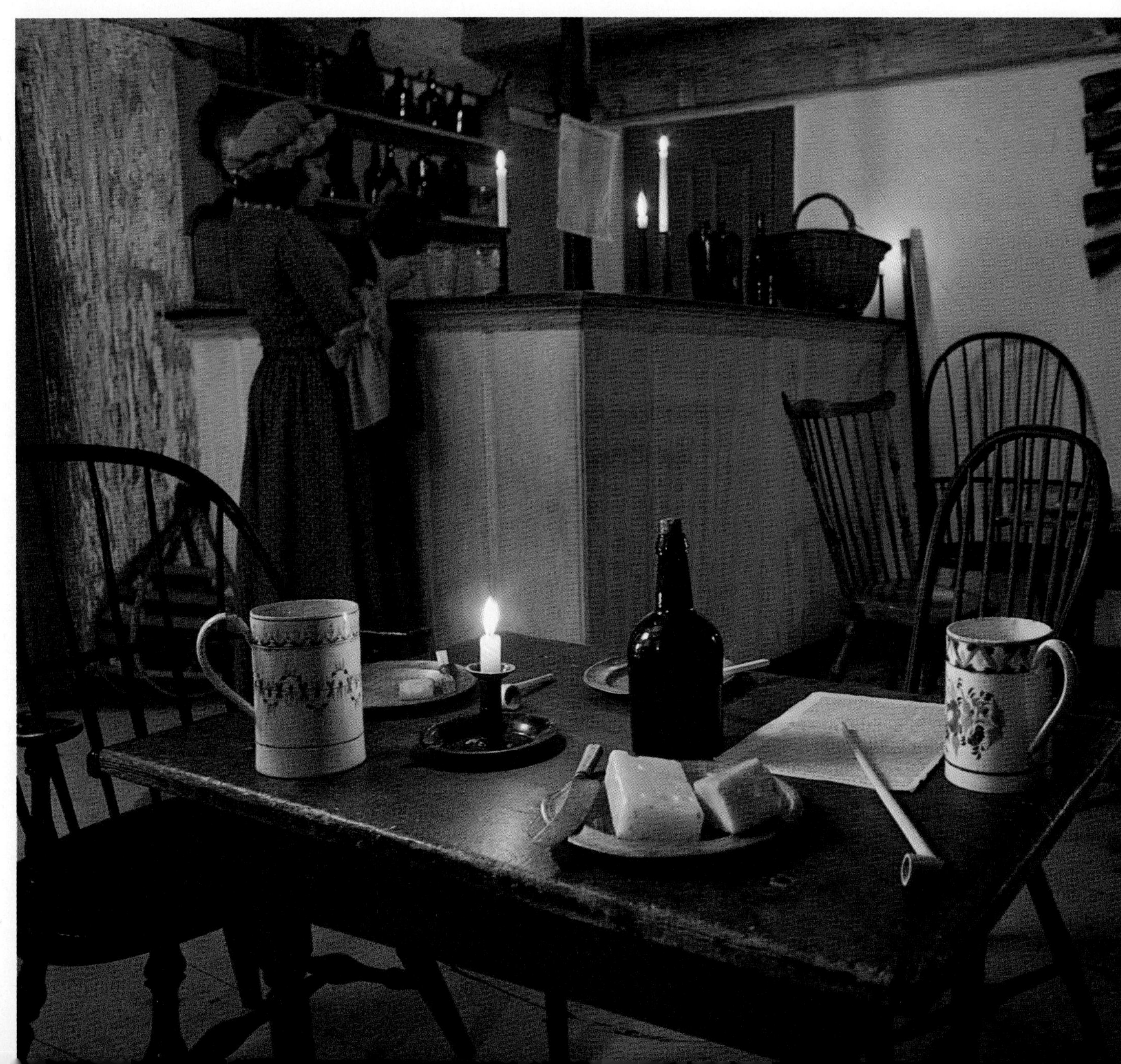

Lexington green looks different today. The meetinghouse that stood where the road forks to Bedford is gone. But Buckman Tavern stands unchanged beside the green. Here in the early morning hours anxious colonials waited in the taproom, some lifting their last tankard of rum. Chat with the guides; you may find a living link with that day, as I did in a young man whose surgeon forebear bound up the wounded.

Walk across the green, past the monument where the slain militiamen lie in a common grave, to the Harrington House. Jonathan Harrington, Jr., who was mortally wounded, crawled to this house and died in the doorway at his wife's feet.

Down the Bedford Road the Hancock-Clarke House harbored fugitives Sam Adams and John Hancock, a wealthy patriot. Both would soon leave for Philadelphia as delegates to the Second Continental Congress.

At the east end of town, Munroe Tavern (Lexington boasted five in 1775) served as a command post for Lord Percy, whose relief column saved the British expedition from

Taproom of Lexington's Buckman Tavern warmed heads and hearts in the chilly dawn of the Revolutionary War. From the tavern (below) militiamen assembled on the green (lower right); a boulder marks the line where they confronted a British column on its way to destroy arms in Concord. One of the Americans was farmer Amos Locke, whose musket hangs third down in the taproom between bayoneted British guns. Visitors can examine a bullet hole in the front door and an upstairs room where Revere watched the action.

IRA BLOCK

annihilation on the retreat from Concord. Here patriot John Raymond, a cripple pressed into service as a bartender, tried to duck out a back door. The redcoats shot him dead.

Patriots' Day pageantry continues at Concord. Banners fluttering, drums rattling, uniformed militia companies from Acton, Lincoln, Bedford, and a dozen other villages converge on North Bridge outside of town, just as they did two centuries ago. Here the Americans, mustering 400 men, held firm and drove the British back, away from the bridge. Redcoats found 500 pounds of musket balls, though, and dumped them in the town pond, now only a memory under the Concord business district.

From Wright's Tavern, still on the square, Major Pitcairn may have unwittingly called down disaster on the entire British force. Stirring an injured finger in a glass of brandy, he boasted that "he hoped to stir the Yankee blood" the same way before the night was out. He did.

From behind trees and fences, from inside houses that still line the route, enraged colonials fired into the bewildered column all the way back to Lexington, leaving Battle Road (Route 2A) strewn with bodies. The slaughter continued to Charlestown, costing the British some 240 dead and wounded.

"I never believed," confessed Lord Percy speaking of the colonials, "that they would have attacked the King's troops, or have had the perseverance I found in them."

In March 1775 Patrick Henry of Virginia had sent a thrill through patriot hearts when he declaimed in Richmond's St. John's Church, "I know not what course others may take, but as for me, give me liberty or give me death!"

At Lexington and Concord, men of Massachusetts backed those words with their lives. Two months later, as minutemen from all over New England mustered at Bunker Hill on the Charlestown Peninsula,

The "Minuteman" by Daniel Chester French guards Concord Bridge. Here, in Emerson's "Concord Hymn," the "shot heard round the world" was fired. His grandfather, William Emerson, watched from the Old Manse nearby.

FARRELL GREHAN

All Americans now, rebels and redcoats recall the drama of Bunker Hill in Charlestown each year. The 220-foot obelisk stands on what is left of Breed's pasture. From inside an earthen redoubt on this spot, Americans twice blunted massed assaults by the king's best troops before running out of powder. Old "Charles Town" hid colonial snipers, so the British burned it.

the sacrifices mounted. On the night of June 16, Americans dug in at Breed's Hill, a lower slope, and awaited a frontal attack by 2,500 of the king's "invincibles." Outgunned and outnumbered, the colonials inflicted a thousand casualties before quitting the hill. They proved that "Yankee doodles" could fight in the prescribed military manner of the day. It might be a long war.

Today the Battle of Bunker Hill is commemorated on Breed's Hill, which still commands a view of Boston across the tops of houses that surround the soaring Bunker Hill Monument. Some 290 punishing steps lead to the top, and on a clear day you can look far to the west and see why the fight was worth it.

Audio markers around the base of the spire deliver a minute by minute account of the battle. Holding a rented receiver to my ear, I made the tour, idly watching some boys a few yards away playing baseball under a sign that read: "Ball Playing Prohibited." Somehow, here on ground where Americans had fought and died, this small defiance did not seem inappropriate.

ROSS BENNETT

IRA BLOCK AND (RIGHT) "BURNING OF CHARLES TOWN," NATIONAL GALLERY OF ART, GIFT OF EDGAR WILLIAM AND BERNICE CHRYSLER GARBISCH

BOSTON

CHARLES TOW

Ben Franklin's Philadelphia

Liberty's sage diplomat, Boston-born Benjamin Franklin matured in Philadelphia from obscure printer to renowned scientist and statesman. In his meteoric rise he epitomized the growth of the dependent British colonies into self-sufficient states. With other patriots he helped create the United States of America here in the Pennsylvania State House—Independence Hall, scene of political debates and decisions indelibly written in the national adventure.

The shot heard round the world ricocheted through Philadelphia the evening of April 24, 1775. Toward dusk, a messenger from Trenton clattered up Second Street, reined his horse before City Tavern, and shouted the alarm; the battles at Lexington and Concord had ignited the powder keg of civil war with Britain. All over town men reached for their muskets; soon they were drilling on every open space. Thirty young Quaker men joined them, forsaking pacifism. Women began planning austerity meals, plain beef and pudding.

At an open-air town meeting in the State House yard the next day, thousands shouted approval of a resolution "to defend with arms their property, liberty and lives against all attempts to deprive them." So Philadelphians voted for war. But not for independence—yet. They sought only the redress of grievances, "ardently panting," in the words of a clergyman at Christ Church, "for a return to those Halcyon-days of harmony" before 1765. The vote for independence would have to wait a full 14 months—a long year of vacillation and wrangling, of propaganda and death.

Today the turmoil has disappeared and, like millions of other visitors, I strain to see the dried and flaking pages of diaries, the letters, the reports behind glass cases in Philadelphia's fine museums. I search for words that capture those turbulent days long past when the temper of the city was "little short of Madness," according to Benjamin Franklin, one of 1775's most astute observers.

Franklin, in fact, makes a fine modern-day guide to his adopted city. Many buildings he knew well still stand as restorations or spanking new replicas of those havens where he and his compatriots charted their course over unexplored political seas.

We travelers today are lucky; we know how the story turns out: 200 years of democratic, constitutional government unique in history. Our forebears enjoyed no such certainty as they took arms against the world's major military power.

On that particular April day, Benjamin Franklin, then 69 years old and going strong, was in the middle of the Atlantic Ocean, returning home after ten years as chief American spokesman in London. He had attempted to settle colonial disputes with British ministers and to make them understand American needs. At last, sensing that the problems were irreconcilable, he sailed for Philadelphia, arriving on May 5.

The city he loved stood proud in the middle of the colonies. With 40,000 people and 6,000 homes, Philadelphia ranked second only to London as leading metropolis of the British empire. Its merchants were, according to John Adams, veritable "nobles," grown rich on illegal trade with the West Indies. Great Conestoga wagons rumbled in from Lancaster, unloading fresh produce at covered markets like that at Second and Pine, where today weekend shoppers find handcrafted items, ethnic foods, and a flea market.

On every hand Franklin viewed civic improvements that he, as a rising printer and publisher, had supported to make life easier for the common people. There in Carpenters' Hall was shelved the "large and excellent" collection of the Philadelphia Library Company, including "every modern author of any note." First free library in the colonies, it well served the First Continental Congress and soon aided the Second.

TED SPIEGEL, BLACK STAR. PAINTING OF BENJAMIN FRANKLIN BY JOHN TRUMBULL, YALE UNIVERSITY ART GALLERY, JOHN HILL MORGAN FUND

HISTORICAL SOCIETY OF PENNSYLVANIA. CENTER: PHILADELPHIA CONTRIBUTIONSHIP. BOTTOM: INA CORPORATION MUSEUM, PHILADELPHIA. OPPOSITE: MARIE-LOUISE BRIMBERG

Survivals of 1776: Humble homes of Elfreth's Alley sheltered artisans, laborers, and small merchants, the backbone of patriot armies. The white steeple of Christ Church towered, then as now, over Second Street (above). Hand-in-hand seal identified the Franklin-sponsored Philadelphia Contributionship, America's oldest fire insurance company. Fire fighters then used hand pumps.

To the west rose the Pennsylvania Hospital, first in America, which Franklin had helped to establish. On the skyline shone the steeple of Christ Church, its tower financed by a Franklin-sponsored lottery. Streets boasted paved centers and brick footpaths. At many corners, four-sided lamps, smoke-free and easy to clean, replaced traditional globes. Many homes displayed a carved sign of interlocked hands, trademark of the city's first fire insurance company. All were Franklin innovations.

But people, rather than public places, were dearest to Franklin. He counted as friends the mighty and the lowly of every political persuasion.

Tradesmen of Elfreth's Alley nodded and waved hello. John Bartram, botanist to the king, welcomed the traveler to warm himself before a stove of Franklin's own design and to linger beneath the grape arbor at the Bartram home, now as then an oasis in the crowding city.

Even Mayor Samuel Powel opened the door of his Third Street mansion, said to be the city's grandest, but only slightly more elegant than Franklin's own home in the center of a city block on Market Street.

It was to this dwelling that Franklin returned. His wife, Deborah, had furnished it to his specifications during his absence, but she did not live to welcome him. His daughter Sally, and her husband and children, filled the rooms with warmth and happiness, an atmosphere captured in the new Franklin Court Museum on the house site. Franklin was "so taken up with People coming in continually, that I cannot stir." But stir he must, on May 6, 1775, for he was appointed by the Pennsylvania assembly to the Second Continental Congress, convening four days hence. As "sundry delegates" arrived, Philadelphians rode to cheer them, bells pealed and bands

"THE DECLARATION OF INDEPENDENCE" BY JOHN TRUMBULL, YALE UNIVERSITY ART GALLERY. OPPOSITE: LINDA BARTLETT

played, until, much fatigued, the men found rest at City Tavern. Recently rebuilt, City Tavern is again a good place for weary travelers to rest and enjoy an 18th-century meal.

At the State House, the colony's finest public building, the Pennsylvania assembly gave up its meeting room to the Continental Congress, unknowingly setting the stage for the site's transformation into the nation's revered Independence Hall.

Amid angry bickering, the delegates organized committees to deal with problems ranging from the creation of an army and navy to the setting of conditions for reconciliation with Britain. In early-morning meetings, often in nearby Carpenters' Hall, Franklin helped plan an American postal system and currency, the manufacture of saltpeter for gunpowder, and the search for foreign allies. For Pennsylvania he helped design defenses along the Delaware: on land, Forts Mifflin and Mercer; in the water, barricades of sunken rafts with projecting timbers topped with "three branches armed and pointed with iron."

As Congress labored behind closed doors, Philadelphians speculated on their own course of action. Lines were drawn and the labels loyalist and rebel were assigned in terms of faithfulness to England or lack of it. Many loyalists saw the war, and Congress itself, as illegal. Others feared loss of property. Franklin's close friend Joseph Galloway found "democratic notions" of the lower classes a greater threat than British tyranny. Loyalists who were too vocal were carted about the city with nooses draped around their necks until they recanted.

Franklin's own son William, Royal governor of New Jersey, refused to follow his father in rebellion, wounding Benjamin more deeply than musket fire. After Congress called for the creation of new state governments, William was thrown into jail and later went to live in England.

Many fence-sitters joined the rebel ranks after reading *Common Sense,* the powerful pamphlet written by Thomas Paine, a Franklin protégé.

On April 15, 1776, Franklin wrote that only "general Consent" was required for independence. "The Novelty of the Thing deters some, the Doubt of Success others, the vain Hope of Reconciliation many. But our enemies take . . . every proper Measure to remove these Obstacles."

"You are now guardians of your own liberties," Sam Adams charged fellow Americans after the adoption of the Declaration of Independence (above). The delegates made the irrevocable break with Britain in the Assembly Room of Independence Hall (right).

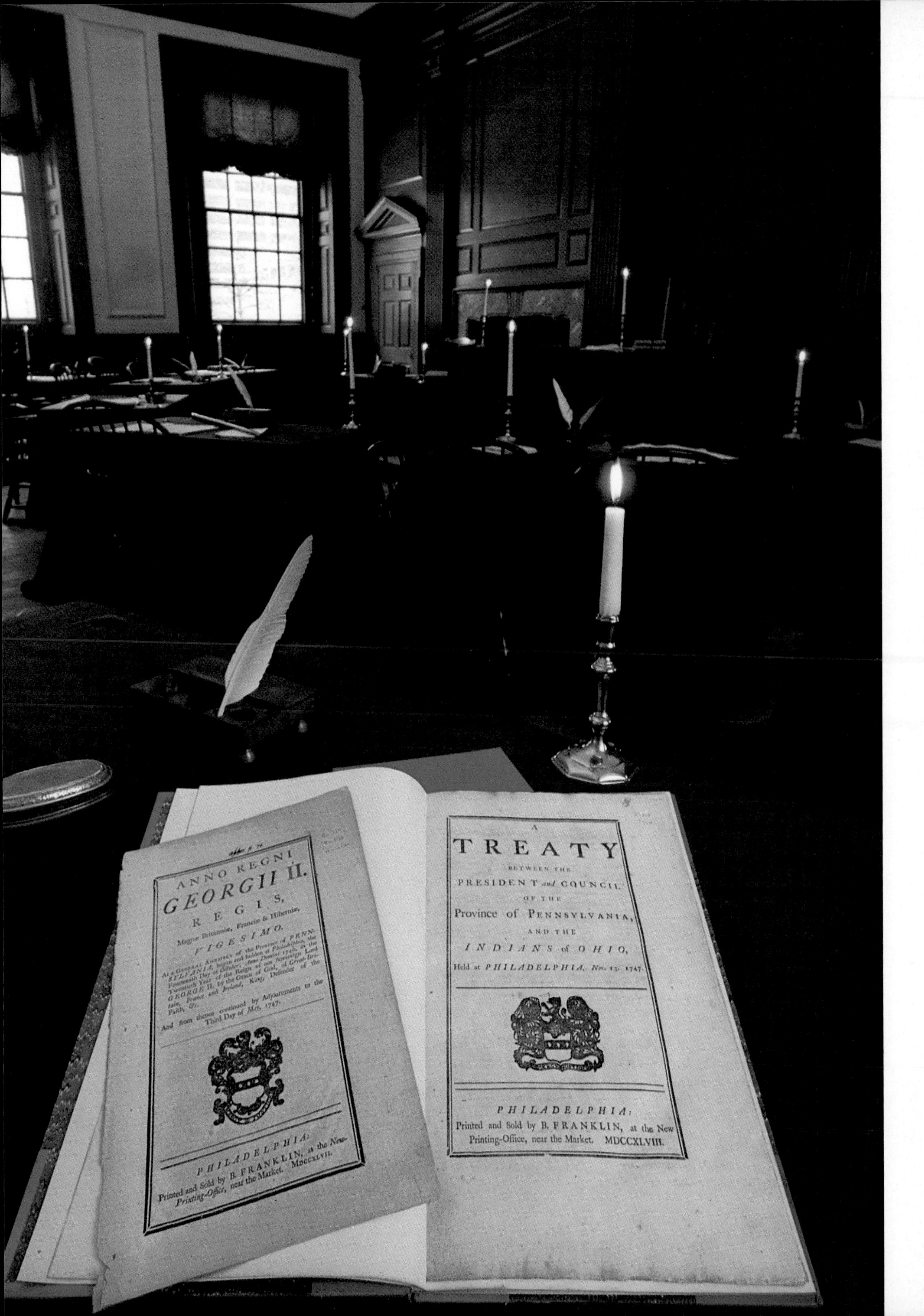
ANNO REGNI
GEORGII II.
REGIS,
Magnæ Britanniæ, Franciæ & Hiberniæ,
VIGESIMO.
At a General Assembly of the Province of PENNSYLVANIA, begun and holden at Philadelphia, the Fourteenth Day of October, Anno Domini 1746, in the Twentieth Year of the Reign of our Sovereign Lord GEORGE II. by the Grace of God, of Great-Britain, France and Ireland, King, Defender of the Faith, &c.
And from thence continued by Adjournments to the Third Day of May, 1747.
PHILADELPHIA:
Printed and Sold by B. FRANKLIN, at the New-Printing-Office, near the Market. MDCCXLVII.
A
TREATY
BETWEEN THE
PRESIDENT and COUNCIL
OF THE
Province of PENNSYLVANIA,
AND THE
INDIANS of OHIO,
Held at PHILADELPHIA, Nov. 13. 1747.
PHILADELPHIA:
Printed and Sold by B. FRANKLIN, at the New
Printing-Office, near the Market. MDCCXLVIII.

He was referring to the British burning of Charlestown, Falmouth, Jamestown, and Norfolk, "with the Flight of Women and Children from these defenceless Places, some falling by Shot in their Flight."

States began instructing their delegates to vote for independence, and Congress appointed a committee of five—including Benjamin Franklin—to prepare a declaration. Chairman Thomas Jefferson, "that young man from Virginia," shut himself up in his lodgings at Market and Seventh to write a draft.

Some revisions were made by the committee. Jefferson sent a copy to Dr. Franklin, at home with gout, asking him to "peruse it and suggest such alterations as his more enlarged view of the subject will dictate." Franklin changed "We hold these truths to be sacred and undeniable" to the sharper "self-evident."

On July 2, by vote of Congress, independence was declared. The delegates then spent two days revising the written declaration, finally approving it on July 4.

Four days later, the stirring words were read to a cheering throng in the State House yard. "The company declared their approbation by 3 repeated huzzas..." and celebrated with "bonfires, ringing bells... Demonstrations of Joy." It "compleats a Revolution," John Adams wrote, that "was in the minds of the people and in the union of the colonies... before hostilities commenced."

July Fourth! To modern Americans the apex of the Revolution. To colonial Philadelphians, just another day in their crisis-ridden calendar. If the year before offered political uncertainty, the year following promised military disaster as the British threatened the city's very survival. Gen. William Howe occupied New York and boasted he would eat Christmas dinner in Philadelphia.

Congress implored other colonies for aid. Philadelphia streets became clogged with wounded and ragged soldiers trudging home after their short enlistments expired. All able-bodied men were ordered to build earthworks to defend the city or else face "sale of goods and chattels" to hire stand-ins. "All in hurry and confusion. Howe is on his march."

Before the British could blockade the Delaware, Franklin embarked for Paris to shape an alliance with England's longtime enemy, the king of France. Before he left, Franklin had mortgaged his home and raised 4,000 pounds, about $200,000 today, to aid the rebel cause.

"In the great cause of Liberty," the First Continental Congress met in 1774 at Carpenters' Hall, where a bivouac recreates militia life. A 1778 London cartoon shows Holland, France, Spain, and America exploiting the English cow of commerce while an Englishman beats his breast, the British lion slumbers, and Howe idles in Philadelphia.

MARIE-LOUISE BRIMBERG. LEFT: THE JOHN CARTER BROWN LIBRARY, BROWN UNIVERSITY

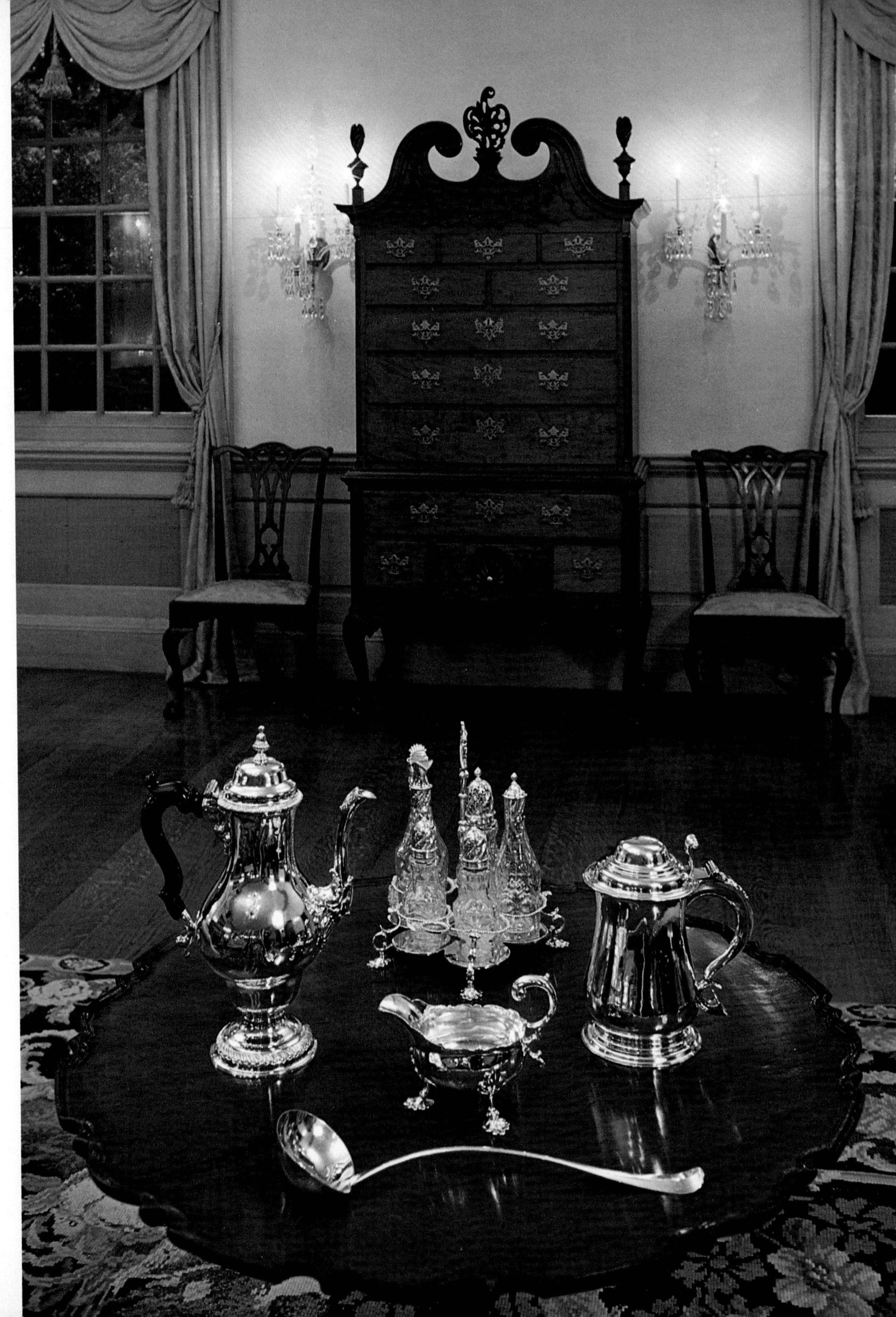

Winter came, granting reprieve, for by the rules of "civilized" European warfare, fighting stopped with the first snow; Howe returned to New York, leaving a Hessian garrison to hold Trenton.

Gen. George Washington broke the rules and gambled all on a Christmas night strike. He plotted the strategy at the Thompson-Neely House, which still stands in Washington Crossing State Park. The words of Thomas Paine fired his men: "These are the times that try men's souls. The summer soldier and the sunshine patriot will, in this crisis, shrink from the service of their country." Few of the 2,500 patriots shrank from duty as they crossed the ice-choked Delaware and marched on Trenton, where the Old Barracks today wears scars of the bitter house-to-house fighting that routed the Hessians. Washington's victory was the finest Christmas gift Philadelphians could have.

The following June, Congress presented the whole nation with a memorable gift—a national flag of 13 stripes and 13 stars "representing a new constellation." Not a word then or for the next 100 years about who designed it or sewed the first banner. Then a grandson's recollection fed the national hunger for explanation. George Washington, it was said, visited Betsy Ross, a flagmaker for the navy, and directed her needle. And thus she became the mother of the national flag.

Visitors come like dutiful children to the simple artisan's home on Arch Street where Betsy may have boarded in 1777 when she could have stitched her flag. Whatever the case, she has woven a fine legend.

Late in the summer of '77, Howe struck again. Skirting Franklin's river defenses at Forts Mifflin and Mercer, he sailed up Chesapeake Bay, then marched his 15,000 men overland. Washington tried to cut off the

THE LIBRARY COMPANY OF PHILADELPHIA

Golden age of Philadelphia shines yet in the artistry of its craftsmen. Silver signed by Philip Syng, Jr., and John David graces the parlor of 18th-century merchant Edward Stiles, re-created at the Winterthur Museum in Wilmington, Delaware. Cabinetmaker Benjamin Randolph embellished his trade card (above) with samples of his work. Furniture inspired by England's Thomas Chippendale reflects an American exuberance, seen in the peanut-shaped carving tucked into the cartouche atop a mahogany highboy (below).

MARIE-LOUISE BRIMBERG (ALSO OPPOSITE)

advance at Chadds Ford, but by September 19 Howe was on the doorsteps of Philadelphia. At 2 a.m. came "a great knocking at peoples Doors and desiring them to get up, that the English had crossed the Swedes ford at 11 o'clock and would presently be in the City.... [Soon] Waggons rattling, Horses Galoping, Women running, Children Crying, Delagates flying, and all together the greatest consternation fright and terror that can be imagined."

Congress, fleeing to Lancaster, ordered that the town's bells be sent to safety, to prevent their being melted down for cannon. The State House bell, later named the Liberty Bell, was hidden in Allentown.

October became the city's "starving time." Though Howe's men repulsed Washington's attack on their main camp at Germantown north of the city, rebels still hounded supply lines. For firewood the British burned the pews of the Presbyterian church called Old Pine, whose minister had been a prime rebel orator.

To open the Delaware, Howe launched a bombardment of Fort Mifflin. The six-day siege destroyed it and killed or wounded 250 rebels. Rather than surrender, survivors set fire to the ruins and carried away the wounded in the dark of night.

Today, when the cannons cease and the smoke clears, muster is over for the costumed militiamen at restored Fort Mifflin. Each Sunday they re-enact a defense that, Washington wrote, "does credit to the American Arms, and will ever reflect the highest honor upon the officers and men of the Garrison."

By Christmas of 1777 the British were in full control of the erstwhile American capital and settled in for a comfortable winter's billet. At Samuel Powel's house, the Earl of Carlisle commandeered the best rooms, pushing the family into a rear wing. But he visited them daily for

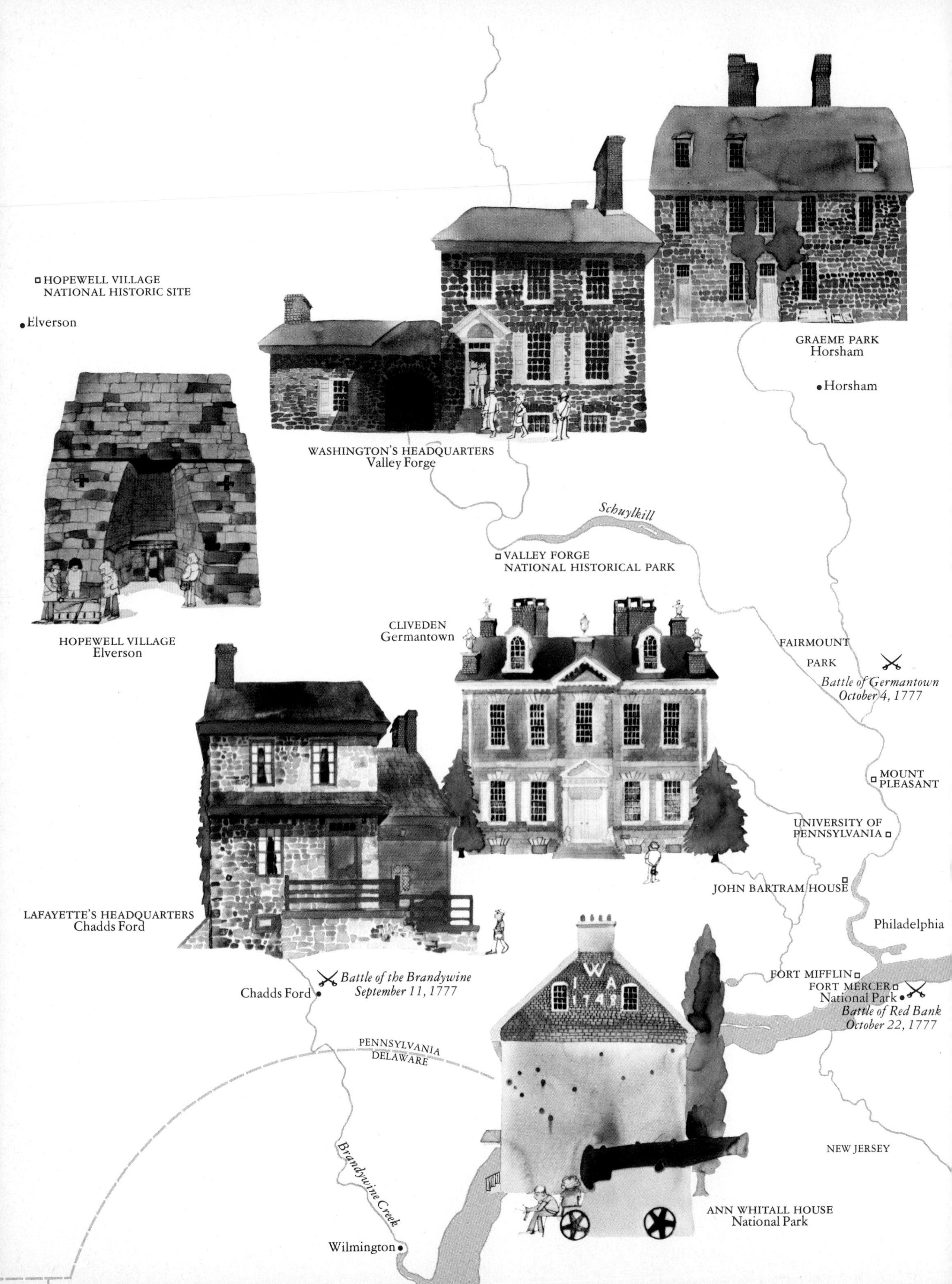

HOPEWELL VILLAGE
NATIONAL HISTORIC SITE
Elverson
WASHINGTON'S HEADQUARTERS
Valley Forge
GRAEME PARK
Horsham
Horsham
HOPEWELL VILLAGE
Elverson
Schuylkill
VALLEY FORGE
NATIONAL HISTORICAL PARK
CLIVEDEN
Germantown
FAIRMOUNT
PARK
Battle of Germantown
October 4, 1777
MOUNT
PLEASANT
UNIVERSITY OF
PENNSYLVANIA
JOHN BARTRAM HOUSE
LAFAYETTE'S HEADQUARTERS
Chadds Ford
Philadelphia
Battle of the Brandywine
September 11, 1777
Chadds Ford
FORT MIFFLIN
FORT MERCER
National Park
Battle of Red Bank
October 22, 1777
PENNSYLVANIA
DELAWARE
Brandywine Creek
NEW JERSEY
ANN WHITALL HOUSE
National Park
Wilmington

HISTORICAL PHILADELPHIA

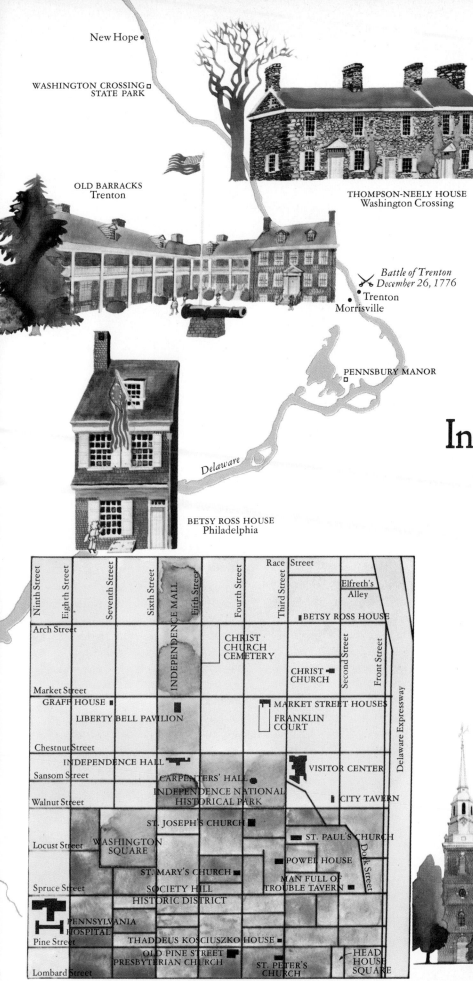

The Revolution turned the tranquil environs of Philadelphia into bloody fields of battle. Many sites evoke wartime sacrifices. The Thompson-Neely House, used by patriots as a military headquarters, recalls the bleak December of 1776 when Washington made plans there to steal across the Delaware River. During a blizzard his ragged army surprised Hessians billeted in the Old Barracks at Trenton and won a vital victory.

In restored Hopewell Village, summer demonstrations recapture daily life at the iron foundry that supplied cannon and shot to the patriots. To cut off such supplies, General Howe marched from the south but was slowed at Brandywine Creek. There, in Gideon Gilpin's stone farmhouse, General Lafayette lodged the night before his first battle.

Independence Town

Washington struck the main British camp at Germantown, but 120 Britishers barricaded themselves in Cliveden, mansion of Judge Benjamin Chew, delaying the patriots long enough to rob them of victory.

At Fort Mercer, now a New Jersey park, 400 soldiers from Rhode Island held off 2,000 Hessians on October 22, 1777. At her home nearby, Ann Whitall refused to interrupt her spinning—until a cannonball pierced the house. Later she nursed the wounded there.

Encamped at Valley Forge, Washington lost 3,000 men to winterkill. Earlier he had been a guest at Graeme Park, although its owner was a loyalist.

In Philadelphia's Washington Square, thousands of soldiers found final rest. Washington's statue keeps vigil over the tomb of an unknown soldier whose epitaph reads: "Beneath this stone rests a soldier of Washington's Army who died to give you liberty."

PAINTINGS BY PAUL HOGARTH

CHRIST CHURCH
Philadelphia

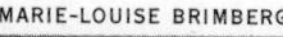

MARIE-LOUISE BRIMBERG

tea, becoming "the best friends in the world." Later, George and Martha Washington resumed their close connection with the Powels, one of the few families to prosper under both regimes.

Franklin's home did not fare well. Capt. John André, later hanged for his part in the Benedict Arnold plot to seize West Point, lodged at Franklin Court while squiring local belles and planning extravagant fetes for officers and loyalists. On his departure André removed Franklin's portrait; books, scientific equipment, and musical instruments also disappeared. Franklin later billed King George III for the missing items but was never reimbursed.

The State House fared even worse, converted into a jail and hospital for American prisoners of war. The British dug a pit nearby to dispose of corpses, both human and horse, creating a stench that hung over the block for months.

For ordinary citizens, British occupation meant suspense and empty promises. Many men were tempted to sign up for duty in His Majesty's service by offers of 50 acres "where every gallant Hero may retire and enjoy his Bottle and Lass."

Meanwhile, Washington's army shared that same dream as they suffered through the cruel winter of 1777-78 at Valley Forge. They never faced battle here, but disease, hunger, nakedness, and icy winds took a ravaging toll: 3,000 dead.

With spring came news and hope. France had signed an alliance, negotiated by old friend Benjamin Franklin, and May 6 was given over to celebration. On orders from London, Howe withdrew from Philadelphia in June. The following years would see Cornwallis surrender and Franklin return, a British peace treaty in hand, to help his compatriots form a lasting constitutional government. Liberty would again ring out over the streets of Philadelphia. Today a new bell, bicentennial gift from Great Britain, swings high above the visitor center of Independence National Historical Park, pealing out the message that freedom, so hard won more than 200 years ago, is still alive in the land.

ALICE J. HALL

"The most elegant seat in Pennsylvania" John Adams called Mount Pleasant, the mansion Capt. John Macpherson built with profits from privateering. Benedict Arnold bought it for his bride in 1779, but neither ever lived there.

The World of George Washington

George Washington spent most of his life in the fertile, wooded wedge of tidewater Virginia that lies between the Rappahannock and Potomac rivers. There he was born, grew to manhood, and learned a trade—surveying. There he took his bride to his beloved Mount Vernon. There, in his 68th year, he died.

Not beyond criticism while alive—"the dishclout of every idle speculation," a senator scolded—Washington in death was venerated as a demigod. An acquaintance, Parson Mason Locke Weems, perceiving "a great deal of money lying in the bones of old George," concocted an apocryphal biography laced with platitudes and self-righteous bravado. A hero-hungry people swallowed the Weems story, cherry tree and all. Nathaniel Hawthorne once drolly commented that the father of his country "was born with his clothes on, and his hair powdered, and made a stately bow on his first appearance in the world."

George, first of six children born to Augustine Washington and his second wife Mary Ball, bowed in—according to the family Bible—in the usual way "about 10 in the Morning" on February 22, 1732. The birthplace was Popes Creek Plantation overlooking the Potomac, not far from where, 75 years earlier, George's great-grandfather John Washington first set foot in America.

Mount Vernon beckons modern visitors as it did such honored guests as Chief Justice John Marshall and General Lafayette. George Washington compared it to a "well-resorted tavern."

MARIE-LOUISE BRIMBERG

Today Popes Creek Plantation, restored to the working farm it was in George Washington's youth, is a living national monument. Behind split-rail fences, oxen lazily grind their cuds. Tobacco and Indian corn ripen in fields Augustine Washington once tilled, and rows of herbs and flowers pattern a colonial garden. Paths young George might have followed wind through ancient red cedars down to water's edge. Ancient too is the lineage of a clump of fig trees, said to be scions of those that bore fruit outside the nursery of baby George.

The house where he was born burned on Christmas Day 1779, apparently when sparks from a chimney blew through a window. Years of neglect all but erased evidence of the ruin. Wild shrubbery and the old fig trees were all that remained.

Efforts to preserve the birthplace met with success in the early 1930's when a memorial house, representative of the colonial period, was erected on foundations unearthed by the U. S. Army Corps of Engineers. Subsequent excavations, however, convinced archeologists that a nearby U-shaped foundation was the actual location. An outline of crushed oyster shells traces the floor plan. In imagination looms the fine house where a child of destiny romped.

Young George's second home was a 2,500-acre plantation on Little Hunting Creek that we now know as Mount Vernon. It was originally patented by great-grandfather John. Over an existing foundation Augustine built a 1½-story farmhouse in 1735. Three years later he moved to

From his library, with "spyeglass" and rolltop desk, Washington ran Mount Vernon. An upstairs bedroom displays pictures of Martha and her children. Throughout the Revolutionary War, George wore her locket around his neck.

TED SPIEGEL, BLACK STAR. OPPOSITE: MARIE-LOUISE BRIMBERG

Ferry Farm on the Rappahannock. There, in April of 1743, Augustine died from "gout of the stomach."

His will provided that George's half-brother Lawrence receive the "patrimonial Mansion" and grounds at Little Hunting Creek. Lawrence renamed the place Mount Vernon, in honor of Adm. Edward Vernon under whom he had fought the Spanish during the War of Jenkins' Ear.

Lawrence, 14 years older than George, filled the void left by Augustine's death. Educated in England, entrusted with public offices, he was to George both hero and mentor. At Mount Vernon, astir with land-rush excitement, the young surveyor found opportunity as well as welcome. There Lawrence's wife Anne Fairfax provided a connection with the cream of landed aristocracy.

At Belvoir, her father's estate, George enjoyed an easy familiarity with ladies and gentlemen of rank and privilege. He was hunting companion to no less than Thomas, sixth Lord Fairfax, proprietor of more than five million acres between the "heads" and "springs" of the Potomac and Rappahannock. Into this princely realm George took surveyor's gear and an appetite for land of his own. Before his 19th birthday he had saved enough to buy 1,460 acres in the Shenandoah Valley.

George Washington's military career began after Lawrence died of tuberculosis in 1752. Though lacking any experience, he sought to follow in his brother's footsteps as adjutant. Lt. Gov. Robert Dinwiddie

Kitchenware for entertaining on a scale befitting a hero crowds Mount Vernon's scullery. Lavish meals—one included "pigg... leg of lamb, roasted fowls, beef"—sated guests. Laid out as the seat of a country squire (overleaf), "the tout ensemble," *a visitor wrote, "bears a resemblence to a rural village."*

MARIE-LOUISE BRIMBERG.
OVERLEAF: VICTOR R. BOSWELL, JR., NATIONAL GEOGRAPHIC PHOTOGRAPHER

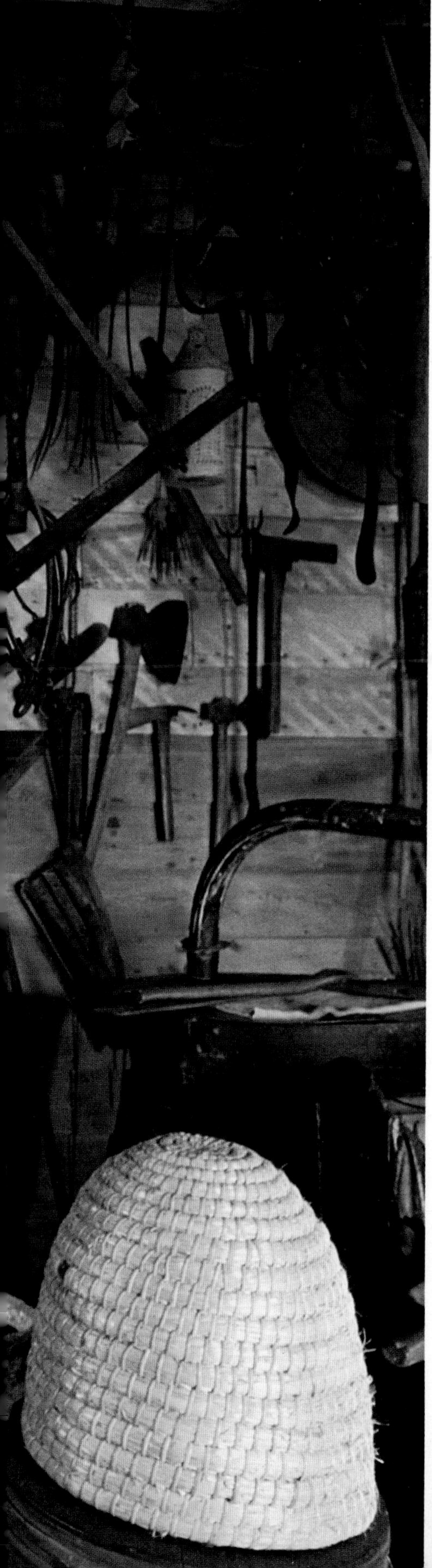

was kindly disposed and commissioned the "braw laddie" a major of militia. He was not yet 21.

In 1753 he crossed the Alleghenies to gather intelligence of French forces in the Ohio Valley, claimed by the crown. An exchange of official messages hardened positions, inviting war. The next spring Washington—now a lieutenant colonel—returned to the wilderness and for the first time "heard the bullets whistle." He led a surprise attack on a French encampment, killing ten, one of whom was the commander, Joseph Coulon, Sieur de Jumonville.

Expecting attack by a superior force of French troops and hostile Indians, Washington prepared for action at his camp in Great Meadows, Pennsylvania, "a charming field for an Encounter." From the center rose a hurriedly built palisade of logs he called Fort Necessity.

On July 3, 1754, "the most tremendous rain" and a "constant, galling fire" forced him to surrender. Powder wet, spirits dampened, he signed the *Capitulation* contrived by Coulon de Villiers, brother of the slain Jumonville. Misled by faulty translation of the document, Washington acknowledged *l'assassinat*—

Discreet dependencies off Mount Vernon courtyard housed slaves, servants, and craftsmen, and provided services to make the plantation self-sufficient, if not profitable. Storehouse (left) held implements doled out and scrupulously accounted for. A 1799 inventory noted "reap hooks," "Plow hoes," and "Scythe blades," along with "1 Elegant French horn." Salthouse (above) displays nets and rock salt echoing days when Potomac fisheries sold shad by the thousands. Slaves, including those who made fabric from homegrown fibers, lived in the Spinning House Quarters.

MARIE-LOUISE BRIMBERG

the assassination—of Jumonville. "Such was the complication of political interests," Voltaire observed of the "little skirmish" in the Pennsylvania wilderness, that a "shot fired in America could give the signal that set Europe in a blaze."

Flash point of a world conflict—the Seven Years' War in Europe, the French and Indian War in America—Fort Necessity survives today as a peaceful roadside park. A pocket-size battlefield with reconstructed stockade, it remains "a charming field" for picnickers and a pleasant rest stop for travelers near Farmington on U. S. 40. Washington, who had a sharp eye for land in peace or war, once owned part of the site.

Close by is Gen. Edward Braddock's grave—a detached segment of the national battlefield. In 1755 Braddock mounted a new campaign against the French. His ill-conceived march on Fort Duquesne cost him his life and very nearly that of his aide Washington, who had two horses shot from under him. Despite "so scandalous" a defeat, as Washington viewed the Battle of the Monongahela, he emerged with honor intact. However, serving without pay and weakened by dysentery, he had "sufferd much in my private fortune, besides impairing one of the best of Constitution's." Balm came in a new commission—commander in chief of the Virginia militia.

His career on the frontier ended late in 1758 with a bloodless triumph at Fort Duquesne, abandoned and burned by the French. As Fort Pitt rose from its ashes, Colonel Washington rode homeward to resign his commission. On January 6, 1759, he married Martha Custis, wealthy widow and mother of two.

His 27th birthday saw him taking his place in the House of Burgesses. In April he introduced Martha and the children—Jacky and Patsy—to their new home at Mount Vernon. To a friend he wrote, "I am now I believe fixd at this Seat with an agreable Consort for Life...."

For the next 16 years George Washington's world was mainly that of a prosperous planter. His sister-in-law's death in 1761 left him sole owner of Mount Vernon, which he

Plan of Alexandria tested apprentice Washington's surveying skills in 1749. The port town soon grew and prospered; visiting ships flew flags from around the world. Captain's Row (right) looks much as it did in Washington's day. Legend holds that Hessian prisoners of war laid the cobblestones.

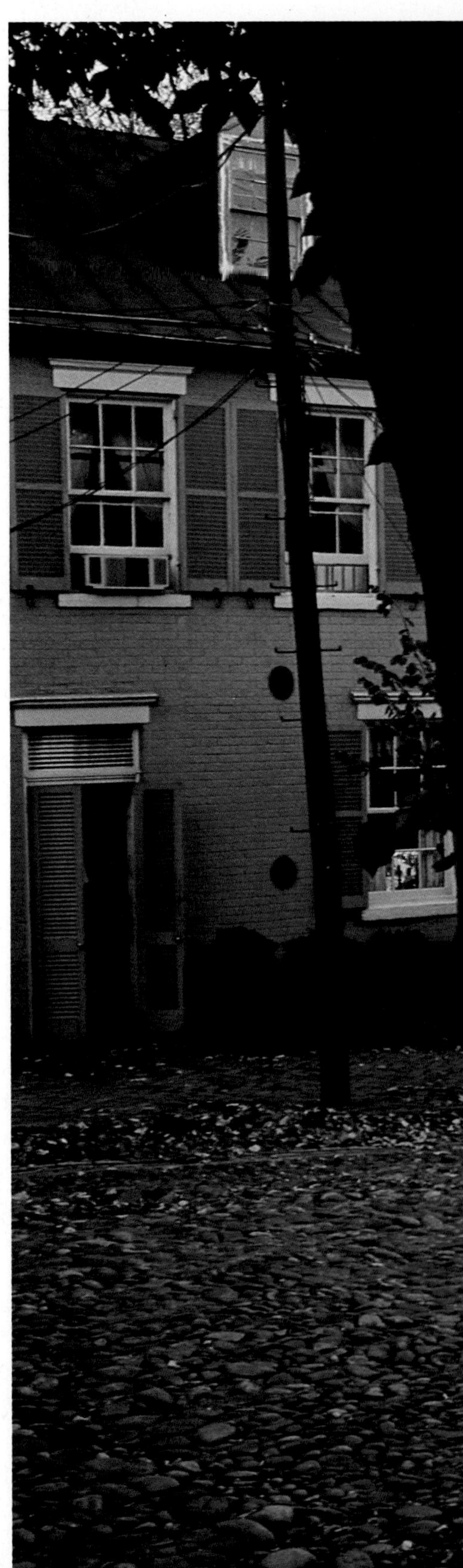

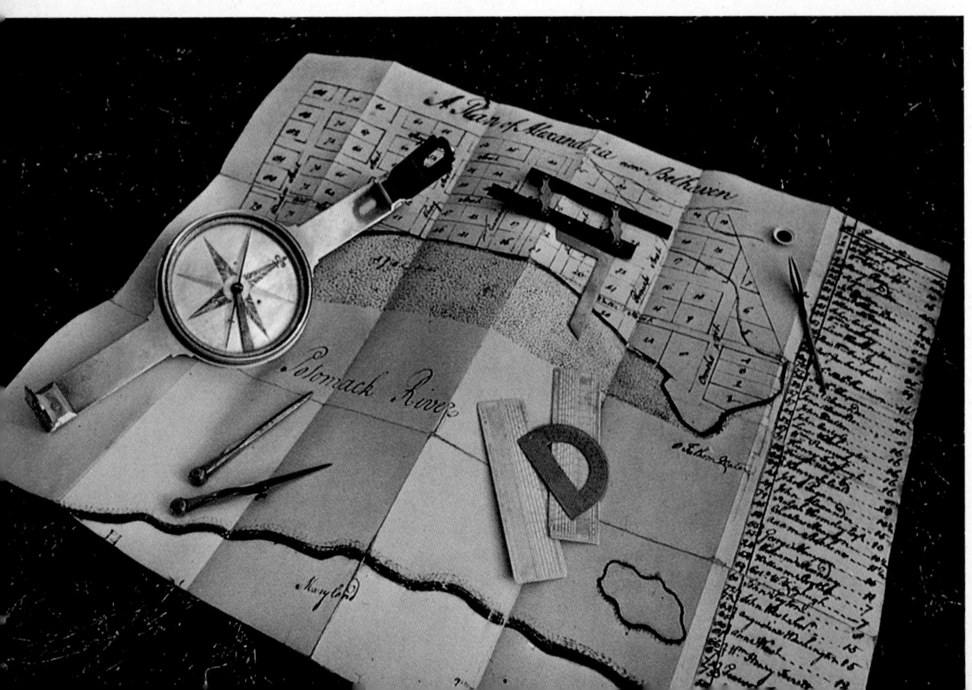

MARIE-LOUISE BRIMBERG. LEFT: TED SPIEGEL, BLACK STAR

MARIE-LOUISE BRIMBERG

gradually expanded until the plantation covered more than 8,000 acres. Though the fields where he planted tobacco and grain have been many times subdivided, the mansion house grounds of about 500 acres remain intact. An unending stream of visitors tour the carefully restored house, the outbuildings, and gardens, before strolling down to the vault where George rests "in the shadow of my own vine and my own fig tree." Beside him lie the remains of his "agreable Consort."

Several miles distant is Woodlawn. The land, a "most beautiful Site for a Gentleman's Seat," was Washington's bequest to Lawrence Lewis, his nephew, and Lewis's wife Nelly Custis, Martha's granddaughter. Farther south is Pohick Church, built in 1772 and since restored. Washington surveyed the land where it stands.

In Alexandria the Washingtons had a pew at Christ Church, still a haven of worship. As a youth, George helped survey the port town. Still standing is John Carlyle's house, where Washington frequently lodged and General Braddock held councils of war. The City Tavern, now known as Gadsby's, was Alexandria's social center; here George and Martha supped and danced.

The pleasures of retirement ended for Washington in 1775, when the Second Continental Congress elected him commander in chief. For the next eight years his was the burden of leading an ill-equipped, undermanned army. He retreated in New York and survived, savored victory at Trenton, endured at Valley Forge. His triumph at Yorktown ended the war and enabled him to "resign with satisfaction the Appointment I accepted with diffidence."

He returned to Mount Vernon in 1783, but his stay was short-lived; in 1789 the electoral college named him the first President of the United States. Washington, Thomas Jefferson recorded, "had rather be on his own farm than to be made *Emperor of the world.*"

At the age of 65, Washington once again beheld the "tranquil theatre" of Mount Vernon, where he could don plain garb and roam his fields. There, he wrote, "Rural employments while I am spared . . . will now take place of toil, responsibility, and the sollicitudes attending the walks of public life." He had little more than two years to live.

WAYNE BARRETT

In Alexandria, the Stabler-Leadbeater Apothecary Shop, now a museum, served George and Martha. It treasures her order for a quart of the "best Castor Oil and the bill for it." At Christ Church, the Washingtons paid a pew rent of "five pounds, Virginia money."

ENGLISH

DAVID ALAN HARVEY. OPPOSITE: PAINTING BY REMBRANDT PEALE, NEW-YORK HISTORICAL SOCIETY

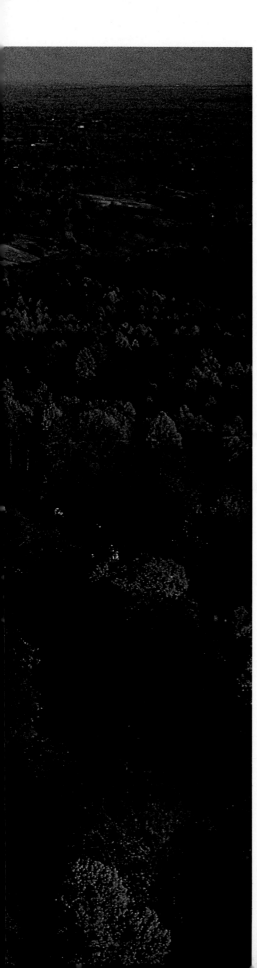

Mr. Jefferson of Monticello

Kicking through snowdrifts two feet deep, snorting great clouds of vapor into the January night, the two horses floundered along a rude mountain trail hacked into the woods of frontier Virginia. Naked branches clawed at the young bride's cloak as she clung to her lurching mount and yearned for the cozy phaeton she and her husband had abandoned eight miles back.

Next day Thomas Jefferson would note in his garden journal "the deepest snow we have ever seen." But to him these hills had been home for all of his 28 years, and so he led his bride unerringly through snow and darkness to the aerie they would share for ten happy years: Monticello, his "little mountain" above the town of Charlottesville.

Upslope they struggled, until at last they reached the summit of Jefferson's hill—and a welcome as cold as the night. The servants had not expected them to arrive at this hour in such weather and so had banked the fires and gone to bed. In a one-room house sometimes called the Honeymoon Cottage, Martha Wayles Skelton Jefferson—widowed at 19, wed again at 23—spent her first night at Monticello.

It was the first of many nights in the little brick house that Jefferson called the South Pavilion. The dawn presented Martha with a chaotic hilltop strewn with mounds of dirt, racks of lumber, stacks of bricks baked on the site. In two years, workers had tonsured the wooded hilltop, leveled its pate, and built the cottage. But the main house, Thomas Jefferson's dream and posterity's mirror of the man, was still only a skeletal shell in 1772.

And what a shell! Soaring over the lowlands where most other

"And our own dear Monticello," exulted Thomas Jefferson over the stately home that so eloquently bespeaks the man. "With what majesty do we there ride above the storms!" But the waves of destiny did break over his wooded hill, bearing him both greatness and grief.

A crystal epergne with sweets nestled in its dangling cups . . . a pair of dumb-waiters flanking a fireplace to hoist fine vintages from an ample cellar . . . a tearoom awash with window light, ablaze with candleglow, alive with talk and music—thus did Thomas Jefferson host endless tides of houseguests despite his failing finances. Modern place settings await an annual Founder's Day dinner by the Thomas Jefferson Memorial Foundation, Monticello's guardian.

patricians chose to erect their stately homes, it gazed down at its neighbors as did its creator, a man of six-foot-two in a world of men averaging perhaps half a foot short of that. Under a shock of reddish hair—which often seemed to need a good combing—throbbed a mind that towered over its time, a multifaceted intellect that could devise a plow's moldboard and a decimal coinage system, play a prized violin and read Homer in Greek, draft both the

MARIE-LOUISE BRIMBERG. RIGHT: LINDA BARTLETT

Declaration of Independence and the Virginia Act for Religious Freedom in a scant six weeks—and design a classical showpiece that outshone the Georgian houses of its day.

It was inevitable that such a mind should be caught up in the birth throes of the infant nation. Time and time again Jefferson left his hilltop to serve his country in the arena of politics. But at each return he would launch anew into "putting up and pulling down"; architecture, he once wrote, "is my delight."

By 1782 the house seemed nearly finished. Great spans of glass welcomed the sun that seemed to follow Jefferson through his day, flooding into his bedroom-study in the morning and into the dining room at day's end. Classical columns bore a pedimented portico on the west front. It was clearly a two-story house, but not yet the domed mansion that it would one day become.

Then tragedy struck. After giving birth to a sixth child—only two of the couple's children lived to maturity—Martha died. Thomas Jefferson was inconsolable. He wrote, brooded, walked for hours. Without his guiding hand and driving energy, construction work ground to a halt. Monticello all but stagnated.

In 1784 the nation's need of him brought Jefferson down his mountain again to serve five years as minister to France. Until then he had known classical architecture only

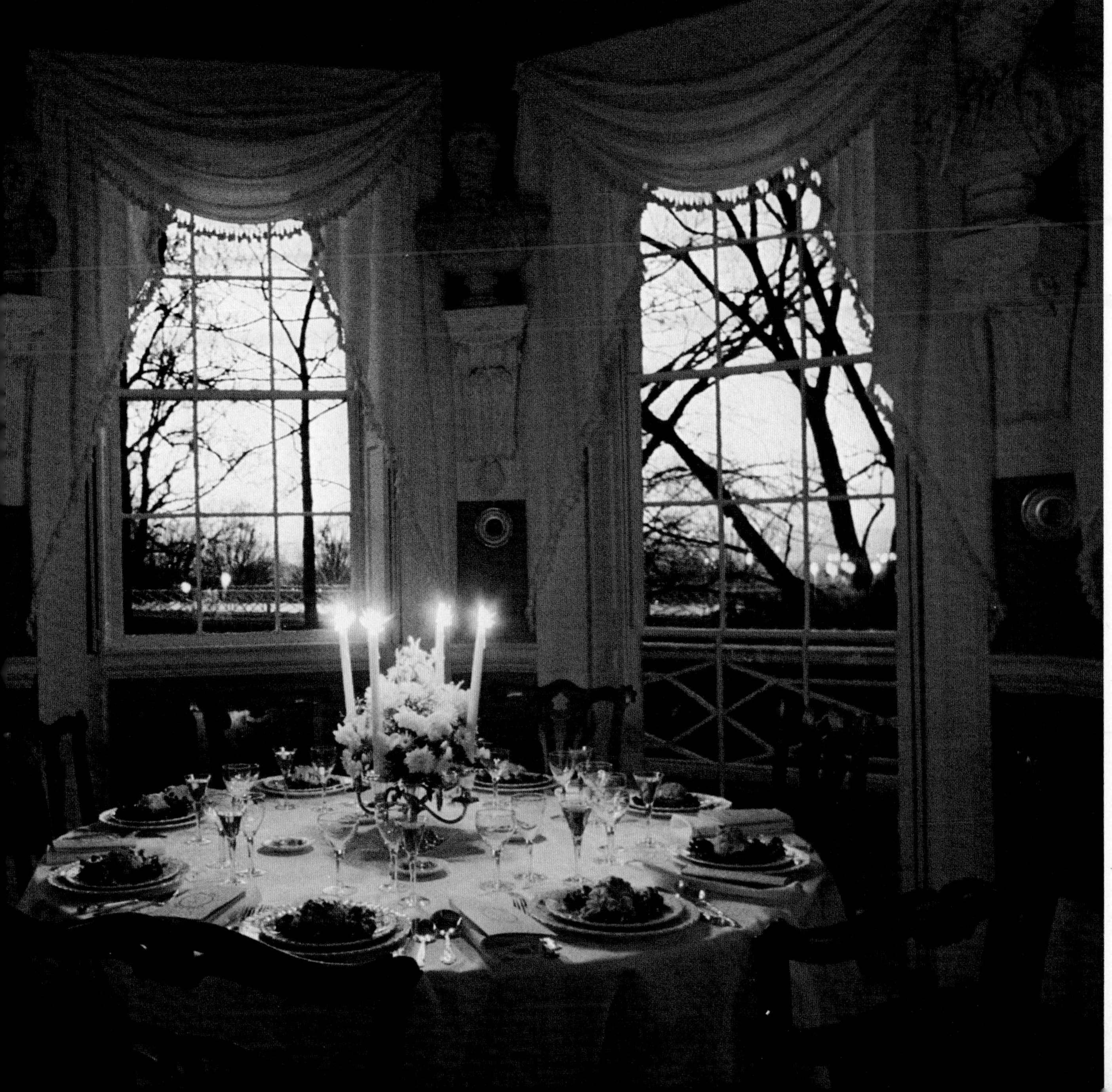

from his beloved books. Now he saw the originals—and came home fired with fresh ideas for Monticello. A dome took shape. A frieze disguised the second story and made the two stories look like one. Forty years after its inception, Monticello at last reached the form we know today.

A visitor to Monticello now sees the house as Jefferson's hordes of guests never did. Some marveled—and others recoiled—at an entrance hall decked with elk antlers, a bison head, Indian maps drawn on rawhide, and a motley assortment of other memorabilia from the Lewis and Clark expedition. As President, Jefferson had doubled his country's size with the Louisiana Purchase, then sent the two explorers to see what the nation had bought. The clutter must have been incongruous in that stately classic chamber, but it must have launched many a lively conversation as well.

Books and letters probably lay about his study at all hours of the day and night. Methodical almost to a fault, Jefferson kept copies of his letters and saved seemingly every scrap of correspondence, notes, and sketches that came to hand. His journals chronicle in longhand the sprouting seed and the falling leaf, the dropping temperatures of autumn and the return of the various migrants in spring. But, sadly, almost nothing remains to tell us of

Gifted gadgeteer, Jefferson invented little but tinkered much. Weights like the cannonballs fired in the Revolution still drive his seven-day clock in the entry, sinking past day markers into holes in the floor to reach Saturday in the cellar. On the entry's ceiling soars an enigmatic eagle. Why 18 stars, some of them six-pointed? No one knows.

His polygraph's twin pens wrote two letters at once. It was, he thought, the "finest invention of the present age."

In a blend of chaise, table, and early swivel chair, Jefferson stretched his lanky frame as he wrote letters in his bedroom. In 1826 he lay abed, stretching his long life to one more dawn: July 4, 1826, freedom's 50th birthday.

MARIE-LOUISE BRIMBERG. LEFT: LINDA BARTLETT

In his prime, Jefferson saw Maison Carrée, *a Roman temple, and designed Virginia's Capitol (below) after it. In old age he founded the University of Virginia, evoking classical themes in its dome and colonnaded student rooms. Saving brick with serpentine walls—curves, not thickness, keep them from toppling—he laid out gardens where students still talk of knowledge and life.*

his beloved Martha. For Jefferson the public man kept his private life as private as he could. Whether in grief or in a simple determination to guarantee their privacy forever, he seems to have destroyed the letters they must have exchanged and even avoided any mention of her name. Scattered accounts written by some of Monticello's numerous visitors during her lifetime give us only a tantalizing hint of a gracious and "pretty lady," charming as a hostess and cherished as a wife by the husband who dubbed her "Patty."

Two daughters grew to womanhood, no thanks to the booby traps created by their father's almost incessant remodeling. In 1797 his newly married daughter Maria fell into the cellar through a floor that wasn't completed, and soon after tumbled out of a yawning doorway. As common as the tinkling of her harpsichord was the thump of hammers and the screech of saws as workers, aided by Jefferson's servants, wrought his latest brainstorm.

Servants? Most of them were slaves, living, sweating symbols of the inability of freedom's champion to unlock the dilemma he knew must rend the nation. Some evidence even suggests that he had several children by his slave, Sally Hemings; the debate on this question may never be fully resolved. Like its creator, the great house keeps its counsel, riding serenely above the storm as it introduces modern generations to Jefferson the man.

DAVID F. ROBINSON

MARIE-LOUISE BRIMBERG. TOP: ALDERMAN LIBRARY, UNIVERSITY OF VIRGINIA

Americans Spread Out

On trails that pierced the heart of Indian country, in ships that sailed through hazards to wealth, along the borders of Spain's embattled empire—everywhere on a bountiful continent, Americans were in motion. Some sought riches, others refuge. All expanded a nation.

RAY ALLEN BILLINGTON

The little band of Revolutionary War veterans who gathered in Boston's Bunch of Grapes Tavern one March night in 1786 listened enraptured as Brig. Gen. Benjamin Tupper spoke. He told them he was just back from a surveying expedition to the Ohio country and had wonders to describe: rich black humus in soil yards deep, fields where a man could plow all day long without once stopping to pick up a rock. God's country, within their reach.

Brig. Gen. Rufus Putnam, who had called the veterans together, reminded them that Congress recently had passed the Ordinance of 1785, which provided for the sale of unsettled lands in 640-acre sections at about a dollar an acre. They had been paid for their military service in "Certificates of Indebtedness," which had shrunk in value to between 8 and 12 cents on the dollar. But Congress had to accept them at face value. Why not, Putnam suggested, turn in their certificates for Continental currency, buy a million acres in the Muskingum River Valley (in present-day eastern Ohio)—and make a fortune? Thus was the Ohio Company born.

When they met a year later, only $250,000 was on hand. Hoping that this was enough for a down payment, they hurried an agent away to New York, where the government was meeting. The Reverend Manasseh Cutler, though a gentleman of the cloth, was a Yankee who would never let scruples interfere with a bargain. So one night he found himself enjoying an excellent oyster supper with Col. William Duer, secretary of the Treasury Board, precursor of the Treasury Department. Duer revealed that he represented a number of congressmen and government officials who not only wanted the Ohio Company to secure its lands but also hoped to share in the transaction themselves.

If the company would ask for 6,500,000 acres instead of only a million, Duer's group would push the measure through Congress, help in the financing, and take a mere 5,000,000 acres as their reward. All was done, and on July 27, 1787, the Ohio Company was given its giant plot of land.

But the Reverend Cutler insisted that settlers would refuse to move unless assured an orderly government. His prodding forced Congress to adopt the Northwest Ordinance. Under this measure, also known as the Ordinance of 1787, the area north of the Ohio and east of the Mississippi was to be carved into three to five "territories."

The territories were to be governed at first by officials who would be named by Congress. As the populations of the territories increased, so would the political power of the people, until each territory would enter the Union on terms of full equality with the older states. Ohio, Indiana, Illinois, Michigan, and Wisconsin became states under the ordinance. Its terms proved so admirable that they were applied to all remaining western territories.

"CHIEF BLACKBIRD" BY ADOLPH A. WEINMAN, GILCREASE INSTITUTE, TULSA, OKLAHOMA;
DETAIL OF A PAINTING BY EMANUEL LEUTZE, NATIONAL COLLECTION OF FINE ARTS, WASHINGTON, D. C.;
PHOTOMONTAGE BY JAMES L. STANFIELD, NATIONAL GEOGRAPHIC PHOTOGRAPHER

The Ohio Company prepared to receive its first settlers by putting aside 4,000 acres at the junction of the Muskingum and Ohio rivers for a "city & Commons." The company also supervised a lottery for eight-acre house lots and larger plots for farming. Transportation was arranged, and a modest sum was appropriated to assist those "who may be otherwise unable to remove themselves thither."

The first colonists landed on the east bank of the Muskingum in April 1788 to begin clearing fields and building cabins. The concentration of Harvard and Yale graduates among them explains their decision to call their outpost Adelphia, a choice soon vetoed by the Ohio Company, which favored Marietta to honor Marie Antoinette, because of French aid during the Revolution. Speculators who had shared in the land purchase lured other pioneers from New England. Soon wilderness beachheads were established at Gallipolis and Losantiville (later given the slightly less awkward name of Cincinnati.)

The Yankees were not alone in the borderlands. South of the Ohio the peopling of Kentucky and Tennessee had been under way since 1775, when a North Carolina speculator, Judge Richard Henderson, hit on the illegal device of buying land from the Indians. During negotiations, he sent a longtime employee named Daniel Boone to blaze a path into Kentucky. With 30 frontiersmen, Boone set out on March 10, 1775, from settlement outposts at the Watauga River in present-day Tennessee. His men cut their way slowly across Powell's Valley, through the flaring portals of the Cumberland Gap, over the hilly country of eastern Kentucky, and finally to the valley of the Kentucky River. There, where the bluegrass grew tall and thick, they erected the cabins of a settlement they called Boonesborough. The judge soon sent more pioneers over the Wilderness Road. Others, defying his authority, planted their own "Kentucky Stations" nearby at Harrodsburg, St. Asaph's, and Boiling Springs.

The stations—palisaded forts surrounding a cluster of cabins—came under repeated attack during the Revolution. Some settlers fled, but after the war most old-timers returned, and newcomers crowded the Wilderness Road. "What a buzzel is this amongst People about *Kentuck,*" wrote a Virginia backcountry clergyman as he lamented his departing flocks. "To hear people speak of it one would think it was a new found paradise." By the 1780's the homes of 20,000 persons dotted the countryside, and Louisville, at the falls of the Ohio, was a thriving community with a rectangular grid of streets and plans for a city park.

Tennessee had fewer people, but they insisted that North Carolina allow their area to become a separate state. When the North Carolinians indignantly refused, the frontier families set up their own state of Franklin. They bombarded Congress with requests for admission to the Union, boasting they would soon "vie with Athens itself" in learning and culture. The Franklinites' expanding population produced a sanctioned claim to statehood, as Tennessee, in 1796.

The spirit of adventure—and lust for profits—that lured pioneers westward was soon challenged by Indians who could be pushed only so far. Several tribes were spurred on by British agents in Canada who still dreamed of recovering all territory north of the Ohio. American expeditions against these Indians ended in disaster. The first, in the Valley of the Maumee in 1790, blundered into an ambush that cost 183 lives. The second, on a branch of the Wabash a year later, was jumped in a dawn attack that left 630 Americans dead and 283 wounded.

Unless the new nation found competent commanders to defend the territory, it would be lost. The threat grew when the British built a new post, Fort Miami, on the Maumee River in undisputed American territory. (The Ohio town of Maumee stands on the site.) President Washington, now alarmed, ordered Gen. "Mad Anthony" Wayne to launch an immediate attack in the fall of 1793. But Wayne chose to spend the winter drilling his army in frontier warfare tactics. In the summer of 1794 Wayne began a cautious advance northward.

The Indians made their stand south of Fort Miami, where a tangle of trees, felled by a tornado, created a natural barricade. Wayne, knowing that

Cumberland Gap, pioneers' way to "a New Sky & Strange Earth," saw 300,000 go west in the late 1700's. Today's highway follows yesterday's Warriors' Path. Ken-ta-ke ("meadow land"), Virginia, and Tennessee meet at the Gap.

BRUCE DALE, NATIONAL GEOGRAPHIC PHOTOGRAPHER

the Indians usually fasted before a battle, leaked the news that he would attack on August 17—and then waited until August 20. When many of the Indians drifted away to seek food, Wayne charged. Within minutes the Battle of Fallen Timbers was over. Few Indians had been killed or wounded, but their spirit was broken. The survivors signed a treaty which surrendered most of Ohio to the United States.

To the south, the Spaniards kept the borderlands in turmoil. They stirred up the Indians, occupied territory claimed by the United States, and threatened to keep Kentuckians and Tennesseans out of New Orleans. When France won Louisiana from Spain in 1800, the situation worsened. President Jefferson began negotiations to buy New Orleans.

Events in Europe played into his hands. By 1803 a Franco-English war was brewing, and this made likely a British attack on New Orleans. Napoleon, recognizing the inevitable, agreed to sell the Louisiana Territory, which encompassed nearly all the Great Plains to the Canadian border.

Even before the treaty was drawn up, the President had been planning an expedition to explore the vast, unknown territory. The leaders of the exploration were 29-year-old Meriwether Lewis, who had learned wilderness ways beneath the shadows of the Blue Ridge, and William Clark, a 33-year-old brother of George Rogers Clark of Revolutionary War fame. They gathered a crew of 49 strapping young frontiersmen at St. Louis and in the spring of 1804 set forth on the nation's earliest exploring enterprise.

From May to November in 1804 the expedition inched its way up the Missouri River in keelboats. The explorers wintered with the Mandans in Dakota, then in the spring pushed on in wooden canoes. They were guided by a remarkable Indian woman, Sacagawea, mate of a French-Canadian

In a mighty merger of rivers, the gilded Mississippi meets the barge-laden Ohio at Cairo, Illinois. The leveed town once was port to 3,700 steamboats. The Ohio also buoys frolickers in history—contestants in a flatboat race. Such boats bore migrants, who then built houses from the timbers.

MARTIN ROGERS

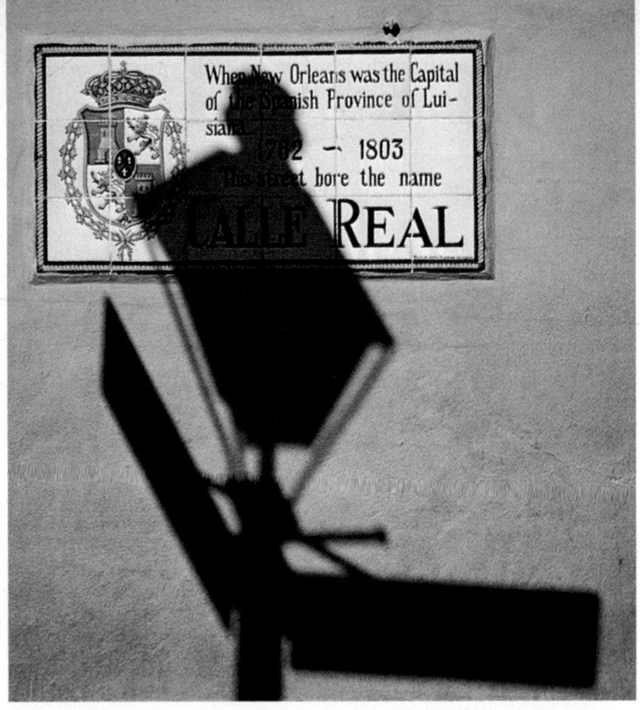

St. Louis Cathedral blesses Jackson Square in New Orleans' French Quarter. Where Spain and France wrote history—and street signs—Americans found a bargain: the three-cents-an-acre Louisiana Purchase, which doubled our territory.

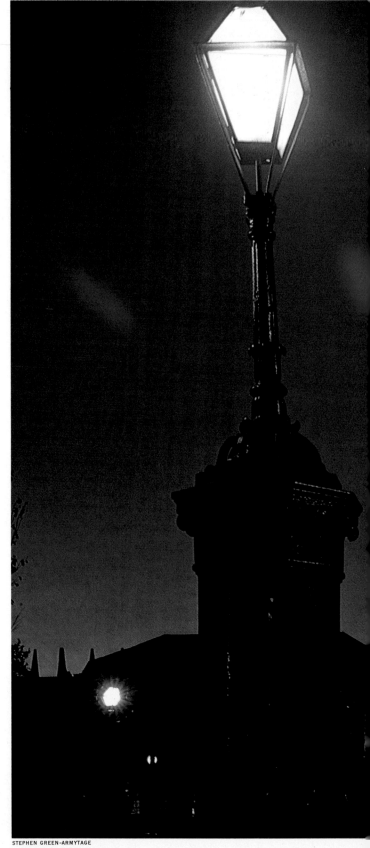

trapper. With her newborn baby boy strapped to her back, she and her husband helped lead the party through the Rocky Mountains. Struggling up the Big Muddy, they portaged around rapids or, "up to our armpits in the cold water," labored the heavy boats onward. They reached the head of the Missouri at Three Forks, then followed the Jefferson River into the country of the Shoshoni. For a time the Indians were hostile, but the presence of Sacagawea mollified them.

With horses procured from the Indians, Lewis and Clark pressed on, crossing the Bitterroot Mountains and descending the Clearwater and Columbia rivers. In mid-November 1805 they reached the Pacific, "reward of all our anxieties." There they built Fort Clatsop, named after an Indian tribe.

The expedition inspired a westward sweep of the farming frontier, which had lagged to the east. By 1812 several hundred thousand pioneers lived on the sunset side of the Appalachians, and all the Mississippi Valley seemed destined to be settled.

Another war delayed that happy prospect. In 1812 England and the United States again resorted to arms, this time over the right of American shippers to sail the seas without interference by Britain's powerful navy. The young nation's "fir-built frigates" outsailed the Royal Navy's best. But the War of 1812 was no triumph for the United States.

America's early attempt to strike at England

STEPHEN GREEN-ARMYTAGE

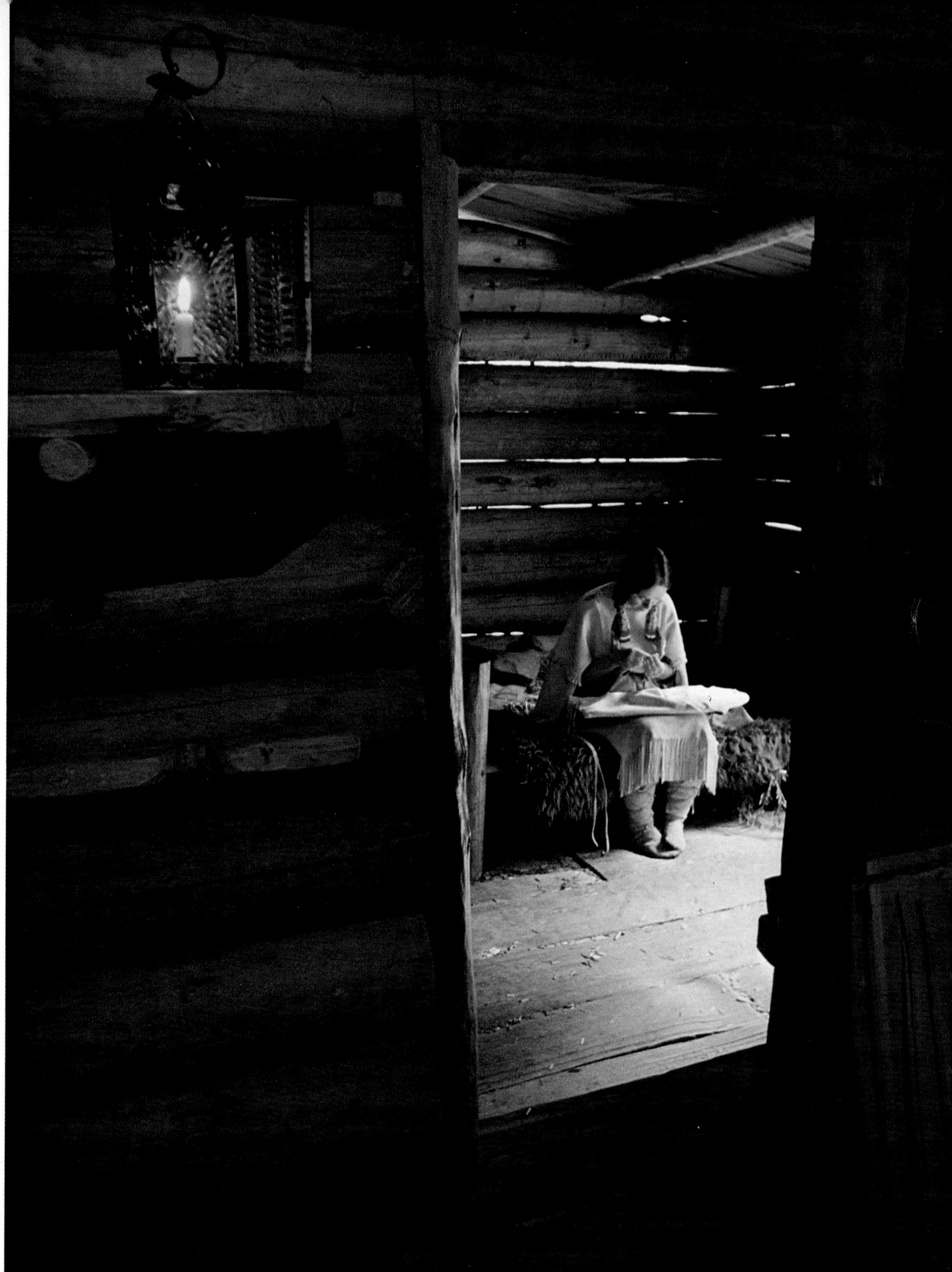

LOWELL GEORGIA

under construction. Spectacular—and impractical—projects were launched. Boston, despairing of getting a waterway through the Berkshires, gambled on a series of small, end-to-end railroads. Pennsylvania's costly system of canals featured inclined planes for the sliding of barges up and down mountains.

Maryland, undaunted by the Appalachians, chartered the Chesapeake and Ohio Canal Company, raised some $3,000,000 in state, federal, and private funds, and began digging on July 4, 1828. When President John Quincy Adams tried to turn over the first shovelful of dirt, he rammed his spade into an unyielding tree root. It was an ill omen.

Baltimore merchants, lukewarm to a canal, backed a railroad—the Baltimore and Ohio, begun in 1828. The B & O helped to doom the C & O. When the project was abandoned in 1850, its cost had hit $22,000,000, and the ditch had reached only to Cumberland on the eastern edge of the mountains.

The canals—and even abandoned canal routes—did serve the nation in another way: by helping to shape the course of migration. New Englanders and New Yorkers, assured a safe and economical journey over the Erie Canal, streamed westward in droves to settle in the upper portions of the Old Northwest, as they called it, and to push into Iowa and Minnesota. Come-outers from the Middle Atlantic states followed the National Road or abandoned canals into the Ohio Valley, then onward to the fringe of states bordering the west bank of the Mississippi. Farmers from the slave states advanced the cotton frontier across Alabama and Mississippi into Louisiana.

Beyond lay the vastness of Texas, Spain's loss and Mexico's gain as a reward of the latter's independence in 1821. The possession was open to anyone who accepted Catholicism and became a citizen. Moses Austin, a Connecticut Yankee and a Missouri frontiersman, won permission that year to introduce 300 colonists. When he died, his son Stephen, a scholarly 27-year-old, took over. Within two years 300 families—the "Old Three Hundred" in Texan lore—occupied the colony that Stephen Austin established on the Colorado River. Mexico, pleased with Austin's success, soon inaugurated the *empresario* system, granting giant tracts to speculators who guaranteed to bring in specific numbers of settlers. The *empresarios* advertised their cheap lands so widely that "Texas Fever" raged throughout the South. By 1830 about 30,000 Americans—and only 3,500 Mexicans—lived there.

This spelled trouble, for irreconcilable culture differences divided the two groups. The bumptious American frontiersmen, many of them social outcasts, resented being governed by "foreigners."

When Mexico made a bumbling attempt to assert its authority over the Texans, they demanded the right to govern themselves as a Mexican state. Rebuffed, they formed a provisional government with a battery of officials and a small army.

Their defiance brought the Mexican president, Gen. Antonio López de Santa Anna, storming into Texas with a tattered army of 6,000. As he advanced on Austin's colony, where the rebels were centered, Santa Anna was blocked at San Antonio by a handful of Texans in the Alamo, a former mission. Santa Anna at first sent only a few hundred men against the Texans. But their commander, Capt. William B. Travis, said the men of the Alamo were determined that "victory will cost the enemy so dear it will be worse for him than a defeat."

The besiegers' army ultimately numbered as many as 3,000; wave after wave of them swept against the mission walls. Finally, on the gray morning of March 6, 1836, the Mexican troops launched an all-out assault.

On their third try they swarmed into the building. The Texans fought desperately with rifle butts and knives. By noon all 187 of them—including such folk heroes as Davy Crockett and Jim Bowie—had fallen. The Mexicans lost 1,544 men.

The cry "Remember the Alamo!" resounded through Texas. Her leaders declared her an independent state and named Sam Houston head of the army. A rough-and-tumble Tennessean and former Indian fighter, Houston led a ragtag army eastward with Santa Anna on their heels. At the San Jacinto River, near the protection of the American border, Houston and his men elected to make their stand.

On April 20, the armies clashed. In 17 minutes the battle was over, with 630 Mexicans dead and Santa Anna a captive, along with 730 of his men.

The Republic of Texas had won independence. But not until 1845 would Congress welcome Texas

DAVID HISER

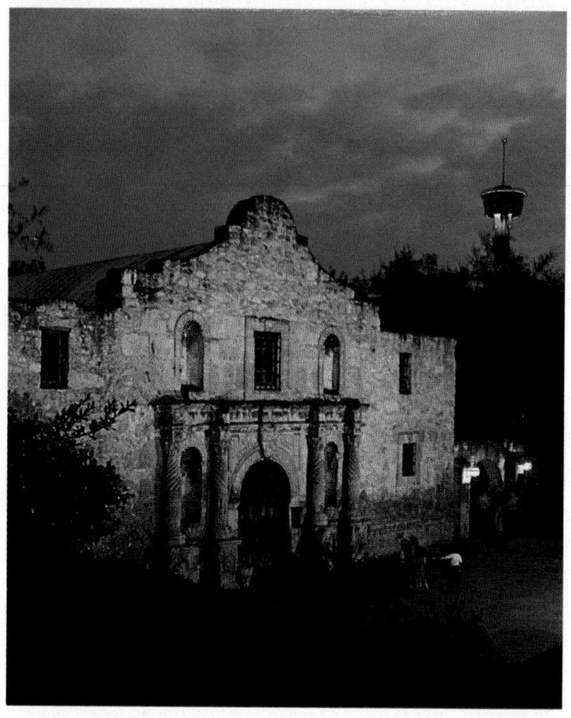

The Alamo, citadel of "high souled courage," stands ever remembered in San Antonio. Cottonwood trees, los alamos, *gave the former mission the name that rallied Texans to freedom. The restored shrine is near La Villita, where adobe walls and the Spanish Governor's Palace recall a Southwest that spoke* español.

into the Union. By then, the Far West was an arena of empire, where the United States would fight and maneuver to realize her "Manifest Destiny"—the patriotic phrase of the day, the impetus for extending her borders to the Pacific. Spain claimed a domain old and broad. She had founded the hamlet of Santa Fe back in 1609. Later, one of her far-roving missionaries, Father Junípero Serra, had planted a chain of missions along the California coast. And England's powerful Hudson's Bay Company claimed the entire region north of the Columbia River.

Trappers led the American thrust into the Far West. The broad South Pass through the Rockies provided easy access to seekers of beaver, much in demand by European hatmakers. Beginning in 1825, many trappers lived in the Rockies, emerging each summer to meet a supply train from the East and barter their "hairy bank notes." These "mountain men" eventually numbered about 600. In search of the animals they all but exterminated, they explored an area that would give the Union new states, from Wyoming to Washington.

The mountain men helped to open—and advertise—rich lands awaiting the plow. They traced the trails and streams that would be the lifelines of survival. They damaged the self-sufficiency of the Indians by trading them firearms and firewater. By the time the men of the mountains began to vanish, the farmers were entering a less wild Far West.

Oregon lured them first. There Dr. John McLoughlin, chief factor of the Hudson's Bay Company, was building an empire. McLoughlin not only sent his brigades of trappers over most of the West but also imported farmers, converted trappers into townsmen, and planted British roots throughout the company's vast realm.

To break this monopoly, the United States relied on the frontiersman's insatiable desire for cheap land. Unexpected American colonizing was also inspired by missionaries. The Reverend Jason Lee, a Methodist, established the first mission in 1834, choosing as its site the Willamette Valley. Among those who followed was Dr. Marcus Whitman. When he failed to cure several Indian children stricken with measles—while curing whites who had better resistance—he, his wife, and 12 others were massacred.

The missionaries won few converts. But in letters home and in money-raising speaking tours in the East, the clergymen converted thousands of farmers to the belief that the Willamette Valley was God's country. There crops could be harvested three times a year, and 640 acres of the best land in the world awaited all comers free of charge.

Migration began in 1839 when the first caravan of covered wagons plodded along the Oregon Trail. They followed the Platte and North Platte rivers westward, crossing the Rockies over South Pass. They then swung slightly southward to restock at Fort Bridger, a trading outpost near the Green River built by one of the toughest of the mountain men, Jim Bridger. (The story goes that when Dr. Whitman removed an arrowhead that had been in Bridger's back for three years, the crusty Bridger said, "In the mountains, meat don't spoil.")

From Fort Bridger the caravan turned north and west to a Hudson's Bay Company base, Fort Hall. There, at first, the wagons were exchanged for packhorses, and the journey continued along the Snake and Columbia rivers to Jason Lee's mission.

Yearly caravans followed the pioneers until by 1845 some 5,000 Americans were in Oregon, most of them in the Willamette Valley (around today's

IRA BLOCK. OPPOSITE: "CONSTITUTION AND THE GUERRIÈRE, IN ACTION" BY MICHEL F. CORNE, 1813, U. S. NAVAL ACADEMY MUSEUM

Salem). The 750 British in the Oregon country were north of the Columbia River. They showed no inclination to surrender the lands they occupied. But the Americans had already pledged "all Oregon or None." In 1843 they established a government to operate "until such time as the United States of America extend their jurisdiction over us."

A wilderness war seemed inevitable. Then, surprisingly, the Hudson's Bay Company shifted its headquarters from Fort Vancouver on the Columbia to Fort Victoria on Vancouver Island, where the company's enormous store of trading goods would be safe. The British government, correctly interpreting this to mean that the company no longer believed that the region was worth fighting for, made known that it was ready to settle the long-standing boundary dispute. In June 1846 a treaty was signed extending the 49th parallel boundary to the Pacific. Land-hungry pioneers had added another sizable chunk of territory to the United States.

More land was soon to come. While Oregon had attracted most of the emigrants, a smaller number had headed for the lower Sacramento Valley of California. The California Trail, branching from the Oregon Trail near Fort Hall in present-day Idaho, had been pioneered in 1841 by a band of 32 men, a woman, and a child. Braving the searing Nevada deserts and the snows of the Sierras, they were the first train to journey from the Missouri to California. By spring of 1846 some 700 Americans lived in California, nearly all of them in the lower Sacramento Valley. Many were veterans of the fur trade, and they were spoiling for a fight.

Mexico and the United States already had begun

Constitution, *oldest commissioned ship in the U.S. Navy, convoys history in Boston, where she was launched in 1797. She won immortality, the name* Old Ironsides *– and the battle against the British frigate* Guerrière *in the War of 1812. Her guns toppled the foe's mizzen (above) in 16 minutes.*

drifting into war over the annexation of Texas in 1845. As both sides flexed muscles, rumors of the impending crisis reached the Americans in the Sacramento Valley. They decided to act. The nearest symbol of Mexican authority was the tree-shaded hacienda of Mariano G. Vallejo, a Sonoma rancher. He was even then working with American agents to deliver California peacefully to the United States.

Led by a rawboned, tobacco-chewing illiterate named Ezekiel Merritt, 33 Americans reached Sonoma after an all-night ride. They were received courteously and invited to partake freely of brandy while breakfast was prepared. This delayed matters until a non-drinking idealist, William B. Ide, convinced his host to surrender California.

And so the rebels crowded into the Sonoma plaza on June 15, 1846, raised a flag bearing a crude symbol of a bear, and listened to Ide read a flowery proclamation. With the Bear Flag Rebellion came a requiem for Mexico's reign in the Southwest.

The Bear Flaggers did not know that a larger conflict had begun in April when forces on the tense Rio Grande border fired on each other. "War has commenced," wrote an American dragoon in his diary. War dispatches were flashed eastward over a new miracle of communication: the telegraph. It was a very satisfactory war for the United States. In the Treaty of Guadalupe-Hidalgo, ratified in March 1848, American military triumphs were translated into a Mexican surrender of California and all the Southwest.

But with the new territory came a new problem: Should the states that would emerge be free or slave? Frontier expansion had created a crisis in a nation hopelessly divided over slavery. Some already said that the issue could be resolved only by civil war. The Mexican War had already tested young military leaders in the crucible of battle. Fellow officers against the Mexicans—Grant and Lee, Sherman and Jackson, McClellan and Jefferson Davis—would meet again in a trial of blue and gray.

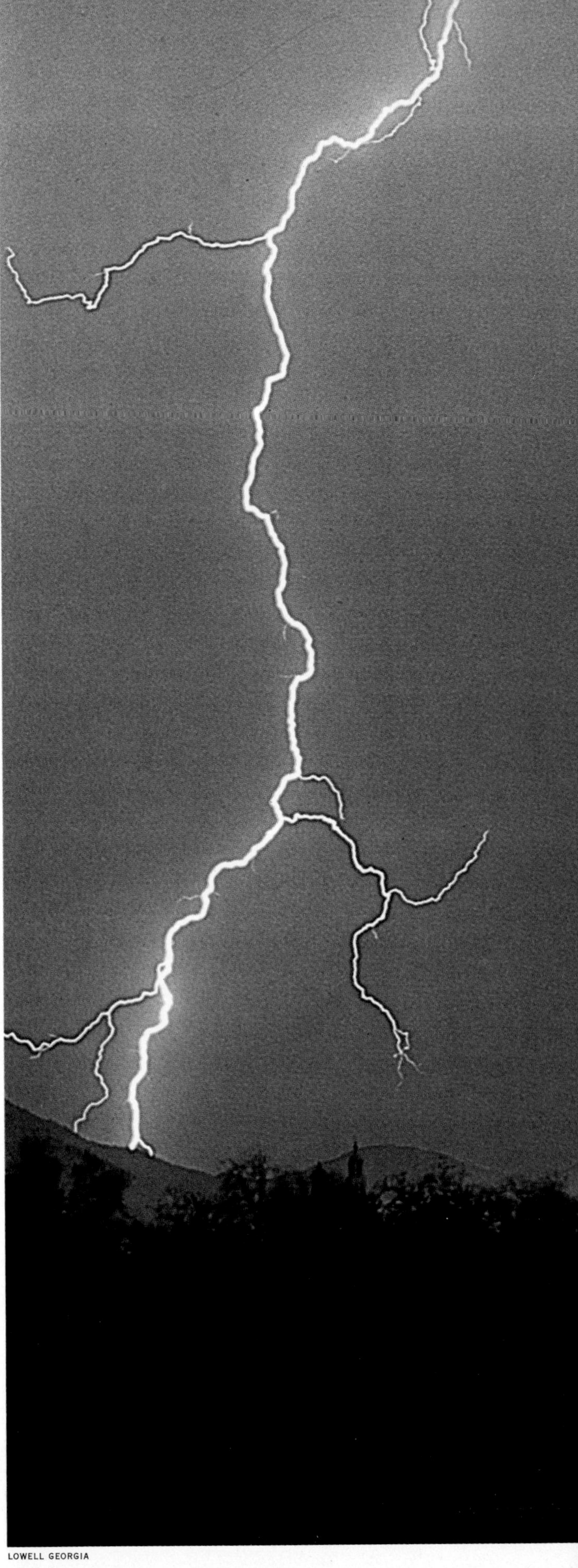

Lightning etches "The White Dove of the Desert," the San Xavier del Bac Mission near Tucson, Arizona. Founded in 1700, it saw the high noon and the fiery sunset of Spanish rule on land that in a new dawn would be the United States.

LOWELL GEORGIA

Wealth from the Sea

"In the moneth of Aprill, 1614," recorded Capt. John Smith, "I chanced to arrive in New-England . . . our plot was there to take Whales." But the hunt proved unsuccessful, and the expedition turned instead to "Fish and Furres." His ships left for Europe with a cargo of some 1,300 furs and 47,000 fish.

Captain Smith's voyage foreshadowed permanent settlements of New Englanders who would claim their share of the sea's bounty. In boats ranging from frail shallops to full-rigged sailing ships, they fished, traded to the world's farthest ports, and learned most successfully "to take Whales." Today the flavor and heritage of those seafaring days live on in Massachusetts towns like Salem, Marblehead, Gloucester, and Nantucket, and particularly at Mystic Seaport in Connecticut.

The Puritans of the Massachusetts Bay Colony were almost forced into seafaring. Their original purpose was to farm, but the stony soil obliged them to exploit more reliable staples: fish and timber.

Governor John Winthrop's bark *Blessing of the Bay,* launched in 1631, traded native products as far south as the town of New Amsterdam. Soon Yankee vessels shuttled between home, the Southern colonies, the West Indies, and Europe in an endless pursuit of the best trade. Return cargoes included West Indian molasses for rum distilleries

Lookout's giddy view frames a Mystic Seaport panorama between the yardarms of square-rigger Joseph Conrad. *Beyond rides the gallant* Charles W. Morgan, *last of the wooden whalers and emblem of the age of sail.*

FARRELL GREHAN

and English manufactured goods—if the captain had not sold his ship as well for a handsome profit!

The colony's chief fishing port at Marblehead supplied many a cargo. Codfish was a specialty—top grade for the European Catholic market, "middling" for various foreign and colonial tables, and "refuse" for slaves on West Indian plantations. The rugged fishermen braved treacherous seas in small shallops or ketches. Handlines, thrown over the side, were often baited with the plentiful, ill-esteemed lobster.

Early Marbleheaders huddled in tiny wooden houses on rocky ledges. Pathways twisted as a man might wander around boulders and streams on his way to the harbor. Eighteenth-century prosperity brought the quaint, low-ceilinged homes which still crowd one another higgledy-piggledy down the narrow, crooked streets of old Marblehead.

Above them rise the luxurious mansions of merchants Jeremiah Lee and "King" Hooper. Lee's stately Georgian home has spacious rooms and a magnificent stairway.

Gloucester ran a close second to Marblehead and finally overtook her. Today, Gloucester fishermen go down to the sea in "draggers," whose sturdy hulls mingle with sleek pleasure craft at Seven Seas Wharf. The smell of fish, the screaming gulls, the hardy fishermen—now dressed in baseball caps, T-shirts, and hip boots—recall Gloucester's 19th-century prime, when her speedy schooners raced "down East" (downwind) to the fishing banks.

Mystic Seaport, an old shipbuilding site on Connecticut's Mystic River, vividly re-creates such a 19th-century port. A whole coastal village is assembled here, complete with working craft shops and shipyard.

The masts are the first thing that catch your eye. Towering masts of majestic square-riggers, festooned with spider webs of rigging. Slim-lined, graceful masts of sloops and

"Not enough to do to keep a man off a growl. . . ." grumbled a skipper in 1842. "I prefer to scrimshone." Scrimshaw, the whaleman's hobby, spelled relief from the aching monotony of long voyages. Wishful thinking inspired vivid scenes, scratched with jackknife and sail needle on sperm whale teeth or jawbone and on walrus tusks. The "shincracker" wheel, mounted on a swinging tiller, steered the whaleship Morgan, *whose eagle-decked stern looms above.*

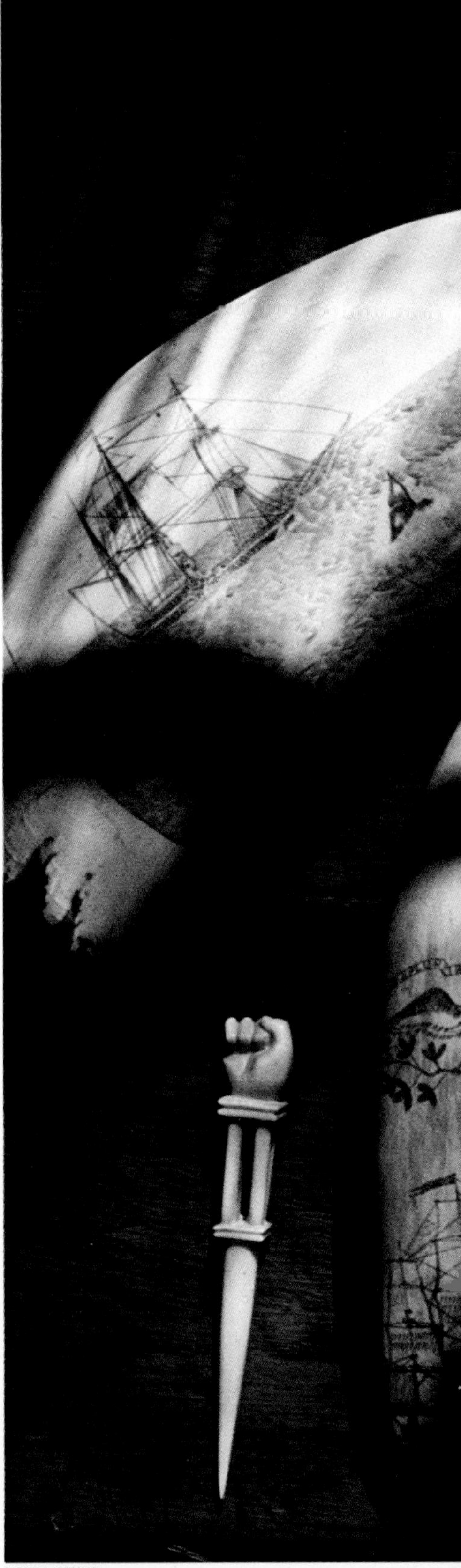

FARRELL GREHAN

schooners—the tallest adorning the *L. A. Dunton,* a Gloucester fisherman that, at sea, "rode like a duck." And around them on the river swoop the brightly colored sails of Dyer Dhows (sailing dinghies in Mystic's youth training program) like a flock of startled water birds.

A sea chantey draws you to the *Joseph Conrad,* where a demonstration team is rhythmically hauling up the yard. The fore-topsail fills, and a shouted "Belay!" cuts off the chanteyman, even in the middle of a phrase, or bad luck will follow.

Heading up Village Street toward the museum buildings, you pass a rope walk, sail and rigging lofts, and a ship chandlery, or supply store. Stop at the doorway of the Spouter Tavern and your imagination jumps straight into the pages of Melville's *Moby Dick.* You can almost hear the "tramping of sea boots" and see a "wild set of mariners" rolling in, fresh off the boat, for a warm-up draft of gin and molasses.

So might the crew of the *Charles W. Morgan* have returned from her "greasy" maiden voyage with 2,400 barrels of whale oil. Built in 1841, the *Morgan* earned 1.5 million dollars during an 80-year career. Her blubber-boiling tryworks are cold now, her wheel untended. But her swift whaleboats, poised on their davits, seem ready to lower away and fly on a wild "Nantucket sleigh ride," towed by a harpooned giant.

For all the romantic tales, crews who shipped from Nantucket or other ports risked three or four rough, underpaid years at sea. Shipowners and officers took most of the

Wooden eyes scan lost horizons in the Ship Carver's Shop, where an ancient art lives on at Mystic. Figureheads and stern carvings decorated sailing ships fore and aft—and were tended with care as good luck guardians.

FARRELL GREHAN

profits. But Nantucketers had little choice. Whaling was their lifeblood. It fed and clothed them and built their homes.

Most Nantucket houses—clad still in silver-gray shingle or white clapboard—mirror the simplicity of their Quaker builders. Many have a rooftop "walk" for horizon-scanning.

Main Street dwellings of the mid-1800's boast richer lines. Joseph Starbuck built the famous Three Bricks for his sons. A daughter lived opposite in an imposing white pillared home. Guides point out the hollow newel-post where by custom the mortgage deed was hidden. The note paid off, owners plugged the hole with a local status symbol—a whale ivory "mortgage button."

Sons of Nantucket's first families occasionally moved "off island." A Macy boy opened a dry goods store in New York. And Joseph Rotch, of a whaling family, helped set up that industry in New Bedford.

There, said Ralph Waldo Emerson, men would "hug an oil-cask like a brother." From a window of New Bedford's Whaling Museum, you gaze down to ships at the still-busy waterfront where whalers once docked. The town's golden age of whaling is long past, but historical societies strive to preserve its aura.

Whaling, fishing, and trading declined drastically during Revolutionary War years. The British navy sank or captured unarmed American ships. Some New Englanders found a patriotic recourse in privateering—and built larger, faster vessels to pursue enemy prizes.

FARRELL GREHAN

The impressive size of her 1819 Custom House reflects Salem's early contribution in shipping revenue to the national treasury. Nearby Derby House displays ship models, navigation aids, rum measuring cups—tokens of a rich trade that swelled the new nation's coffers.

PEAKS ISLAND

FARRELL GREHAN

"In sculpture he had no rival in New England." So it was claimed of master carver and architect Samuel McIntire—witness the superb woodwork of the 1782 Peirce-Nichols House in Salem. McIntire's carving style is visible in draped classical urns, elegant interior details, and pieces of furniture. The knocker may have summoned Jerathmiel Peirce, whose ships docked on the North River behind his house.

Other merchants and captains built tall mansions on Washington Square, Essex Street, and beautiful Chestnut Street, filling them with handsome furnishings and Oriental luxuries, perhaps even a turbaned Indian houseboy.

Seeking postwar profits for their new ships, owners sent them to the Orient. New York merchants exported ginseng, a wild root valued by the Chinese as a panacea and aphrodisiac. Bostonians traded glossy sea otter pelts and other furs to the mandarins. And in successful rivalry, ships with mixed cargoes sailed from the little port of Salem.

Elias Hasket Derby's *Grand Turk,* out of Salem, arrived in Canton in 1786. The Chinese emperor graciously permitted "foreign devil" Capt. Ebenezer West to load tea and chinaware. His return brought fabulous profits to Derby. Soon lucky Salem women, dressed in China silk gowns, sipped tea from their own sets of Canton "china." Derby's ship rosters listed famous Salem names, among them Nathaniel Bowditch, whose *New American Practical Navigator* became a seaman's other bible.

Salem's Peabody Museum depicts a great East India trade. China was only part of the story. Ships on the favored eastern route around Africa picked up Madeira wine, African gold dust and ivory, Indian cottons and spices. In 1797 Capt. Jonathan Carnes' pioneer cargo of Sumatran pepper cleared a 700 percent profit. Salem became known as the world's leading pepper port.

The windows of Derby's 1762 brick house stare emptily down the now-grassy finger of Derby Wharf, once lined with busy warehouses and East Indiamen. Nearby stands the Custom House where novelist Nathaniel Hawthorne served as port surveyor. He described the bypassed seaport of 1849, wharves crumbling and customs officers dozing while trade was siphoned off to the larger harbors of Boston and New York.

But old Salem's waterfront still throngs with ghosts of an era that gave her a brave town motto: "To the farthest port of the rich East."

MARY H. DICKINSON

BILL STRODE

Utopias in the Wilderness

A procession of religious and social idealists streamed toward the Mississippi in the early 1800's, eager to build their particular utopias, their heavens on earth. In the vanguard tramped three Shaker missionaries. Sent into the wilderness to win converts to their communal, monastic sect, they set out from upstate New York on New Year's Day 1805, their beacon the campfires of Kentucky's Great Revival.

South through Pennsylvania and Maryland, Virginia and Tennessee the Shakers journeyed, then north again and through the Cumberland Gap, coming at last to Kentucky, where the wild woods rang with the hymns and sermons of camp meetings. The Shakers, once called "Shaking Quakers" for their frenzied rituals, won converts among the frontier faithful, who danced, shouted, and even barked in pursuit of salvation. Soon thriving new Shaker settlements grew in the west—one was Pleasant Hill in Kentucky's rolling bluegrass. Here gathered "families" in the simple Shaker way, believers in the social gospel of Jesus.

By mid-century the Shakers and zealous thousands from other sects had brightened the prairies and forests with neat villages which, like Pleasant Hill, even today delight travelers. Some utopians sought religious haven; others set up communities to make life better for working people. All communally fed, clothed, and directed members. Some sects enforced celibacy, believing with Saint Paul that he "that is unmarried careth for the things that belong to the Lord." Many believed in the millennium of the New Testament book of Revelation, the

"'Tis the gift to be simple," sang the Shakers of their God-given freedom from worldliness. The heavenward-soaring staircases which grace the 1839 Trustees' Office at Pleasant Hill, Kentucky, show their worship-at-work. Shakers consecrated their earthly homes, ever sweeping and brightening. "There is no dirt in Heaven," said leader Ann Lee. In the celibate Shaker way, serene brothers and sisters filed through separate doorways into the Meeting House (above) and the dining room in a Dwelling House (top). But the sexes were equal—woman's work, like man's, included trades and the ministry.

BILL STRODE

"New Jerusalem" America promised.

Some of the earliest utopians had been welcomed by William Penn's colony. In 1732 these Pietists, wanting to live as ancient Christians, established the cloister of Ephrata some 50 miles west of Philadelphia. Men and women alike dressed in monk's robes. In the gabled, medieval-style buildings, today's visitors climb steep stairs, thread passages "strait and narrow," and stoop in doorways built low to enforce a bow of humility. On summer weekends they hear hooded choristers re-create ethereal music of the past. Books, at first printed by Benjamin Franklin, after 1743 emerged from Ephrata's own press in a publishing enterprise unique in colonial America.

In 1777 war's misery came to the peaceful community when General Washington, routed at Brandywine, entrusted hundreds of ill and wounded soldiers to the charity of Ephrata.

Between the Revolutionary War and the Civil War, utopians founded more than a hundred communities in the United States. In 1804, some 600 farmers and artisans, under a charismatic leader, George Rapp, broke from Germany's state Lutheran church and came to America. Within 25 years the Harmonists, as

The Shaker sister's year-round labors with spinning wheel, dye pot, loom, and needle kept not only her own village clothed and carpeted. Often she headed a complex industry which created fine textiles and garments for sale to "the world." Shakers raised their own flax and (opposite) spun it into linen for summer dresses and rough tow for horse blankets. With walnut leaves they dyed wool for "trowsers" (left). Cotton they wove into coverlets (top) or into bright tapes for chair seats. Silk and linen made a dress fine yet sturdy enough for daily use. And to air their handiwork, Ohio Shakers invented the clothespin.

they called themselves, had built three towns. Their first, Harmony, Pennsylvania, was a bustling village where girls sang as they spun wool, and tailors, carpenters, and farmers all worked for the common cause.

A dozen of Harmony's original houses remain. Visitors now stroll through the diminutive neighborhood where steep-pitched roofs once were thatched, linger in the museum, and wander to the walled cemetery at the edge of town where graves are unmarked; all were equal in the sight of God.

In 1814-15, seeking better trade routes, the Harmonists moved to their second Harmony—on the Wabash River in the Indiana Territory. Dozens of their sturdy buildings are still in use. Industries hummed, storing up wealth for the day when these

Hands to work and hearts to God made perfectionists of Shaker craftsmen. At Pleasant Hill the joiner smooths a cherry table—in its wooden drawer knob and natural finish he seeks utility. A stave for applesauce bucket or cider noggin takes shape under the cooper's drawknife. In the joy of work Shakers invented cut nails, a circular saw, the flat broom—and a vise, the better to sew it.

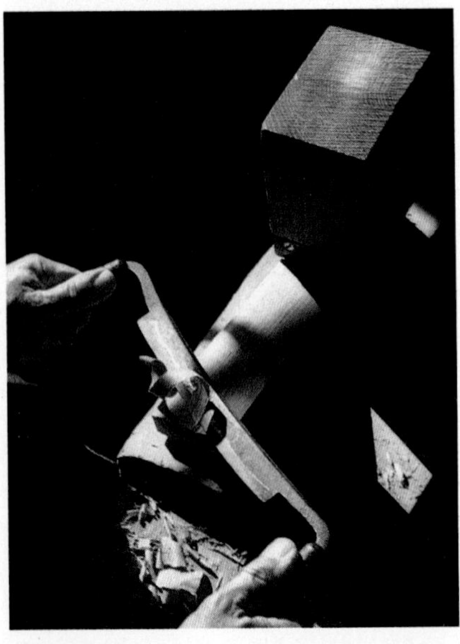

BILL STRODE

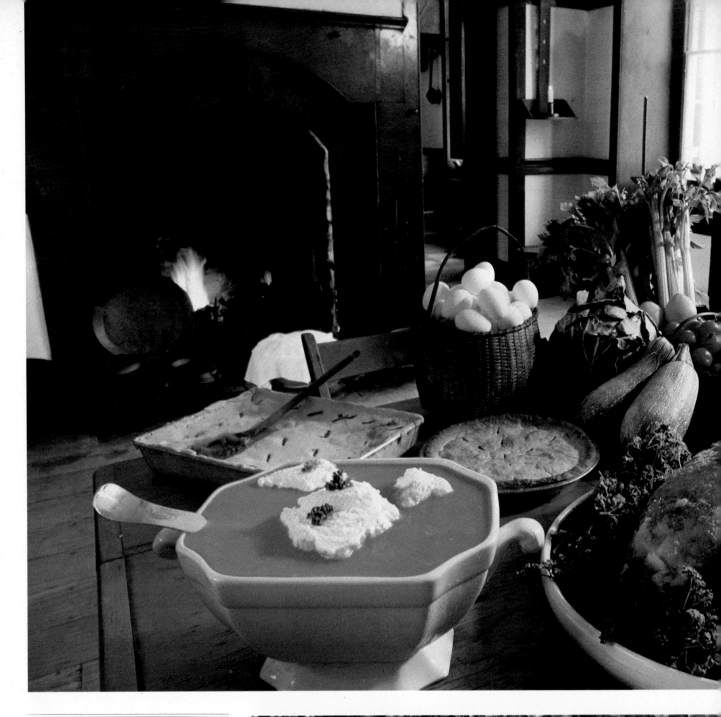

Shakers venerated God's earth — and by progressive farming reaped its bounty for their tables, for hungry wayfarers, and for eager markets. Throughout the 1800's soberly clad brothers set out from Shaker towns by foot, wagon, flatboat, or steamboat with the wares that brought them fame as golden-rule peddlers of seeds, herbs, jeans, chairs, brooms, baskets, and prize livestock. Today sheep again graze along the stone fences at Pleasant Hill, and visitors who feast from the gardens hear the old caution against waste: "Shaker your plate."

millennialists hoped to go to Jerusalem to meet Christ.

But their best markets were in Pennsylvania, and ten years later "Father" Rapp took them back. There, in Economy (now Ambridge), his Great House marks their success. Step through the Georgian front door; enter the office with its big iron safe. Visit the Trustees' Room, where Gertrude Rapp served currant wine and ginger cakes as callers listened to the melody of two pianos.

The Harmonists sold their Indiana town to Robert Owen, a wealthy British socialist reformer. In 1825 Owen came to Washington and, before Congress and Presidents James Monroe and John Quincy Adams, described his dream: New Harmony would show the world a free intellectual life. Recruits hastened to the village on the Wabash. In the laboratories of his son David Dale Owen, the U. S. Geological Survey was born. Owenite zeal led to a public school system, Indiana's first trade school, and a cultural "golden age" flourishing anew in the contemporary theaters and galleries that mingle with lovingly restored Harmonist and Owenite sites.

In 1817 another German sect came to America. Philadelphia Quakers lent them money and sped them on Pennsylvania's new road to Ohio. There they cleared land for their "quiet Zoar farm" and laid out the tidy village on the Tuscarawas.

Today descendants of the original Zoarites greet visitors to their still-living town, escort them through workshops, and point out the log cabin where leader Joseph Bimeler preached his first sermon. Zoar's settlers planted a "Garden of Happiness." Now one can pace flower-lined paths which converge to symbolize life's journey to Christ.

The Inspirationists, also German, had already settled in western New York when, in 1854, they received through their mystical leaders a divine command to seek a "goal in the West." Their new home on the Iowa prairie—Amana—grew to a cluster of seven villages. As in other utopias, daily routines expressed spiritual ideals. Amana's restored communal kitchen evokes the old sociability, when 15-gallon kettles of beef stew bubbled on the huge brick-and-iron stove, and when 50 to 60 villagers gathered, men at one long table, women at another, to share the harvest of fields and gardens tilled by all. Visitors can watch for hours as Amana workers in original buildings turn out fine woolens and handmade clocks and furniture.

From Sweden in the 1840's and 1850's more than 1,000 followers

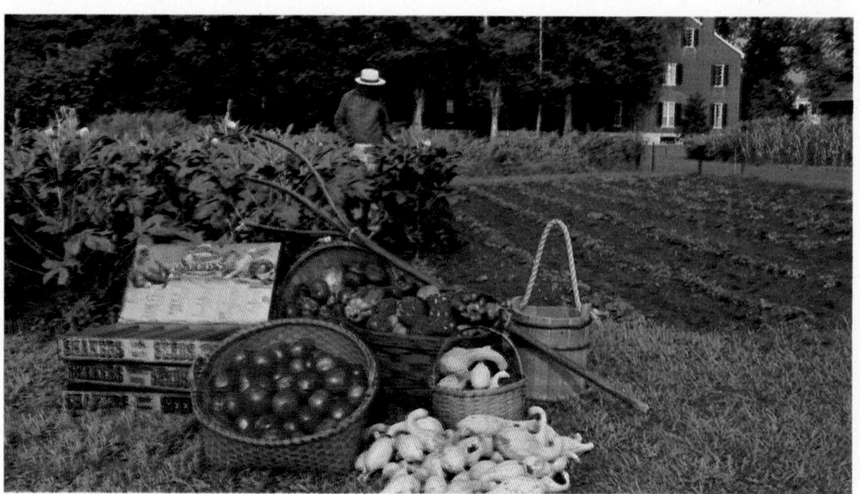

BILL STRODE

of Eric Janson sailed to New York. On the Erie Canal some of these Jansonites rode boats so crowded that many stood for days, or plodded along the towpath, picking corn and apples on the way. Others walked 350 miles from Toledo to Bishop Hill, their colony in western Illinois. There, cabins and log-lined mud caves were their first shelters so dark, damp, and crowded that death scarred almost every dawn.

Soon the Bishop Hill colonists built a communal home of four stories with 96 rooms, Big Brick, a pioneer condominium. Big Brick is gone now, and youngsters slam homers toward the ravine where their ancestors dug in for the winter. But one can still explore the elegant Steeple Building and the gambrel-roofed, white frame church, lighted by graceful wrought-iron chandeliers.

Back East, Yankee utopias dotted New England. In West Roxbury, Massachusetts, Brook Farm tried to dignify labor with a life of culture, and met encouragement from Ralph Waldo Emerson, the great transcendentalist. Bronson Alcott led a flight to Fruitlands, an old red farmhouse in the village of Harvard, Massachusetts. In *Transcendental Wild Oats,* Louisa May Alcott gently poked fun at her father's experiment and the sparse vegetarian diet of "solar seeds" and "bowls of sunrise."

The red farmhouse, now a museum, welcomes visitors, who may see the attic room of the "little women," where the rain, said Louisa, "made a pretty noise on the roof." The Brook Farmers have left us no historical shrines. Their legacy stands on our library shelves, in the literature created by disciples such as Hawthorne, Thoreau, and Whitman.

When the Civil War came, pacifist Zoarites watched their sons run off to fight, and gentle Kentucky Shakers fed the ragged, bloody hordes of both armies, sometimes a thousand in a day. Canals, then railroads, had opened up once-secluded towns. Summer visitors came to stare. Simple communal economies faltered and failed. The strong leaders died, and children of the millennialists awoke to the lure of a new nation.

MARGARET SEDEEN

Shaker spirits rise again as the Louisville Ballet Company re-creates a sabbath devotion. Worshiping Shakers of old—sometimes joyful, sometimes solemn—stamped and whirled, shrieked and sang, and shook the evil out.

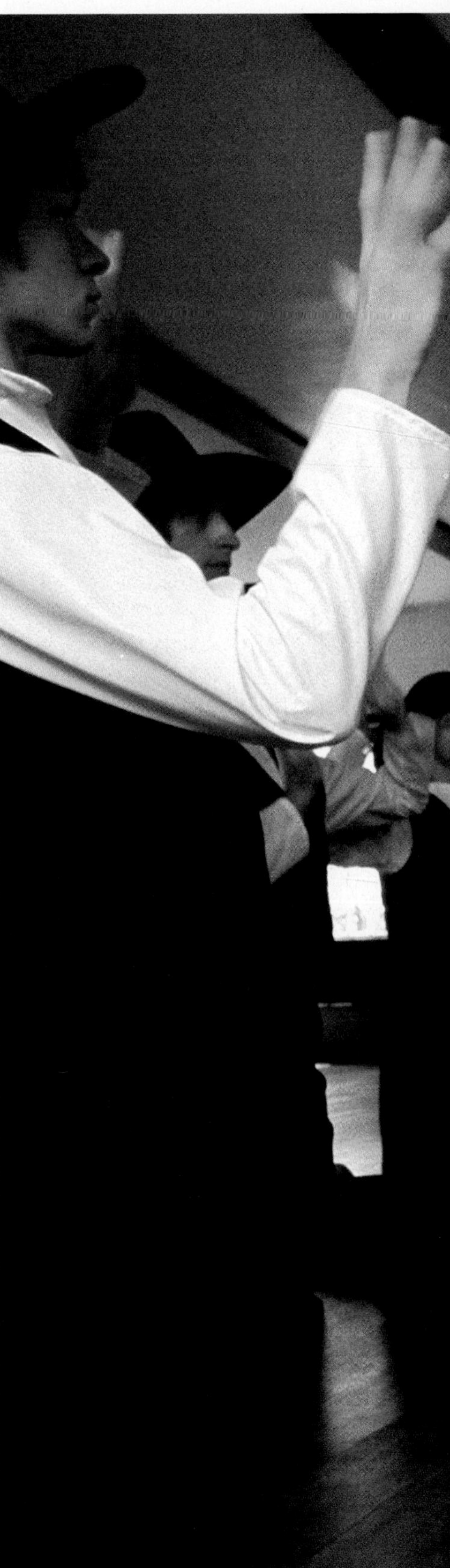

BILL STRODE

Santa Fe to San Francisco

It's William Becknell, all right. Franklin, Missouri, hasn't set eyes on him and his companions for five months, not since they headed west with a packtrain in September of 1821 to barter with the Indians. Now they're back, like flotsam sloshed ashore by that endless sea of grass. The tiny frontier town pours out of shops and homes and saloons to see how the traders fared.

One of them yanks out a rawhide pouch, tosses it to the ground, and knifes it open. Out jangles a glittering cascade—coins! Silver ones, the stuff not of Indian hagglings but of the fabled and forbidden reaches of New Spain far to the south. Forbidden no longer; Mexico has won her independence from Spain and the right to trade with her American neighbors. And Becknell has won a niche in history as the trader whose footfalls—and glowing accounts afterward—turned an Indian trail into the Road to Santa Fe.

Today we call it the Santa Fe Trail. We glimpse a few faded feet of it in Missouri towns that once succeeded each other as its starting point: Franklin, Independence, Westport, Kansas City. The grasslands remember it more clearly; there the eye can skid to the horizon on a broad, shallow depression arrowing to the southwest, its grass a bit greener than the rangeland it bisects.

What greener pastures awaited the traders who poured down that trail! One of Becknell's companions

Made of mud and faith, the Church of St. Francis near Taos, New Mexico, rang with the prayers of Spanish padres of the 1700's who won Indians of the Southwest for cross and crown.

LOWELL GEORGIA

S.FRANCISCO de ASIS

turned an investment of $60 into a $900 bonanza. Becknell went back the next spring with a freight wagon; soon rugged freighters were rolling down the 800-mile trace in great caravans, four abreast to discourage Indian raids. And soon the traders were returning with braying strings of mules to sell as the dependable engines of those two-ton wagons.

There was more than profit waiting in Santa Fe. There was rest and food and safety after the rigors of drought, quicksand, Indians, and two months of loneliness. There were cockfights, card games, and drinking-dancing-brawling marathons called fandangos, fueled by a fiery brandy dubbed Taos Lightning. There were customs officials far from their overseers in Mexico City; everyone knew that only a half—or maybe a third—of that $500-a-wagon levy would ever find its way into government coffers. And ah, there were those beautiful señoritas in their low-cut blouses and high-hemmed skirts, puffing on *cigarritos* of tobacco rolled up in corn husks. Santa Fe was another world—and one that should be entered properly.

A few miles outside town, the incoming wagon train would creak to a halt. Seasoned teamsters knew

Banners as colorful as its past bedeck the Palace of the Governors in Santa Fe. Gone are strings of human ears that festooned it in days of raid and revolt. Gone is the oxcart's creak and the bragging bullwhacker who could lash across three yoke of oxen to whip a fly off the lead beast's ear. Santa Fe means "holy faith"—and that endures, still whispered in Spanish accents, still celebrated in fiestas nearly as old as the town. Taos Pueblo (overleaf) also endures; so did Indian gods when converts saw counterparts to them in the saints.

LOWELL GEORGIA (ALSO OVERLEAF). BELOW: ADAM WOOLFITT

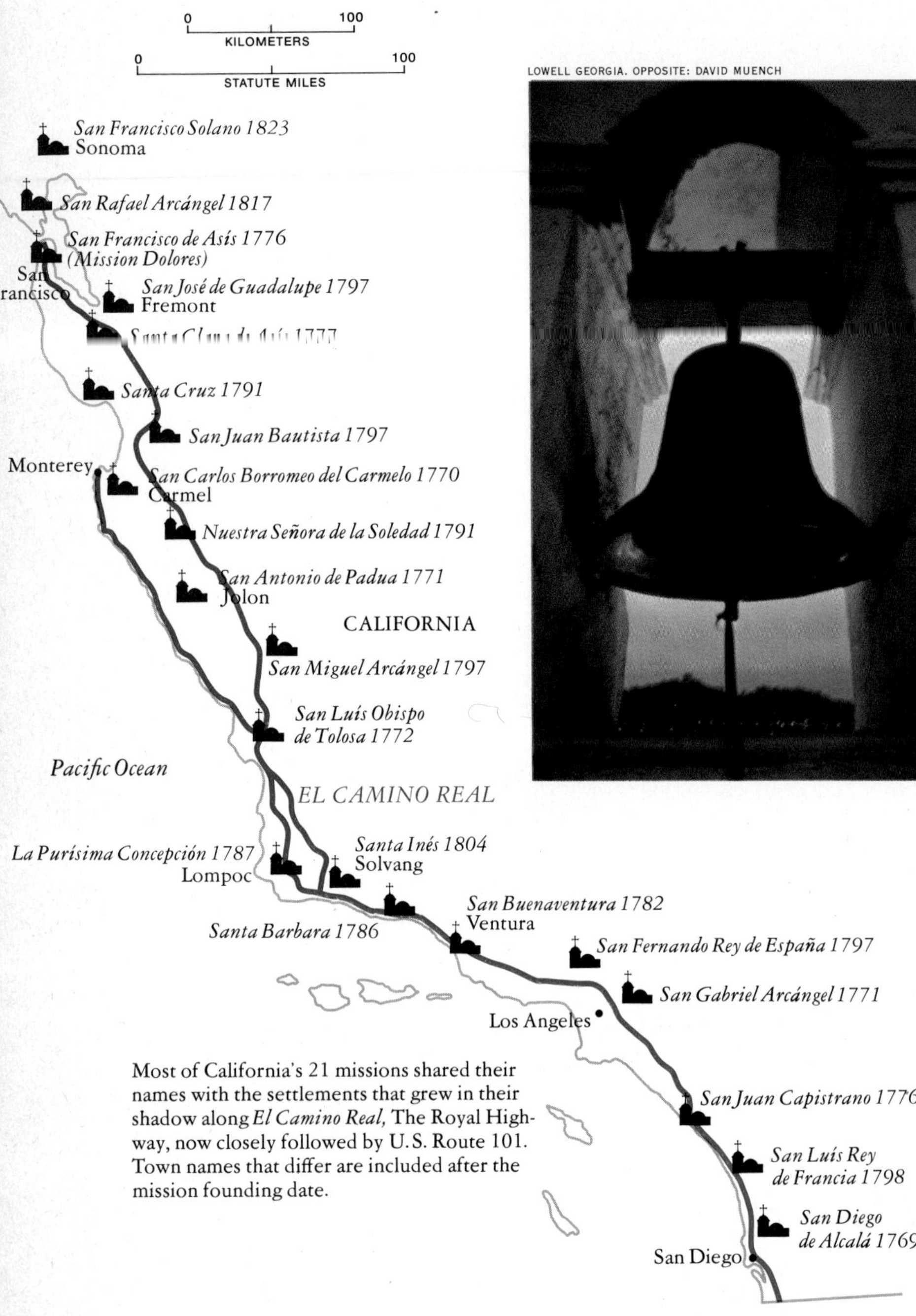

Most of California's 21 missions shared their names with the settlements that grew in their shadow along *El Camino Real,* The Royal Highway, now closely followed by U.S. Route 101. Town names that differ are included after the mission founding date.

LOWELL GEORGIA. OPPOSITE: DAVID MUENCH

An isle of amazons, rich in pearls and gold—that was California in an old Spanish novel. Sea dogs lit out to find it, and thought they had when they came on an "island" where natives threw away oyster shells with pearls inside. Baja or "Lower" California proved to be an arid waste; missions there sputtered and died. Alta or "Upper" California seemed no better to captains weak with scurvy and desperate for a harbor in its craggy shoreline, or to soldiers grubbing for treasure among huts of adobe and brush. But Father Junípero Serra sought a "rich . . . harvest of souls" to build and work the missions and asistencias *(outlying stations) along the coast. Now he walks in the beauty of doves and bougainvillea at Mission San Juan Capistrano. And a bell at San Diego de Alcalá, first of the nine missions he founded, echoes his prayer that the Angelus rung in California "be heard around the world."*

they'd be taxed by the wagonload, so they heaped the goods from two or three wagons into one and left the empties behind. A hasty shave, a clean shirt, a new cracker on the bullwhip, and in they rolled.

Veteran trail hands guffawed when greenhorns spotted "brick kilns" outside the city. That *was* the city, a haphazard scattering of adobe cubicles, none more than a story high, though some embraced a courtyard, and one—the Governor's Palace—stretched for some 300 feet along one side of the town plaza.

It still does, reigning modestly as the oldest government building in the United States. Today Indians from miles around array the palace's block-long portal with their wares: massive silver buckles and necklaces, rings set with turquoise, breads and tortillas baked in outdoor beehive ovens that the conquistadors would recognize. Those Spanish conquerors might know the old palace, too; working with Pueblo Indians, they built it in 1610 as an outpost of Spain's New World empire.

With a few thousand soldiers and incredible good luck, Spain in the 1500's had subjugated some 11 million Indians, largely by seizing the reins of the Aztec and Inca empires. But Spain lacked the funds and soldiers to yoke the tribes in the rest of her vast claim—the part that stretched north from Mexico and west to the Pacific. So she sent in a new breed of conqueror, clad not in burnished helm and breastplate but in robe and rosary.

The missionary's job was to put himself out of business: build a mission, make Christians and farmers of the neighboring Indians, and in ten years turn the mission over to parish priests and parcel out its lands as farmlets for Indian peons. Teamed with each mission was a presidio, a small fort whose handful of soldiers were supposed to guard against

threats from without and sin from within. They put a special zeal into tracking down backsliders for a taste of the lash; some miscreants were forced into slavery or even executed. But the soldiers were no saints. Time and again the exasperated padres railed at the evil influence of the lewd and bawdy soldiery, and more than one mission was relocated to deliver its converts from temptation.

One mission rose near the centuries-old Taos Pueblo, today a tourist magnet some 70 miles north of Santa Fe. The pueblo's peaceful face belies the sad chronicle of Spanish oppression, the sporadic Indian revolts, and finally the bloody uprising that poured from a kiva in 1680 and engulfed Santa Fe in flame. The Indians kept the plaza and palace but erased all else that was Spanish. To Apache raiders went the Spanish horses—and on them the Apaches raided as never before. In a dozen years the weakened pueblos around Santa Fe began to slide back under the Spanish thumb. But the Apaches and their neighbors the Comanches discouraged settlement outside the

From two priests and a two-room hut, San Luis Rey grew to become richest of the missions. Gargoyles adorned its waterworks; California's first pepper tree still shades its garden. But only riches of soul glorified a padre's cell.

LOWELL GEORGIA

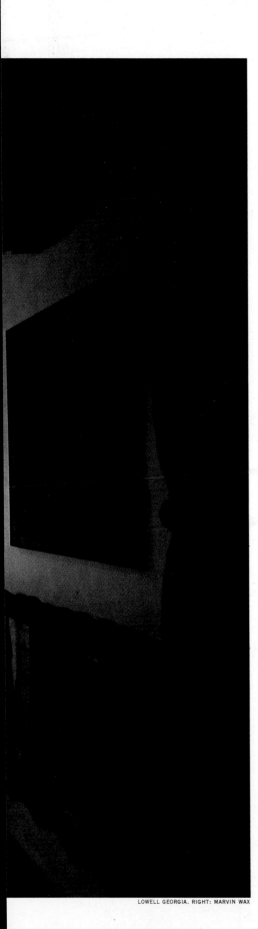

LOWELL GEORGIA. RIGHT: MARVIN WAX

Amid grandeur he never knew in life, Junípero Serra slumbers beneath the floor of Mission San Carlos Borromeo at Carmel, second of the nine he founded. At his feet in this memorial lies a grizzly, symbol of the state that began with the missions of the padres. They herded in the first cattle and sheep; they planted vineyards that sprouted into a great wine industry. Remembering the icons they left behind in Spain, they taught neophytes to carve santos*—but Indian hands drew from the wood a St. Benedict (above) and a Madonna and Child that still gaze at Carmel with faces more Indian than Spanish.*

Rio Grande Valley for years to come.

By the early 1700's the mission system had reached into present-day Arizona and Texas. In the 1760's a new threat seized Spain's attention. Russian and English ships were probing the bays and beaches of California, and the Russians had built Fort Ross—now reconstructed as a state park some 100 miles upcoast from the Golden Gate. Spain had made virtually no use of California; if she didn't fill the vacuum, and fast, someone else would.

On a hill east of what is now San Diego, an unlikely conquistador reined his mule to a halt in 1769. How had this frail stick of a friar survived the arduous trek from the Baja, burdened with his 55 years, his ulcerated leg, and the reedy wheeze of asthma? In pain and adversity, Father Junípero Serra would plant nine California missions during his last 13 years. By 1823 the missions numbered 21, strung like rosary beads along *El Camino Real,* the Royal Road that stretched from San Diego to Sonoma.

A visitor today can see all 21 as Junípero Serra never did. Those that rose before his death began as squat chapels of sticks and mud; only as they prospered could they rear the echoing churches and arched cloisters that pilgrims tread today. And only in the mission of San Juan Capistrano is there a chapel still standing in which Father Serra is known to have said Mass.

Around the missions, each then about one day's journey from the next, blossomed the languid life of Spanish California. It was slow to bloom; early padres often hovered near starvation while infrequent supply ships clawed their way up from the Baja against ornery winds and tides. By the time Mexico won her independence in 1821, the Californios were prospering on cattle but mustered only a sparse population and no manufacturing. In New Mexico, Spain's vital fender against Indians and land-hungry Americans to the north, the missions of the mid-1700's had degenerated into mismanaged slums where record books we would consider priceless today were used to plug up windows and roll cigarettes. The garrison at Santa Fe was still armed with 16th-century flintlock blunderbusses. And Texas to the east was filling up with Americans, brought to Mexico's doorstep by the Louisiana Purchase of 1803.

Unable to keep them out of Texas, Mexico granted land and citizenship to some of these Americans in hopes they would settle peaceably. But soon they were demanding schools, jury trials, and a say in government. Denied these, they demanded independence—and in March of 1836 a small garrison of them fought and died for it at the Alamo in San Antonio. To Sam Houston's troops that scarred old mission church gave a new battle cry as they routed Santa Anna's army on the plains of San Jacinto: "Remember the Alamo!"

With Texas lost, the rest of the old Spanish West grew restive under Mexican rule. In Sonoma in 1846 a band of Americans proclaimed California a republic. On their crude banner stood a grizzly bear; history would dub their brief adventure the Bear Flag Rebellion.

From porches and facades around the town's big plaza the bear flag still flutters. But war with Mexico at last shook loose the remnants of the old Spanish West and made of them bright stars in America's ensign.

David F. Robinson

A Moorish dome, a classical door, an old Spanish bell booming from a tower designed by a Mexican stonemason ... like all the early missions, San Carlos at Carmel blends the varied cultures that enrich the heritage of the Spanish West.

LOWELL GEORGIA

Wagons West

Two curving ribbons of metal thrust up from the Midwestern earth. One soars in a gleaming arch that enframes the skyline of St. Louis. The other, a wagon wheel's rim, spans a lonesome grave.

The message of the Gateway Arch is triumph: Technology sweeps you to the top in four minutes. From an air-conditioned room 630 feet above the Mississippi you can look over rolling fields where the West begins. The monument celebrates the trek of some 300,000 men, women, and children in history's greatest overland migration. The Oregon Trail. Manifest Destiny.

Now come down to earth and head west to seek the grave of Rebecca Winters, for it can be found—and that is the message of the humbler memorial: The trails exist.

The land still remembers those who crossed it. We can see landmarks they prayed that they would live to see. We can trace in the soil the ruts etched by their wheels. We can read their names, carved on rocks: *S.H. Patrick June 6, 1850, G.O. Willard Boston 1855.* We can follow them by using their own guides: "you ascend another bluff.... Look out for toads with horns and tails." We can endure with them: "The snow was getting deeper and it was growing colder.... and when I awoke I found my long braids frozen to the ground. They had to be cut off to release them." We can go west with the people of the trails.

Ever since French fur traders settled St. Louis in the 18th century, the river town had been a jumping-off place to the wilderness. Lewis and Clark bought supplies there, as did early missionaries and the trailblazing families of the 1840's. Later emigrants said goodbye to the East in St. Louis, and from there began their journey to the Oregon Trail.

They loaded their wagons and belongings and stock aboard steamboats which churned upriver to the confluence of the Mississippi and the Missouri. Four hundred miles or more up the Big Muddy the voyage ended at a river town—first, Independence, later Westport and St. Joseph, all in Missouri.

There the westering families off-loaded the wagons, probably trying to remember the reason for moving so much stuff. The trusty guidebook warned against "useless trumpery." Why then that claw-footed table or this carved-oak bureau?

The travelers were also told to use oxen, not horses, as a wagon team. But many had horses for riding or for trade. And there were milk cows, which in a pinch would tolerate being yoked with oxen.

A typical train consisted of 50 or more wagons covered by canvas or waterproof drill. The train's captain was elected—for this was a rolling democracy—and the hired guide was usually a mountain man. At the edge of the river town the train headed west on the 2,000-mile adventure called the Oregon Trail.

Some who migrated took a trail they called their own. They were Mormons, and among them was Rebecca Winters. Well organized and highly literate, they left journals that illumine the saga of all who turned westward in hope.

The story of the Mormon exodus begins in Nauvoo, a trim little Illinois town about 170 miles upriver from St. Louis. You hear the first chapters in the visitor center. Then guides—all inevitably well-scrubbed, dark-suited young men—will show you around the stern brick houses

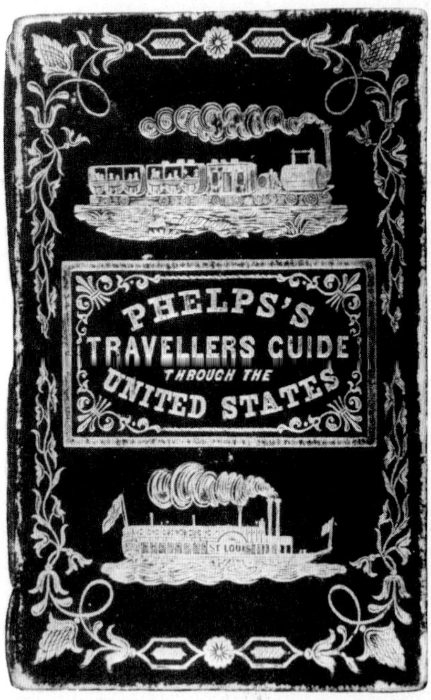

Stainless-steel rainbow arching over St. Louis links the vision of Jefferson with the deeds of westering pioneers. His Louisiana Purchase, doubling our land, made the fur-trade depot of St. Louis an American outpost— and soon a gateway, symbolized by Eero Saarinen's arch. An 1847 guide (above) —"containing Upwards of Seven Hundred Rail-Road, Canal, and Stage and Steam-Boat Routes"—got people to the end of the line. The anonymous walked, with or without a mule. Unlettered and in a hurry, they couldn't keep journals, as better-off wagoners often did.

OPPOSITE: DAVID HISER. RIGHT: SMITHSONIAN INSTITUTION

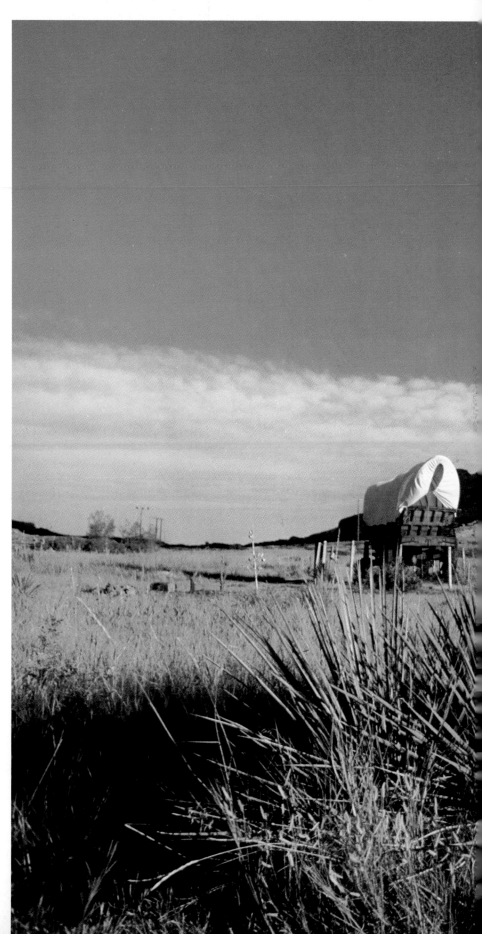

and shops of a town built by Mormons, abandoned, and in recent years proudly restored by Mormons.

Missionaries all, the guides earnestly tell about their religion. You don't have to be a Mormon to appreciate this American story. Historian Daniel J. Boorstin compares the members of the Church of Jesus Christ of Latter-day Saints with "the well-organized Puritans of early New England, who had also tried to build Zion." And, like the Puritans, the Saints helped open a wilderness.

Long before they marched westward, their religion was looking west. Vermont-born Joseph Smith, acting under what he said was a revelation from God, launched the religion in upstate New York in 1830. He and his followers next headed for an outpost of the frontier, Kirtland, Ohio. There the Mormons—including a young carpenter named Brigham Young—erected their first temple,

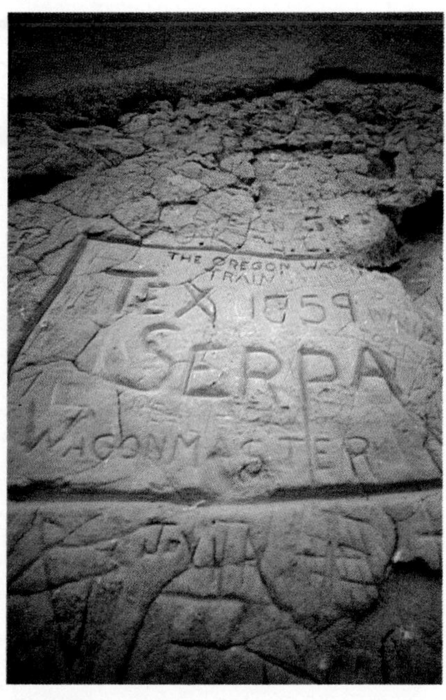

Landmark of the Oregon Trail, Scotts Bluff stands as a national monument today. Farther west, the soft stone of Register Cliff gave travelers a chance to leave their mark in history.

LOWELL GEORGIA

LOWELL GEORGIA

which still stands in Kirtland, now a Cleveland suburb. A bank failure helped propel the Mormons out of Ohio and into Missouri. But the proud and prospering newcomers did not fit in; they were too friendly toward Indians and did not support pro-slavery forces. Soon after Joseph Smith's arrival in Missouri in 1838, a mob massacred several Mormon families. The governor then ignited a crusade against the Saints.

The Mormons fled to Illinois, where, in 1839, with the aid of a rising politician named Stephen A. Douglas, they got a charter to settle a swampy, run-down town optimistically called Commerce. They renamed it Nauvoo, which they said meant "Beautiful Place," and they made it just that. They drained its swamps for farmland, laid out a grid of streets, built brick houses and meeting halls, and raised a stone temple rivaling in size any building west of the Alleghenies.

All that remains of the temple is an outline of stones on a grassy plot. Elsewhere, though, are the sturdy buildings restored to evoke Nauvoo when it was the largest city in Illinois.

Nauvoo began to crumble in 1844. From the outside came the battering of "Gentiles" who resented its wealth, disliked its independence, and feared its well-armed, 4,000-man Nauvoo Legion. From the inside came the criticism of Joseph Smith by Mormons who opposed his plan to run for President and accused him of immorality. When he ordered his legion to smash the press of a Mormon newspaper that criticized him, anti-Mormon forces arrested him—and mobilized to move against him and his followers.

On June 27, 1844, less than a month after the first (and last) issue of the newspaper, Joseph Smith and his brother Hyrum were murdered by a mob that broke into the Carthage, Illinois, jail. The site is now a Mormon shrine.

The Saints kept building their temple, but more mobs, more raids made withdrawal inevitable. Under a new leader, Brigham Young, they began planning the exodus of 20,000 men, women, and children. They would leave Nauvoo—but they would finish their temple. In February 1846, the first group of wagons started lumbering to the ferry landing for the crossing of the Mississippi.

Their trail is dim across Iowa today. But in Garden Grove, 150 miles west of Nauvoo, there is a patch of earth where unnamed Mormons lie.

A westward-spun web bound heartland to continent's edge. From the 18th century's Old Spanish Trail to the Butterfield Overland Mail of 1858-61, these routes scribed the message of Manifest Destiny: expansion. The Oregon Trail became a historic etching in such places as Guernsey, Wyoming (above). Highways follow the trail still.

LEWIS AND CLARK ROUTE
Fort Mandan
NORTH DAKOTA
MONTANA
Three Forks
Yellowstone River
Lembi Pass
Rocky Mountains
IDAHO
Fort Hall
WYOMING
SOUTH DAKOTA
Missouri
MINNESOTA
WISCONSIN
Grand Portage
Lake Superior
SUBLETTE CUTOFF
Casper
North Platte River
Register Cliff
Guernsey
Fort Laramie
Scotts Bluff
South Pass
Independence Rock
Great Salt Lake
Fort Bridger
Salt Lake City
Chimney Rock
Ash Hollow
Ogallala
NEBRASKA
MORMON TRAIL
OREGON TRAIL
Fort Kearny
Platte
South Platte
Council Bluffs
Omaha
Mt. Pisgah
Garden Grove
Nauvoo
Carthage
IOWA
ILLINOIS
OLD SPANISH TRAIL
UTAH
Denver
COLORADO
Pikes Peak
St. Joseph
Westport
Kansas City
Independence
Franklin
St. Louis
KANSAS
SANTA FE TRAIL
Council Grove
Florence
Fort Scott
Bent's Old Fort
MOUNTAIN ROUTE
Fort Dodge
Raton Pass
CIMARRON CUTOFF
MISSOURI
Pipe Spring National Monument
Taos
Mission of St. Francis of Assisi
Santa Fe
Pecos
Albuquerque
Cimarron
Arkansas
ARIZONA
NEW MEXICO
OKLAHOMA
ARKANSAS
Mississippi
Gila
Tucson
Tumacacori National Monument
El Paso
BUTTERFIELD OVERLAND MAIL
Pecos
TEXAS
LOUISIANA
Austin
San Jacinto Battlefield
Houston
New Orleans
The Alamo
San Antonio
Rio Grande
0 200 KILOMETERS
0 200 STATUTE MILES

Here was the first of a string of advance bases set up to sustain the exiles. Here the graves begin.

The dead help mark the way for those who seek the route of the trails heading west. The graves are old enough now to invoke a sense of history, not grief. And yet.... To see a white monument jutting from Iowa earth, tolling the names of the dead, or to stand in a Nebraska graveyard and read names and pathetic ages—*John Cummins 4, Charles Parcket 6 days, Sarah A. Coventon 20 Mos.*—is to learn who it was who made our history and how many, many they were.

The monument stands at Iowa's Mount Pisgah, another base set up to feed and care for the migrants. About 150 people died there in six months. But thousands lived to trek on. At Mount Pisgah, Brigham Young sought to foster better relations with the federal government by personally recruiting 500 soldiers for the Mexican War.

The recruits said goodbye at the next base, now Council Bluffs, near a Lewis and Clark camp of 1804. Captain Pitt's brass band, which would march the Saints west, tootled at the farewell dance: "French fours, Copenhagen jigs, Virginia reels... executed with the spirit of people too happy to be slow, or bashful...."

The Mormon Battalion, whose pay went to the church, reached San Diego, about 2,000 miles away, in 199 days. But no battle occurred. Discharged, most of them turned around and walked to Salt Lake City.

At Council Bluffs, the Saints crossed the river, and in what is now Florence, an Omaha suburb, Brigham Young drew his scattered flock together. They would spend the cold months there, in Winter Quarters.

More than 600 did not live to see the spring of 1847. They lie now in the Nebraska earth, their names on bronze. Adjacent to the burial ground is a garden where cabbages and beans grow from that same earth. This was at least part of what the trekking and the dying was all about: land, a place for new roots.

LOWELL GEORGIA

In Nebraska, the Mormon Trail—and the Mormon saga—begin to blend into the westering mainstream. History again and again took this trail: the Mormons in 1847, the first transcontinental telegraph line in 1861, the route of the Union Pacific, the pioneer automobile's Lincoln Highway (today's U. S. 30)—our first transcontinental road.

U. S. 30 parallels the Mormon and Ox Bow Trails to Grand Island, near Fort Kearny, where the Platte River Valley became the superhighway of migration. James Clyman, the great mountain man, called the broad, flat, untimbered valley "as firm a road as any in the Union or even in the world."

The Mormons took trappers' trails along the north bank, avoiding Gentiles traveling the Oregon Trail on the south bank. All trails melded into the Great Platte River Road, multi-laned today as Interstate 80. To see bits of history, take an exit:

At Fort Kearny, a telegram: *Send company of men here as quick as God can send them one hundred 100 Indians in sight firing on ox train.*

At Gothenburg, an original Pony Express station.

At North Platte, Buffalo Bill's Scouts Rest Ranch and a movie: His Wild West Show comes to town in a film made by Thomas Edison to get a patent on his movie machine.

At Ogallala, a cow town's boot hill

Fort Laramie, fur-trade depot turned guardian of the way west, watched over migrants who paused here before challenging the Rockies. Beyond, wagons encamped "outside the boundaries of Uncle Sam." By July 1850, the fort had registered 37,171 men, 803 women, 1,094 children. Now travelers find soldiers reliving days when "the law wore army blue." A baker offers samples of bland "ration bread," a guard patrols cells that cooled off celebrants of the fort's six-a-year payday bashes. Ask a cavalryman (opposite) and he'll claim troopers won the West. But in Indian wars, the infantry often marched as far as the cavalry rode: 40 miles a day. No battle was ever fought at Laramie.

LOWELL GEORGIA. UPPER: NATIONAL PARK SERVICE

and reconstructed, wicked "Front Street." Here the parallel Mormon and Oregon Trails head northwest, under, or sometimes beside, U. S. 26.

To travelers today, the Oregon Trail becomes vividly real at Ash Hollow, a steep canyon named for its ash trees. The place was both an obstacle and an oasis. The descent into the hollow was a brutal test of wagon and stock. But the reward lay in the "beautiful vale," with its spring, grapes, gooseberries—and trees. Ahead, wood was scarce for fueling fires and repairing wagons.

They'd need repairs after descending wistfully named Windlass Hill. There a wagon was eased down, not with a winch but with a prayer and a scheme: "We detach all the oxen from the wagon except the wheel yoke, lock the two hind wheels"—and hitch oxen to the rear, to pull against gravity, along with a dozen men holding ropes taut.

The ruts gouged by the wheels never healed. You can walk in them on the top of Windlass Hill, look across the endless, rumpled prairie, and see faint signs of the Oregon Trail on the hills ahead.

Drivers on the trail today can mark off the hours—even the minutes—by the landmarks that paced the days and the weeks of the wagon trains. Chimney Rock, a spire of sandstone, volcanic ash, and clay, juts 500 feet above the North Platte. It became the most famous sight on the trail. About 20 miles ahead looms Scotts

Frontier shopping center, Laramie's post trader's store (top and far left) charged 60 cents for a loaf of bread that cost 10 cents in Chicago. Whiskey was dear at a dollar a pint, and the poker game never stopped. Kit Carson and Buffalo Bill were customers. The torn flag in post headquarters evokes the Sioux wars, which ebbed when another customer, Red Cloud, signed a treaty.

JAMES L. AMOS, NATIONAL GEOGRAPHIC PHOTOGRAPHER. OPPOSITE: J. BRUCE BAUMANN

Bluff, a massive brow of rock overhanging a pass, where thousands filed through, walking, riding west. Nearby, in the town of Scottsbluff, lies the grave of Rebecca Winters, whose life spanned so much of our past. Her marker arches alongside a railroad track—shifted to spare her grave. And her roots recall the Revolution: Her father had been a drummer boy for George Washington.

When she died of cholera, William Reynolds bent a wagon wheel and chiseled on it, *Rebecca Winters, Age 50.* His daughter, Ellis, then 5, held a torch at graveside in the prairie night. We will meet Ellis again at the end of the trail.

The Mormon vanguard of 1847—Young, 142 other men, three women, and two children—crossed the Platte to the Oregon Trail at Fort Laramie. Then a fur-trade center, later a key army post in the Indian wars, it is now a national historic site that musters costumed incarnations of the 19th century for visitors of the 20th. The magic works, because Laramie still is an outpost on an empty plain.

The Mormons spent their first night on the Gentiles' trail near Register Cliff, where you can read the carved names or initials of pioneers (and such latecomers as *Bob & Ginny, 1970*). Nearby, wagon wheels have cut ruts so deep that to walk the trail is to walk a trench.

Travelers also left their marks on Wyoming's Independence Rock, a black hump 193 feet high and nearly half a mile long. You can climb to the top—as did Mormons and other trekkers—and stand on a great hub of the plains. On summer days in 1852 the wagon trains would stretch beyond sight, a procession of hope 500 miles long.

On June 27, 1847, three years to the day after the murder of Joseph Smith, the Mormon pioneer company reached South Pass, a crossroad of the frontier. Driving through it today on Wyoming 28, you can appreciate explorer John C. Frémont's description: The approach is so undramatic that "the traveller, without being reminded of any change by toilsome ascents, suddenly finds himself on the waters which flow to the Pacific Ocean."

At South Pass, wagons hurrying west took the Sublette Cutoff; the Saints stayed on the Oregon Trail's branch to Fort Bridger. There they followed a haunted path—the Hastings Route, named after the California promoter, Lansford Hastings.

The year before, a group out of Springfield, Illinois, had taken Hastings' shortcut. Eighty-two people got as far as the Sierra Nevada. Trapped by snow, they began a long ordeal that would give them grisly notoriety as the Donner Party. Thirty-five died, along with two Indians trying to save them. Many of the survivors had stayed alive by eating the bodies of the dead.

The Mormons followed the path that the Donner Party had hacked

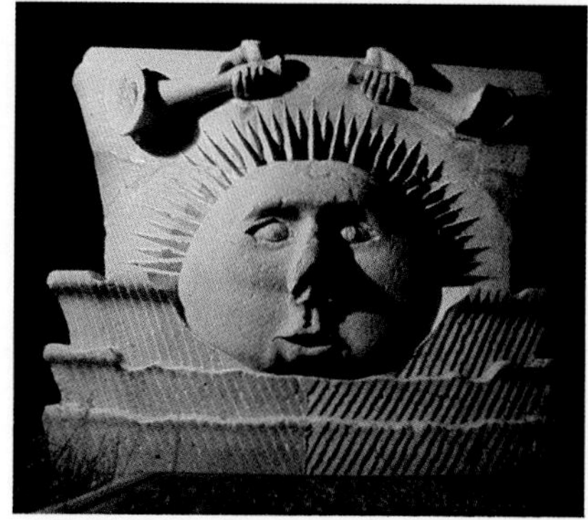

Mormon tragedy and triumph in 1848: In Nauvoo, Illinois, foes destroy a temple only two years old; salvaged "sun stone" bears the promise of horns of plenty. In Salt Lake City, birds appear and devour crickets threatening the pioneers' first spring crops. Seagull Monument in Temple Square honors the gull, now Utah's state bird.

LOWELL GEORGIA. LOWER AND OPPOSITE: JAMES L. AMOS, NATIONAL GEOGRAPHIC PHOTOGRAPHER

From his Beehive House in Salt Lake City, Brigham Young ruled a religious empire and a polygamous domain. The beehive, symbol of Mormon diligence, adorns newel-posts and cupola. There in the abortive "Mormon War" he placed a telescope to watch federal troop movements. At the adjacent Lion House (named for a portico carving) many of his wives lived in community. He kept wife-counters guessing; estimates range from 17 to 27. Dolls in Beehive House remind visitors that the majority of his 56 children were daughters. They wore yokes to improve their posture and, with their brothers, went to an all-Young school.

through the rugged Utah canyons. On July 19, at a Salt Lake City site now marked by a heroic monument, the seekers of Zion saw their promised land: "a broad and barren plain hemmed in by mountains... the paradise of the lizard, the cricket and the rattlesnake."

Within months the first pioneers would be welcoming 2,000 more. They and those who kept following would make the desert "bloom like a rose" and build Salt Lake City.

There, in the Daughters of Utah Pioneers Museum, you can see in homey objects the life of one of the builders: Ellis Reynolds, the girl at Rebecca Winters' grave. She danced with Brigham Young at 17, married at 19, became a physician at 31, had ten children, and wrote poetry. In one life, the sampler of a people dedicated to work and family.

Some pioneers were European converts on a church-financed migration: by ship to America, by train to Iowa City, by foot the rest of the way. Pulling or pushing the jerry-built handcarts, the first group—many of them old and some of them blind—trudged west in five brigades, beginning in June 1856.

Three reached Salt Lake City by October. Snows entombed the later brigades, and about 225 died. But the handcarts rolled on until 1860; nearly 3,000 immigrants walked the 1,400 miles to Zion.

Mormonism not only endured; it prospered—though church and nation clashed, and federal troops once massed for war against the Mormons. After the Saints proclaimed a ban on polygamy, however, the Gentiles accepted them. In 1896 the land of Zion became Utah.

The Mormons' long struggle ended where so much was to begin: in the West, that magnetic realm. At trail's end, Mormon and Gentile alike found what they had sought.

THOMAS B. ALLEN

Oasis become monument, Pipe Spring in Arizona keeps green the memory of the Mormon empire, Deseret. Visitors see a fortress-like ranch where cheese and butter still are made. It once guarded cattle given to the church "on Tithing"—a tenth of their wealth that Mormons still give in cash, goods, or labor. Besides Utah, Deseret encompassed what would become much of Nevada, Arizona, Wyoming, Colorado, and parts of Oregon, Idaho, New Mexico, and California. Within a decade of founding Salt Lake City, Brigham Young had established 100 towns. Mormon telegraph linked outposts of Deseret—a blossoming land that "the Lord has given to us without price."

LOWELL GEORGIA

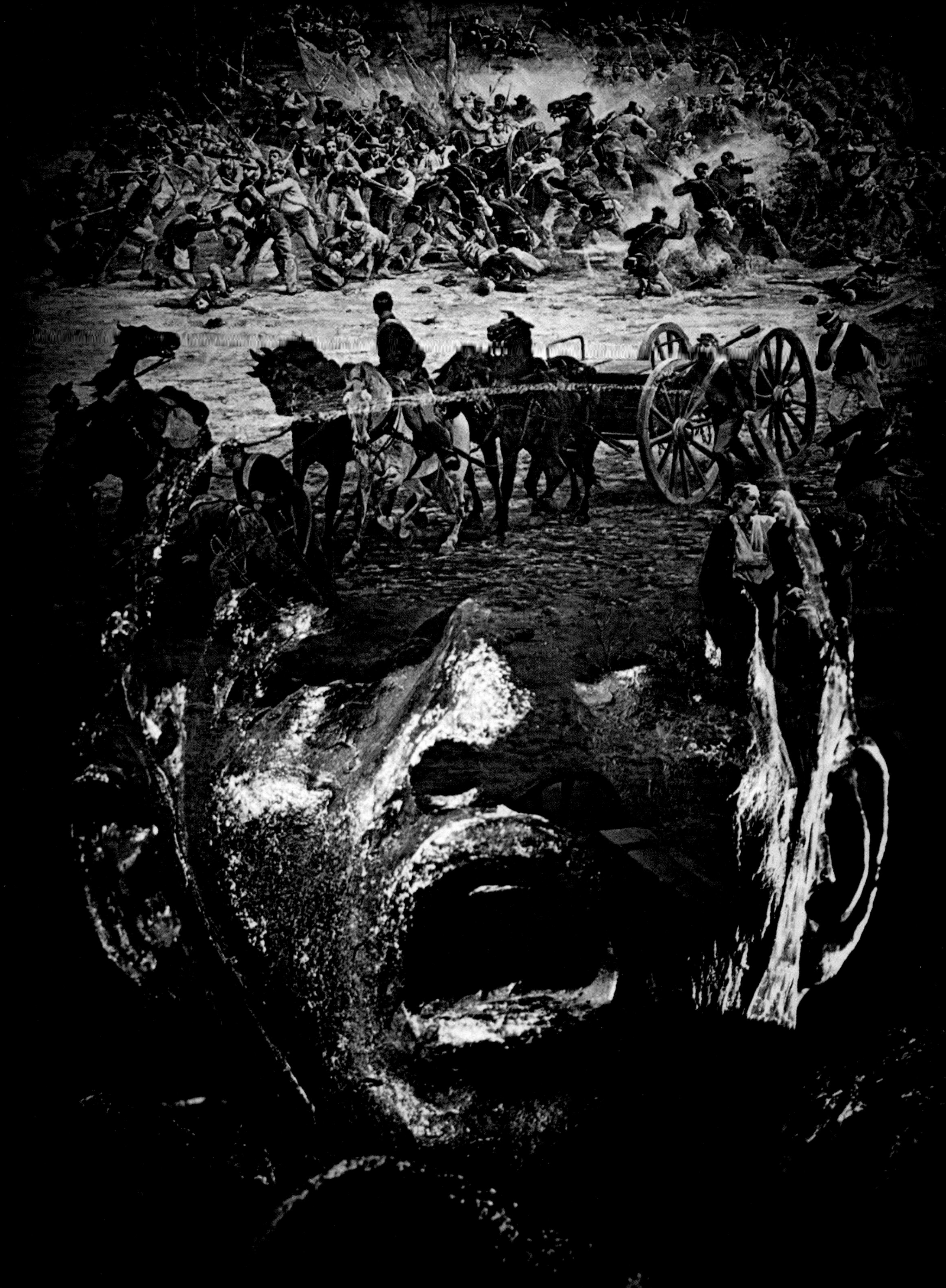

Hallowed Ground

While the North industrialized, the South evolved a planter aristocracy borne on the backs of slaves. Abolitionists could not stomach that "peculiar institution"; slave owners could not abandon it. Slowly, painfully, the house divided—and only blood could again cement the Union.

CHARLES PIERCE ROLAND

It was an unlikely vantage point for a glimpse of the fury to come. Sited where the Shenandoah flows into the Potomac, Harpers Ferry, Virginia (now West Virginia), more nearly resembled a Rhine village than a community of the American South. It lay outside the main plantation area and had only a few slaves. Yet here the erratic visionary John Brown tried to force emancipation by violence. On an October night in 1859, he and 18 followers seized the United States Armory and Arsenal at Harpers Ferry and issued a call for a slave uprising. Ironically, not a single slave rose to his cry for revolt.

Brown and his small band holed up in the armory's enginehouse. A company of marines marched in under the command of U. S. Army Col. Robert E. Lee, a hero of the recent Mexican War and soon to become the paladin of the Confederacy. His aide was Lt. James Ewell Brown Stuart, later the dashing Jeb Stuart of the Confederate cavalry.

After battering down the door, the troops wounded Brown as he shielded a dying son. He was tried and hanged at nearby Charles Town. But he had struck a spark that could not be quenched, and the South responded with fear and rage. He had promised to purge the land in blood. Alive, he failed. But dead and "a-mouldering in the grave," John Brown realized his fiercest hope.

The Civil War was the forge of modern American nationhood. It burned away many remnants of the old federalism and began tempering America into a consolidated national state, set squarely on the path to a more balanced economy of industry, agriculture, commerce, and banking. It ended slavery and exalted wage labor and family farming. It heralded equality for blacks. And it gave Americans our own Iliad, an epic of valor on both sides.

The stage was set at the raw little outpost of Jamestown in 1619 when a ship sold the colonists "20 and odd" Negroes as indentured servants. From that small beginning, slavery spread for nearly two centuries. Then at Mulberry Grove, a plantation near Savannah, Georgia, Eli Whitney built a gin to separate the lint from the seed of the ordinary cotton plant. His fellow Yankees had already copied England's spinning machinery; his cotton gin was all the nation needed for a burgeoning textile industry. The demand for fiber spread the plantation system across the South. By 1860 the Cotton Kingdom, supported by four million slaves, stretched from the Atlantic to eastern Texas, infecting yeoman farmers with dreams of landed estates, faithful slaves, and columned mansions.

All 13 colonies had slavery, but it never took deep root in New England or the middle colonies. A few Southern idealists such as Thomas Jefferson favored gradual emancipation, but only if coupled with removal of the blacks. So slavery was abolished in the North but not the South. And from these

DETAIL OF CYCLORAMA AT GETTYSBURG NATIONAL MILITARY PARK; DETAIL OF SCULPTURE BY HENRY M. SHRADY; PHOTOMONTAGE BY JAMES L. STANFIELD, NATIONAL GEOGRAPHIC PHOTOGRAPHER

attitudes grew two different societies: the Cotton Kingdom and slavery in the South, and an empire of towns, factories, stores, wage labor, and independent farms in the North. By the mid-1800's the North was one of the world's leading industrial and commercial communities as well as a major agricultural producer; it was receiving the bulk of the great waves of immigrants; it was far ahead of the South in population and wealth.

Unable to end the South's "peculiar institution," radical abolitionists in the 1830's joined with moderates who sought instead to stop slavery's spread into the new federal lands. Every time another territory was added, the slavery question flared up and had to be dampened by compromise. In 1850, veteran statesman Henry Clay of Kentucky held aloft a splinter said to be from George Washington's coffin, a "precious relic," and pleaded with his fellow senators: "I conjure gentlemen... solemnly to pause... at the edge of the precipice, before the fearful and disastrous leap is taken into the yawning abyss below." Aged Senator Daniel Webster spoke "today for the preservation of the Union" by compromise. John C. Calhoun of South Carolina, too old and sick to talk, sat with half-closed eyes as a colleague read his somber warning of national dissolution if a course acceptable to the South were not charted. Calhoun died a few weeks later, mourning for "the South, the poor South."

During the next decade, sectional hostility boiled as the compromises fell apart. Events pointed to tragedy with the fated certainty of a Greek drama—events such as the prophetic violence at Harpers Ferry. Then the voters of 1860 split along sectional lines and elected Abraham Lincoln to the Presidency. He had said a nation divided on slavery could not endure; as President, he intended to stop the spread of slavery, hoping that would eventually snuff it out. His election precipitated secession and war.

Charleston belied the tranquil beauty that marked its streets then as now. Behind its white churches and gracious waterfront mansions it seethed with disunion. There on December 20, 1860, the South Carolina secession convention voted unanimously to sever the state's ties with the Union. Townspeople went wild. Cannons boomed, bells tolled, military companies paraded, ladies waved handkerchiefs, old men ran shouting into the streets. From his shaded sepulcher at St. Philip's Church, John C. Calhoun might have looked on with sorrow.

The action set off the dreaded chain reaction of secession. The Confederate States of America was hastily formed, with Jefferson Davis of Mississippi as President. On February 18, 1861, Davis stood between the tall Grecian columns of the Alabama State Capitol and told an inaugural crowd that the Confederacy would keep its sovereignty and territory by peaceful means—or if necessary by arms.

The war's opposing Presidents were both sons of Kentucky's rugged hill country. They were born of yeoman farm families only about 100 miles apart, Lincoln near present-day Hodgenville and Davis at present-day Fairview. Today an imposing temple holds a simple log cabin said to be Lincoln's birthplace, while the Sinking Spring that supplied water to the family still gurgles at the foot of the hill. And at Fairview a towering obelisk marks Davis's birthplace.

Early in each man's life the families moved, the Lincolns north to Indiana and then Illinois, the Davises south to Louisiana and Mississippi. Lincoln became a lawyer and an opponent of slavery; Davis became a soldier, then a cotton planter and slave owner. From nearly identical roots, each was molded by his adopted environment.

In his March 4 inaugural, Lincoln appealed to the South to rejoin the Union. But he was firm in declaring secession illegal and vowing to hold the federal property in all the states. One such property, and one of the few in a seceded state, was Fort Sumter, South Carolina, today a national monument on a tiny, sunbaked, man-made island in Charleston Harbor. On April 12, 1861, Confederates fired on the fort. In two days the garrison surrendered. Lincoln at once called for 75,000 troops to suppress the rebellion; Davis called for even more to defend the Confederacy. The rebel capital now moved to Richmond, *(Continued on page 270)*

"Had I so interfered in behalf of... the powerful... it would have been all right," John Brown told the court that doomed him. "Now, I am done." Not so; his spirit fired Union troops and inspired this painting of his final steps. In fact only soldiers watched—among them John Wilkes Booth.

"THE LAST MOMENTS OF JOHN BROWN," BY THOMAS HOVENDEN; METROPOLITAN MUSEUM OF ART

JODI COBB (ALSO OVERLEAF)

"A pleasant and picturesque place formerly"

The Yankee writer was dismayed at Harpers Ferry in 1865. "War has changed all," he lamented. "The town itself lies half in ruins.... rubbish, filth and stench."

Like the rails and rivers that met at its feet (pages 266-67), the tides of war converged at Harpers Ferry. Now the North held it, now the South. In victory soldiers helped themselves to what they needed; in defeat they torched whatever the foe might use. Most townsfolk fled. Some joined one army or the other, some sought new jobs when factories went up in smoke.

Now armies of visitors invade the town, risen anew as a national historical park. Here stands the enginehouse where John Brown took his stand against slavery and presaged civil strife. St. Peter's Church (above) still keeps vigil on a hillside, remembering when war clouds cast a shadow as worshipers prayed for peace.

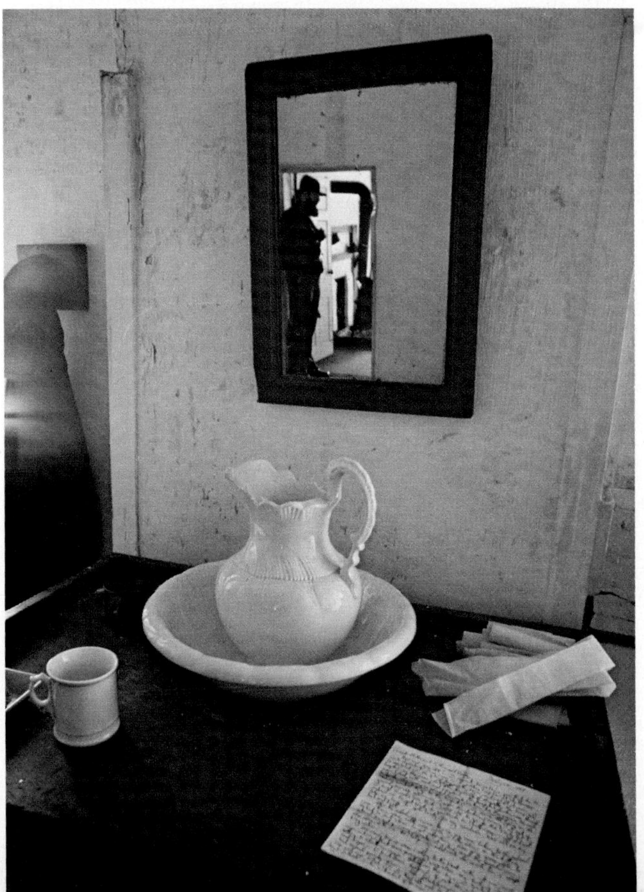

'Scuse me, ma'am, while I examine this here recruit. Now then, mister, how many fingers am I holding up? Can you balance on one foot? Which is your right hand? Got two teeth that meet when you bite? You'll need 'em to rip open them paper cartridges, y'know.

Today at Harpers Ferry such a "physical" gets you a souvenir enlistment certificate. A century ago it would have gotten you into the Union army. And that could have landed you in a sickroom like the one behind the recruiting office—a haven not just for the wounded but for the many more felled by disease.

Summer's sun slowly fades the ready-mades in Harpers Ferry's clothing store, tipping the HATS on the windowpane as it lights up a sale inside. Across Shenandoah Street, one of the main thoroughfares, townsfolk stroll the shaded flagstones past the tailor shop and the recruiting office. At the dry goods emporium many tarry to mail a letter, inspect the pumpkins or the pork chops, perhaps settle down for battle on the checkerboard and a word on the weather with Mr. Engle, the shopkeeper. A jetliner murmurs overhead, but no matter. Here a hundred years ago is only yesterday.

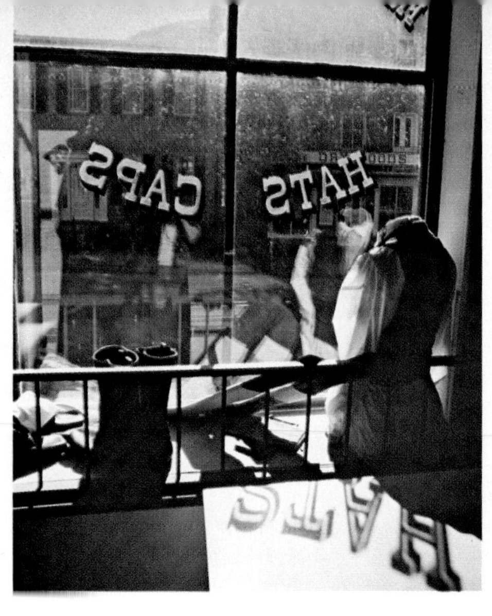

JODI COBB

SMOKERS and CHEWERS will
please spit on each other
and not on the stove
or floor.
HAM

where the Virginia State Capitol, designed by Jefferson, housed the rebel congress and the Brockenbrough Mansion became the chief executive's home. Today the State Capitol still serves Virginia, and the mansion houses the Confederate Museum.

Thus the ancient issue came to trial by combat. The advantage was the Union's; it mustered 23 states and 22 million people, of whom perhaps 1.5 million saw duty in the army. The Confederacy counted only 11 states and 9 million people—and 3.5 million of them were slaves. Its army enlisted about a million men during the course of the war.

The Union was far stronger in wealth, railroads, and industry. Many of today's business giants rose out of the Civil War: Philip Armour made millions speculating in pork, and from the Pittsburgh iron industry grew the Carnegie steel empire and later the United States Steel Corporation. In 1860 the North could outproduce the South—in dollar value—by 32 times the guns, 30 times the boots and shoes, and 24 times the locomotives. "It was mainly for want of these [resources]," wrote the United States census taker after the war, "and not for lack of courage, will, or skill, that the revolt failed."

Witness to history, the Custis-Lee Mansion—now Arlington House, the Robert E. Lee Memorial—has seen Union troops drill and hoop skirts swirl. Begun in 1802, it hosted Lafayette and saw Lieutenant Lee take a bride. From its hill it watched the nation's Capital rise. Now fallen heroes find rest in Virginia's Arlington National Cemetery at its feet.

MARIE-LOUISE BRIMBERG. LEFT: NATIONAL ARCHIVES

But the Confederacy had advantages too. A defensive war requires fewer soldiers, less equipment, and shorter lines of communication than does an offensive war. And the Southerner was defending his hearth and home, while the attacking Northerner had to fight and die for more abstract causes: preserving the Union, emancipating the slaves.

"The whole nation," said Confederate Gen. Robert E. Lee, "should for a time be converted into an army, the producers to feed and the soldiers to fight." But the new nation, caught in its birth throes and dependent on a lopsided economy, was never quite able to sustain its effort, despite prodigious achievements. The extensive Tredegar Works in Richmond turned out huge quantities of iron and arms, especially cannons; by 1863 a chain of factories was able to supply all the army's munitions needs. Southern women and slaves grew enough food for all. Yet there was widespread hunger because of inadequate transportation, and widespread shortages as fledgling industries fell far behind the demand for both military and civilian goods. The government had to rely on treasury notes backed only by its own good faith; perhaps two billion dollars' worth were printed. As hope and resources dwindled, they became literally not worth the paper they were printed on. By 1865 the Southern economy lay prostrate.

Paradoxically, Lincoln, the military novice, turned out to be a better war leader than Davis, the experienced soldier. Lincoln was less doctrinaire, more unconventional, less touchy about fine points of authority and official prerogative. Ultimately he quit trying to fashion Union strategy and delegated the task to Gen. Ulysses S. Grant.

Davis had served with distinction as an officer in the Mexican War and as Secretary of War. He yearned for military renown and took full advantage of his title of commander in chief of Confederate armed forces. He could not bring himself to appoint a general in chief until forced to by the Confederate Congress only a few weeks before war's end. By then, he was turning over to General Lee a lost cause.

Perhaps Lincoln's greatest advantage was simply his ability to get along with people and express himself in language that touched their hearts. Once he said that a temporary use of extraordinary Presidential authority in war would no more create a permanent taste for dictatorship than would the use of an emetic by a sick man create a taste for emetics —and his constituents understood exactly what he meant. Davis seems to have been incapable of such down-to-earth analogies. And while Lincoln was willing to accept a snub from his ranking general if only the general would give him victory, Davis could not abide the slightest lapse in protocol.

The first two years of the Civil War were indecisive, but the Confederacy had reason for optimism. The first full-scale battle, called First Manassas, erupted on July 21, 1861, in Virginia. For the Union, it was a fiasco. The South was jubilant; the North recoiled and braced for a long and bitter fight.

A series of Union generals went down before the brilliant Lee and his great lieutenant, Gen. Thomas J. "Stonewall" Jackson. Second Manassas in August 1862 . . . Fredericksburg in December . . . Chancellorsville in May 1863—each victory kindled pride and confidence throughout the South. Its generals and their armies seemed invincible, despite the death of Stonewall Jackson at Chancellorsville.

But the victories were mainly on the eastern front. In the broad, stream-threaded area west of the Appalachians, Union armies aided by gunboats

Antietam, 1862: Lincoln poses stiffly with detective Allan Pinkerton and Gen. John McClernand. His query: Why won't General McClellan pursue Lee? His answer: "He has got the 'slows.'" A reluctant strategist, Lincoln in time let General Grant run the war. But rebel President Davis (above) itched to lead armies; his office was a "disappointment."

LIBRARY OF CONGRESS. ABOVE: NATIONAL ARCHIVES

and river steamers cut ever deeper into the Confederate heartland to more than even the score with a tally of Union victories: Forts Henry and Donelson in February 1862 . . . Shiloh in April . . . New Orleans, captured April 29 without a battle. The Union navy forced New Orleans to surrender; its ships were beyond challenge. Its blockade of Southern ports grew rapidly tighter, and its support of assaults along coasts and rivers more dangerous.

In 1863, the Union triumphed at Gettysburg in the east from July 1 to 3 and took Vicksburg in the west on July 4. These back-to-back victories marked the turn of the tide: Vicksburg severed the South along the Mississippi River; Gettysburg so crippled Lee's army that it never again threatened invasion. Still, the Confederacy was politically intact and formidably armed. Almost two years of war remained, including some of the fiercest fighting.

Lincoln helped steel the North for the stern effort needed for victory. On November 19, 1863, at Gettysburg National Cemetery, with graves still fresh about him, he read the two-minute address that so eloquently identified the Union cause with liberty, equality, and self-government. Re-elected in 1864, he showed in his lined face the heartache of war as he stood before the Capitol with its great new dome to deliver his inaugural address. With its generosity ("With malice toward none, with charity for all"), its deep religious overtones (" 'Woe unto the world because of offenses' "), and its ringing determination to continue if God willed "until every drop of blood drawn with the lash shall be paid by another drawn with the sword," it ranks with the Gettysburg Address in loftiness and power.

Emancipation and the use of blacks in the army also bolstered the Union effort. About 186,000 blacks, a majority of them former slaves, served in federal uniforms and more than 38,000—perhaps

Under the guns of Lookout Mountain, the Tennessee River wraps an arm around Chattanooga. Union troops in 1863 found no respite as rebels who beat them at nearby Chickamauga besieged them into near-starvation here. Parks now preserve field and ridge where General Grant's relief force wrested from Confederates this gate to Southern heartlands.

EMORY KRISTOF, NATIONAL GEOGRAPHIC PHOTOGRAPHER

as many as 68,000—died. Lincoln's Emancipation Proclamation had no immediate effect on the slaves and was ridiculed in many quarters, but it took effect as Union armies penetrated the South. And it strengthened the moral tone of the Union cause by making the war a crusade for human freedom.

Despite heroic Southern resistance and sacrifice unparalleled in American history, Confederate unity and resolve faltered under the burden of the political doctrine of states' rights and a growing distrust of the Davis Administration. Some governors believed the mobilization of Southern men and resources ought to be mainly up to the states; they strenuously resisted such vital measures as conscription and the impressment of supplies. Davis was accused of both weakness and high-handedness. "Oh, for a man at the helm like William of Orange," one critic wrote, "a man of... heroic character and genius... fertile in resources, equal to emergencies."

Meanwhile Grant's appointment as general in chief gave the North the unity of command it needed to win. His strategy was attrition: attacking relentlessly on all fronts until Confederate resources were exhausted. Lincoln called it "dogged pertinacity."

During most of 1864 and early 1865 Grant hammered at Lee's army in Virginia while Generals William Tecumseh Sherman and James H. Wilson ravaged the lower South with marches and cavalry raids. The navy kept up its strangling blockade and assaults on coastal installations. Its most spectacular feat was the victory at Mobile Bay on August 5, 1864. Braving the deadly fire of Fort Morgan and ignoring the underwater mines—"Damn the torpedoes! Full speed ahead!"—Union Rear Adm. David G. Farragut steamed his fleet into the bay and overwhelmed the lighter rebel flotilla.

By April 1865 the Confederacy was utterly beaten. The most dramatic scene of the war, and possibly of the entire American experience, unfolded on April 9 in the McLean House in the village of Appomattox Court House, Virginia. There Lee, the Virginia patrician, surrendered to Grant, the magnanimous tanner's son who had vanquished him.

Lee's surrender sealed the Confederacy's doom. On May 10, Davis was taken prisoner while fleeing through Georgia; on May 26 the last Confederates laid down their arms. The Civil War was over.

President Lincoln did not live to enjoy victory. Five days after Lee's surrender the great war President was shot by actor John Wilkes Booth during a play in Ford's Theatre, a few blocks from the White House. He was taken to the William Petersen house across the street, where he died the next morning at 7:22. Plays still brighten the restored theater's stage. But from the curtained Presidential box—and from the House Where Lincoln Died, now preserved as a national shrine—the tall shadow of tragedy still stretches across American history.

Two great questions, slavery and secession, were permanently settled by the Union victory. But hard new questions arose to take their places. What would be the role of the South in the triumphant Union? What place would blacks hold in American life? Reconstruction answered these temporarily by readmitting the Southern states to national political participation—under conditions dictated by Congress—and by bestowing citizenship and the franchise on the blacks. The overthrow of Reconstruction by the resurgent white South altered this settlement for a century. Not until the mid-1970's were both the South and the blacks in a position to reassert themselves fully in national affairs.

Four score and seven years ago our fathers brought forth, upon this continent, a new nation, conceived in Liberty, and dedicated to the proposition that all men are created equal.

Now we are engaged in a great civil war, testing whether that nation, or any nation, so conceived, and so dedicated, can long endure. We are met here on a great battle-field of that war. We have come to dedicate a portion of it as a final resting place for those who here gave their lives that

South from Gettysburg limped Lee's army, its northward jab parried, its wounded writhing untreated in wagons lashed by rain and hail. The armies tallied 50,000 casualties—and the town counted one: Jennie Wade, killed by a stray bullet while she baked bread. She stands in stone near where Lincoln vowed "... these dead shall not have died in vain."

FARRELL GREHAN. ABOVE: LINCOLN'S SECOND DRAFT OF THE GETTYSBURG ADDRESS, LIBRARY OF CONGRESS

Cane and Cotton Kingdoms

By elegant carriage or private riverboat, fashionable guests arrive at Parlange Plantation on the False River, an arm of the Mississippi. Inside the candlelit chateau, ladies in silk and brocade pose on little sofas. Slaves bring steaming dishes to tables already "laden with... beef, game... terrapin, tropical... fruits... sweetmeats, wines of every vintage."

Violinists strike up a lively tune, couples whirl onto the galleries, into the garden, down to the river's edge. The hour grows late, and the revelers sit down to the hot gumbo and black coffee that will help make bearable the long journey home, while the young bachelors gather in their own guesthouse to play cards and sip brandy until sunup.

These festive partygoers of the 1840's have long since vanished, but some of the patrician mansions they built along the rivers and winding bayous of a verdant valley still stand. You are welcomed to these symbols of the Old South, where a leisurely, hospitable way of life works its beguiling magic.

To visit Parlange is to encounter ghosts of the pleasure-loving Creoles whose portraits gaze down from the walls. Their carved furniture and gold-leaf mirrors, shipped from Europe to New Orleans and brought upriver by steamboat, still adorn the cool, shadowy rooms. In a spidery script, plantation records detail family treasures of every imaginable sort—dueling pistols, jewels, malacca canes, even "50 pairs of Pantaloons of divers kinds." Inside the house rest poignant reminders of slavery: manacles that shackled runaways and slave-made andirons and furniture. But most of the sprawling quarters that were home to the blacks, here and on other plantations, have burned down or fallen into ruin.

Louisiana's Creoles, white descendants of French, Spanish—and a few German—settlers, "lived more in sensation than reflexion," noted a traveler in the 1820's. Like the owners of Parlange, they brought a little of the Old World into the New.

Very early, the French entered the lower Mississippi Valley. In 1682 La Salle explored the great river, claiming the entire Mississippi Basin for Louis XIV. To honor the king, he named it "Louisiana." Nearly 40 years later, Sieur de Bienville founded New Orleans. In succeeding decades aristocrats and slaves mingled with earlier immigrants. Troubles plagued the colony, and Louis XV ceded New Orleans and Louisiana west of the river to Spain. But Napoleon took it back.

After the United States purchased Louisiana in 1803, a new rush of settlers added a zesty American tang to the Creole gumbo brewing in the lower valley. Rough pioneers from Kentucky and Tennessee pushed in—and collided head on with the cultivated Creoles. "Yankees, and what is worse, Kentuckians," a traveler wrote in 1828, "spread all over the country.... These people are the horror of all creoles, who when they wish to describe barbarity, designate it by the name Kentuckian."

The money crops, cane and cotton, had begun to pay off in the 1790's, when Eli Whitney invented his gin to separate the seeds from the cotton fibers, and a planter, Etienne de Boré, successfully granulated sugar. De Boré showed how to boil cane juice in open kettles until the water evaporated and crystals formed. Molasses and tafia—a kind of rum—were profitable by-products.

Mississippi River country bustled with prosperity before the Civil War. Steamboats laden with cotton and sugar churned down the river highway to New Orleans. Though many a planter lived in a humble cabin on a diet of hog and hominy, a few acquired little fiefdoms with slaves, a big house, perhaps a racetrack and stables. In a good year the cotton nabobs could net $50,000; those who craved city life built mansions in Natchez. A romantic rambler veiled in wisteria, Linden was built about 1785, with the 98-foot gallery added later. Steaming past riverside Natchez, the stern-wheeler Delta Queen *takes passengers on a nostalgic journey back to antebellum days.*

STEPHEN GREEN-ARMYTAGE. TOP: LIBRARY OF CONGRESS

Sumter to Appomattox

"Strike a blow!" fiery Virginia Congressman Roger Pryor exhorted from a balcony in Charleston, South Carolina. The crowd cheered, eager for action against the United States garrison at Fort Sumter.

"The firing on that fort will inaugurate a civil war greater than any the world has yet seen," warned Georgia's Senator Robert Toombs. Jefferson Davis was unmoved: If Fort Sumter was not evacuated, he would "proceed . . . to reduce it."

Less a threat than an insult to the Confederacy, the island fort numbered 85 soldiers ready to fight, perhaps a dozen guns ready to fire. Food was running low. Commanding officer Maj. Robert Anderson ruefully admitted that if rebel guns "do not batter us to pieces we will be starved out in a few days."

That desperate condition stemmed from a bungled attempt to supply Sumter. On January 9, 1861, the unarmed steamer *Star of the West,* bearing food and reinforcements, turned back when cadets from the Citadel, a South Carolina military college, bracketed her with cannon shot.

Within three months rebel shore batteries ringed Charleston Harbor. Gen. Pierre Gustave Toutant Beauregard, seeking "to avert the calamities of war," dispatched terms for a peaceful withdrawal. Anderson knew this dashing Creole well; Beauregard had been his prize pupil in artillery at West Point. But that was years ago. Anderson, himself a Southerner, could not betray his trust: ". . . my obligations to my government prevent my compliance."

At 4:30 a.m. on April 12, a mortar shell from Fort Johnson burst above Sumter. Zealous Roger Pryor had declined the honor of pulling the lanyard: "I could not fire the first gun of the war," he later admitted.

Beauregard's "circle of fire" spat 4,000 rounds in 34 hours. So sporadic was the response that rebels cheered when Sumter's guns did reply. Anderson, his flag in shreds, his barracks aflame, surrendered.

Confederates took over the fort and turned it into a Gibraltar. When federal ironclads attacked in 1863, they "met with a sad repulse." On nearby Morris Island, Union troops dug in and blasted Sumter with cannon, ripping holes in five-foot-thick walls. A Union soldier noted that "shot and shell seemed to be mixed through the mass as thick as plums in a pudding." Men blackened with grime tunneled through the rubble and survived in tomblike bombproofs. "That ruin is beautiful," a Confederate officer wrote of the fort, ". . . in some respects an image of the human soul."

The old image lingers, beckoning throngs in tour boats. Visitors wander among the silent cannon and hear a distant thunder; they gaze at spent shells wedged in brick walls and sniff the breeze for a hint of burnt powder. They lift their eyes to Old Glory and relive the moment when Anderson lowered his tattered flag, the moment, too, when he triumphantly raised it four years later.

Between ran the dreadful course of war, from Sumter to Appomattox. The strategy in the summer of 1861 was the same for both sides: Seize the other's capital city. "Forward to

Fort Sumter, rising from a shoal in Charleston Harbor, South Carolina, looks across a man-made island to Fort Johnson on a far riverbend. There in 1861 Confederates fired the first shell at Sumter, starting the Civil War.

COTTON COULSON

Richmond!" thundered the New York *Tribune.* The Confederacy "must possess the city of Washington," asserted a Georgia newspaper.

Generals scanned charts and issued marching orders. Near the sleepy rail junction of Manassas, Virginia, a testing ground awaited.

In mid-July, Union Gen. Irvin McDowell moved his army of 34,000 south across the Potomac. The pace was slow, the weather hot; troops dawdled to pick berries and fill canteens. Carriages crammed with sightseers—including congressmen and their ladies—brought up the rear. Confident of Union victory, they spread their picnics on grassy slopes and waited for battle to begin.

Sumter's hero, Beauregard, deployed 24,000 men along a meandering creek called Bull Run. On July 20, he was joined by the Army of the Shenandoah, about 9,000 strong. Next morning Union soldiers, blackberry stains on their lips, swarmed across Bull Run. The rebels wavered. But Thomas Jackson's brigade stood firm—"like a stone wall." When federals drew close, he ordered his men to "give them the bayonet. And when you charge, yell like furies!"

Tall in the saddle, "Stonewall" Jackson in bronze surveys the battleground, now a parkland an hour's drive from Washington. Lost in the echoes of time are the rebel yells that unnerved Northern soldiers.

Placid Bull Run twice lent its name to battle, the second time in August 1862, when Jackson again prevailed. He swooped down on Gen. John Pope's supply hoard at Manassas Junction and put it to the torch—but not until his hungry soldiers had sampled such delicacies as canned lobster and pickled oysters, washed down with good Rhine wine.

As armies jockeyed for position, Pope, anxious to "bag the whole crowd," found himself between two fires—Jackson on his right, Gen. James Longstreet on his left. The rebels threw everything they had—including rocks—into the battle and chased the federals back across Bull Run, back to Washington. Poor Pope, "kicked, cuffed, hustled about, knocked down, run over, and trodden upon," had had enough. Lincoln turned to Gen. George McClellan "to reorganize the army and bring it out of chaos."

McClellan knew how it felt to be kicked and cuffed. He was still smarting over the licking he had taken from Gen. Robert E. Lee on the peninsula between the York and James rivers; he had held Richmond in his grasp and let it slip away.

The new turn of events began at

Death reigned at Bloody Lane and Burnside Bridge along Antietam Creek in Maryland. A three-hour fight for the Sunken Road alone killed 4,000 men. In the wake of battle Clara Barton bandaged the wounded. Later she would found the American Red Cross.

FARRELL GREHAN. FAR LEFT: LIBRARY OF CONGRESS

Hampton Roads on March 8, 1862, when the Confederate ironclad *Virginia* (the Union's scuttled *Merrimack* raised and rechristened) made short work of wooden Yankee ships blockading the James River. That evening the armored U.S.S. *Monitor* steamed in, and the *Virginia* met her match. Next morning the ironclads hammered each other until noon, then broke off the fight, content with a draw. But that was good enough for McClellan. With the *Virginia* neutralized, he loaded his Army of the Potomac onto some 400 transports and sailed for Fort Monroe, situated on Old Point Comfort near the mouth of the James.

While McClellan's ponderous army of 100,000 inched up the peninsula, Lee turned loose Jackson's "foot cavalry" in the Shenandoah Valley. Jackson's "sudden and heavy" blows, Lee reasoned, would deprive McClellan of reinforcements.

Roaring up the valley, Jackson crushed the Union garrison at Front Royal, Virginia, and slashed through nearby Winchester. Doubling back, he triumphed at Cross Keys and Port Republic. In all, a month's work. "All Old Jackson gave us was a musket, a hundred rounds, and a gum blanket," recalled one campaigner, "and he druv us like hell."

McClellan, meanwhile, had plodded to the outskirts of Richmond. Lincoln wired him to lob a few shells into the city, but Little Mac wasn't ready. He cursed the weather, lofted observation balloons, and fretted over reinforcements.

Rain was "Confederate weather," and on May 31 the rebels waded in at Seven Pines, their bullets 'humming deadly songs." In two days, more than 11,000 men fell, among them the rebel field commander. Jefferson Davis replaced him on the spot with Lee.

Although he wished "that mantle had fallen upon an abler man," the wellborn Virginian knew exactly what to do: Take the offensive. First he sent cavalryman J. E. B. Stuart—a dandy in plumed hat, flowing cape, and jackboots—to scout McClellan's rear. Stuart's troopers did better, circling the entire Union army. He found the federals' right flank "in the air"—vulnerable.

On June 26, Lee lashed out at Mechanicsville, reeled under heavy fire, and pushed on to assault the blue line at Gaines's Mill. McClellan, forced back across the Chickahominy River, realized his siege of Richmond was broken. Abandoning supplies and wounded, he retreated to the James River, where Union gunboats waited. But Lee's pursuing rebels paid dearly at Savage's Station, Glendale, and especially at Malvern Hill, last skirmish of the Seven Days. Massed Union artillery slammed against the attackers, littering the

Muskets flash at close range in an assault on Battery Wagner, near Charleston. The U.S. Navy blockaded key Southern ports and, after Vicksburg fell in 1863, controlled the Mississippi.

Confederates fought mainly on home soil. Two exceptions, Antietam and Gettysburg, sapped Lee's strength and forced him onto the defensive. He faced Grant, whose bulldog tactics in the West had won Lincoln's support. While Sherman ravaged Georgia, Grant drove Lee south and cornered him at Petersburg. Richmond fell, and a week later Lee surrendered at Appomattox.

OPPOSITE: FRANK VIZETELLY, ILLUSTRATED LONDON NEWS, DECEMBER 5, 1863

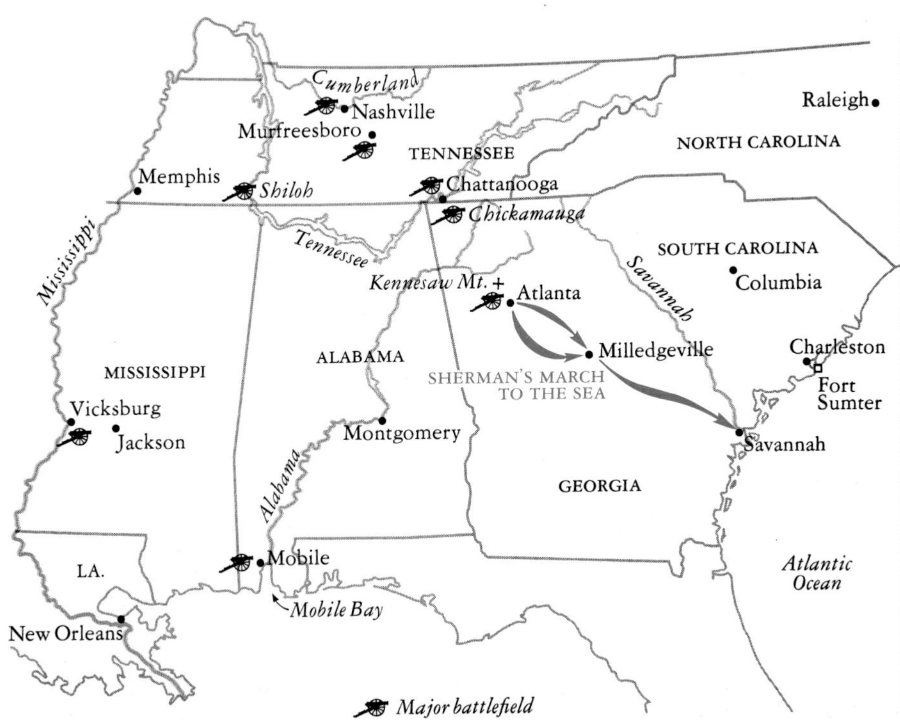

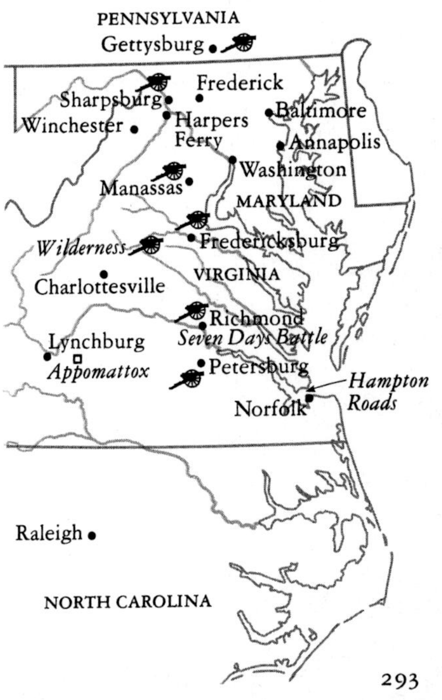

hillside with 5,000 bodies, "enough of them ... alive and moving to give the field a singular crawling effect."

Lincoln believed that the way to win the war was to strike "with superior forces at *different* points, at the *same* time." While McClellan aimed at the South's heart in Virginia, Ulysses S. Grant attacked the South's soft underbelly in the Tennessee Valley. In early 1862 Fort Henry, shelled by gunboats, fell quickly. A few miles away, Fort Donelson National Military Park near Dover, Tennessee, honors men who put up a better fight—but they too bowed to Grant. There some 14,000 rebels laid down their arms.

Grant, a failure in farming and real estate, had jumped at the chance to command an Illinois regiment. He whipped it into shape and won a promotion. When his father heard the news, he cautioned: "Be careful, Ulyss, you're a general now; it's a good job, don't lose it."

Grant risked exactly that when he dropped his guard at Pittsburg Landing on the Tennessee River. On Sunday morning, April 6, eager young rebels charged "like an Alpine avalanche." Federals camped around Shiloh Chapel, a Methodist meetinghouse, grabbed muskets and left breakfasts for the invaders to finish. The retreating Yankees might have been driven into the river, but one division rallied along a "sunken road" and viciously fought back. Rebels called the spot the Hornets' Nest; a Southern soldier wrote how awful it was to "hear the clatter of small arms and the whizing minny balls and rifle shot and the sing of grape shot...."

That afternoon a ball severed an artery in the rebel commander's leg, and he bled to death. Beauregard took over. Massing 62 fieldpieces, his men raked the Hornets' Nest with grape and canister, and after two hours forced its surrender. When darkness brought a respite from battle, he wired Richmond that

Dogwood blooms on Marye's Heights, looking down on Fredericksburg. Here Confederate guns belched "a continuous sheet of flame." Overgrown trench and "terrible stone wall" keep vigil below, where federals charged and died. Miraculously, the shooting stopped when rebel Richard Kirkland, the "Angel of Marye's Heights," brought water to the wounded.

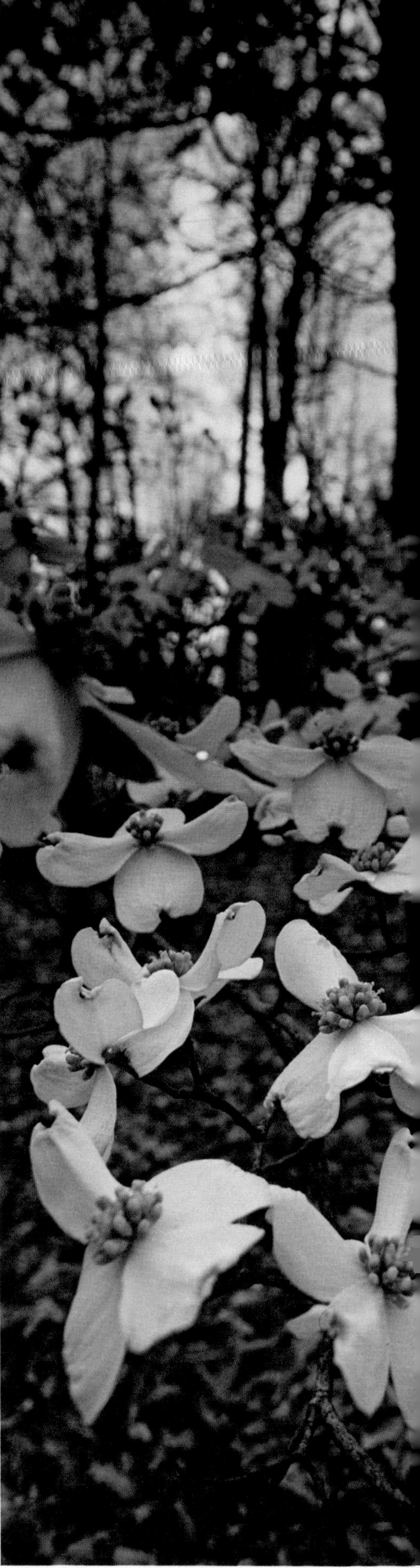

FARRELL GREHAN

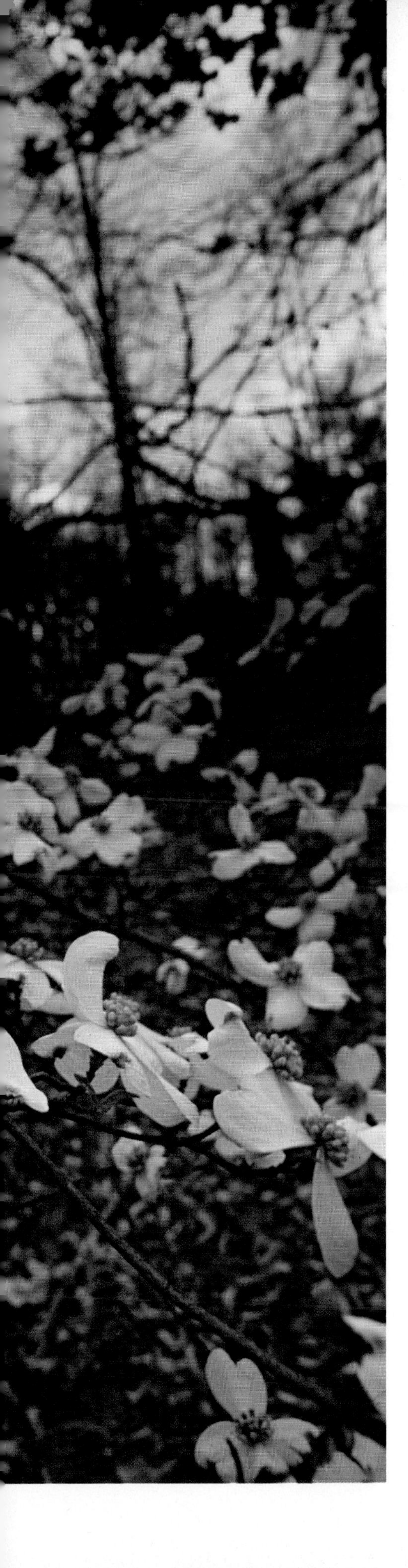

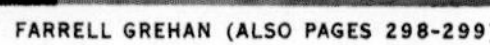

FARRELL GREHAN (ALSO PAGES 298-299)

Garbed in gray or blue, Civil War buffs stage a noisy game of war at Gettysburg. Fully authentic—there are no zippers on these all-wool uniforms—elite units even mimic 19th-century language styles. Mock engagements involve hundreds and portray life in camp as well as on the field. The eve of battle finds men boiling coffee, mending a shirt, reading the Bible. An officer of the First Ohio Artillery sights targets through his range finder. OVERLEAF: *The Union line, an Irish Brigade in the fore, blunts Pickett's Charge in a re-enactment. "We gained nothing but glory," a Virginia veteran wrote of July 4, 1863, "and lost our bravest men."*

he had won "a complete victory."

Not quite. The men in the Hornets' Nest had bought time for reinforcements to land. "Tomorrow," Grant promised, "we shall attack them with fresh troops and drive them, of course." Then, wrapped in a poncho and ignoring a driving rain, he fell asleep under an oak tree.

Shiloh means "place of peace," and so it is. Stroll its dappled paths in silence broken only by bird trill and windsong—and try to imagine the moans of 20,000 dying and wounded. Mayflies dance on a mirror pool named Bloody Pond in this national military park. A leafy canopy shades the Hornets' Nest. Over there the Peach Orchard bloomed and, shivered by gunfire, showered pink petals onto the dead.

Grant was as good as his word. On April 7 he chased the gray from the field. But he was blamed for losing too many men and drinking too much liquor. "Old Brains" Henry Halleck replaced him; some congressmen thought he should have been fired. But Lincoln thought otherwise: "I can't spare this man," he said later. "He fights."

Paralleling Grant's campaign, Union ironclads moved down the Mississippi. On June 6, 1862, they destroyed a thinly armored Confederate fleet at Memphis, an encore to Adm. David Farragut's resounding victory at New Orleans.

In the East, autumn found Lee on the move. "We cannot afford to be idle," he wrote, and pointed his army north toward Maryland. Numbering 50,000—not 120,000, as McClellan believed—they were, said one observer, "the dirtiest men I ever saw, a most ragged, lean, and hungry set of wolves." Gambling against time, Lee divided his force, sending Jackson to knock out Harpers Ferry while he sparred with McClellan at South Mountain. Finally battle lines were drawn along Antietam Creek, which snaked past the hamlet of Sharpsburg in northern Maryland.

In the misty dawn of September 17, Union artillery crashed into a cornfield where rebels crouched. "Again and again," a survivor described, "the field was lost and recovered, until the green corn that grew upon it looked as if it had been struck by a storm of bloody hail." Fighting surged down a sunken wagon road—Bloody Lane—and across a stone span remembered today as Burnside Bridge; each is now a stop on a self-guiding battlefield tour. "The sun seemed almost to go backwards," a rebel soldier recalled, "and it appeared as if night would never come." When it did, more than 23,000 lay wounded or dead—the bloodiest day of the war.

The defiant Lee waited all next day for the attack that never came, then withdrew across the Potomac. McClellan, who "always saw double when he looked rebelward," chose not to pursue. That was the last straw; Lincoln dismissed him.

McClellan's successor, Gen. Ambrose Burnside, lasted for only three months. In that time he led the Union to its most crushing defeat. A torturous crossing of the Rappahannock River, a suicidal assault across a frozen plain, a hurricane of fire from Marye's Heights—that was the scenario at Fredericksburg, Virginia. Lee, watching the slaughter in disbelief, remarked: "It is well that war is so terrible—we should grow too fond of it."

Along the quiet streets of Fredericksburg, motorists follow markers to battlefields. One route leads to Chancellorsville, where "Fighting Joe" Hooker boasted, "I've got Lee just where I want him."

Lee had other ideas. He split his forces, sending Jackson wide to Hooker's right. The flanking march ended in rebel yells and Yankee soldiers running for their lives.

MARINERS MUSEUM. LEFT: JAMES P. BLAIR, NATIONAL GEOGRAPHIC PHOTOGRAPHER

The Mississippi hides its bloodstained past and flows, in Lincoln's words, "unvexed to the sea." In 1863 Union gunboats, shielding transports, roiled the waters as they ran the rebel guns at Vicksburg. After a 42-day siege, the stronghold surrendered on July 4, the day Lee withdrew from Gettysburg.

Jackson, eager for the kill, rode into the night with his staff to scout the enemy's position. Edgy rebels mistook them for Yankee cavalry and opened fire, mortally wounding Jackson. "Wild fire, that, sir; wild fire," he muttered.

Shock, amputation, pneumonia followed. "He has lost his left arm," Lee moaned, "but I have lost my right." As he lay dying in Chandler's Cottage at Guinea, Jackson said: "It is the Lord's day... I have always desired to die on Sunday."

In early June, Lee again turned north. He moved so briskly that his forward units had "breakfast in Virginia, whiskey in Maryland, and supper in Pennsylvania."

Hooker had seen enough of the wily Lee. Gen. George Meade, Lincoln's fifth commander in less than a year, took up the chase.

Long lines, one of butternut, one of blue, touched at Gettysburg on July 1, 1863, sparking the war's greatest battle. For three days it raged. Waves of rebels beat against Union strongholds on high ground, fell back, and surged forward again, leaving in their wake a scatter of human debris. The two sides were so close, one soldier recalled, that "hostile gun barrels almost touched."

An outdoor battle museum, Gettysburg bristles with cannons, statues, markers, observation towers. By foot or car, tourists follow the battle: into Devil's Den, where rebel snipers holed up; onto Little Round Top, where "blood stood in puddles in some places on the rocks." In slow cadence they follow George Pickett's Virginians up the long, grassy incline of Cemetery Ridge to its crest, the northernmost summit of the South's attainment.

"The army did all it could," Lee reflected. "I fear I required of it impossibilities." The fearsome toll: 28,000 casualties, more than one-third of the army's total strength. Meade suffered almost as many, but the field was his.

Hours later Vicksburg, Mississippi, fell. Besieged by Grant's army and

Union gunboats, the city was so tightly surrounded, said a rebel soldier, that "a cat could not have crept out... without being discovered." The defeat cost the South some 9,000 killed, wounded, or missing.

In September, rebels tasted victory in the thickets along Chickamauga Creek in Georgia. When the Union army escaped to Chattanooga, Tennessee, the rebels laid siege. Grant came to the rescue. Troops stormed up Lookout Mountain, clawed up Missionary Ridge—and secured the town. Now Gen. William Tecumseh Sherman had a springboard to the Deep South. He beelined for Atlanta and left it in flames, then headed for Savannah.

In March 1864, Lincoln had summoned Grant to finish off Lee. The dogwoods were blooming when the Army of the Potomac crossed the Rapidan and clashed with Confederates waiting in the Wilderness, near Fredericksburg. Despite heavy losses, Grant continued southward. His troops cheered.

Spotsylvania, Virginia, was a savage brawl of swinging muskets and slashing bayonets. So close was the fighting that once the "flags of both armies waved at the same moment over the same breastworks."

Trenches, edges smoothed by the years, zigzag through dark woods at Cold Harbor. Here Grant lost 7,000 men in half an hour. He pushed on. South of Richmond he besieged Petersburg, digging in for nine months of "hell itself."

The noose tightened. Admiral Farragut closed Mobile Bay. Sherman invaded the Carolinas. Sheridan had scourged Virginia's Shenandoah Valley; then, on April 1, 1865, he stung Lee at Five Forks, exposing his flank. Grant pounced. He shadowed Lee's retreating troops to Sayler's Creek and took 6,000 prisoners. "We grew tired," a Yankee admitted, "but we wanted to be there when the rebels found the last ditch of which they had talked so much."

On Palm Sunday, April 9, 1865, Lee asked Grant for a conference "with reference to the surrender of this army." They met in Appomattox, Virginia, at the house of Wilmer McLean, and agreed to terms.

After handshakes, goodbyes, and tears, James Longstreet—Lee's deputy and Grant's friend from West Point—wondered: "Why do men fight who were born to be brothers?"

WAYNE BARRETT

Lee surrenders as Grant watches. "We walked in softly," recalled Grant's aide, Horace Porter, "very much as people enter a sick chamber." Restored McLean House enshrines the meeting on April 9, 1865, at Appomattox.

"SURRENDER AT APPOMATTOX" PAINTED FOR NATIONAL GEOGRAPHIC BY TOM LOVELL. OPPOSITE: FARRELL GREHAN

Travels with Lincoln

From log cabin to the White House—along a familiar route of Presidents, the "Rail-Splitter" mauls a wedge in an 1860 campaign poster. Abe Lincoln's fateful trail begins in hardscrabble country. At Knob Creek farm, Kentucky (right), he endured five boyhood years of "stinted living." Slowly he rose, freedom his stepping-stone. "Advancement," he insisted, "is the order of things in a society of equals."

When Illinois Republicans offered their favorite son to the nation in 1860, boosters appeared with fence rails supposedly split by the candidate himself. Such Presidential timber! The [illegible] convention went wild. Soon hawkers were offering canes and cigar holders made from "authentic" Lincoln rails. One is minded of the peanut craze a century later, and of all the ways that politics can craft an appealing image.

But some images are true. The "humble rail splitter" lived half his life in a log-cabin world. He remembered the wilds of Indiana: When he was seven, "an axe was put in his hand; and with the trees and logs and grubs he fought until he reached his twentieth year."

The struggle steeled that sinewy frame for life. Visiting the Washington Navy Yard in 1862, the President hefted an ax at arm's length—by the helve, the head straight out. No one around him could match the feat. It seems easy. Try it some time.

Something of the raw world that challenged Abe Lincoln, and shaped him, lingers in the Kentucky hills, the Indiana woodlands, the relic towns and burgeoning cities on what once was Illinois prairie. The trail bespeaks a restlessness—not that of the frontier rovers who banged away at game and got claustrophobia at the sight of a neighbor's cabin, but the restlessness of folk dreaming of better land, stability, a place to take root and prosper.

Tom and Nancy Hanks Lincoln, Virginia-born and Kentucky-bred, worked three homesteads before Abe reached eight. The Abraham Lincoln Birthplace National Historic Site commemorates his birth in a dirt-floor cabin near Hodgenville, Kentucky, on February 12, 1809.

COTTON COULSON. LEFT: CHICAGO HISTORICAL SOCIETY

COTTON COULSON

Two years later the family moved to a more promising spread ten miles away along Knob Creek, hard by the old Cumberland Trail.

Though Tom could scratch his name, Nancy signed with her mark. But they sent Abe and sister Sarah, two years older, trudging two miles to a schoolhouse. Like all the schools Abe would attend—four in all, intermittently, totaling about a year—this one was a "blab" school. Pupils blabbed their lessons aloud. Quiet signified slackness; remedial action might include the rod.

Abe was quick to grow and quick to learn. Neighbors remembered a "tall spider of a boy" who "set everybody a-wonderin' to see how much he knowed, and he not mor'n seven."

A land-title suit threatened to eject the Lincolns. In Indiana the government ran the surveys; there a man was less likely to lose his land in a maze of lawsuits. In 1816 the Lincolns headed for the territory soon to become the 19th state.

Near Troy, Indiana, they ferried the Ohio, already a great thoroughfare upon which wondrous "chariots of fire" steamed. The Ohio was also a great divide. Here the Founding Fathers drew the line, banning slavery to the north in the Northwest Territory. Thus the Founders, including some slave owners like Jefferson, had set the nation's course. Where slavery existed, they could do little to uproot it. But they curbed its spread, and they envisioned its end. Lincoln would follow that course, wherever it led.

Homegrown and handmade is still the rule at Lincoln's boyhood home in Indiana. Frontier fare includes biscuits and bacon, vegetables, and wild plants. Abe climbed to bed on wall pegs like those behind the woman kneading. When his mother died here in 1818, the boy whittled the coffin pegs.

The rippling farmland of southern Indiana today bears little resemblance to the wild forest that confronted the Lincolns. For twelve miles they threaded a wagon trace, then hacked through the brush for another four. Lincoln recalled nothing harsher in his boyhood than this wilderness trek.

Their land—Tom would claim 160 acres for $320, mostly on credit—lay close by Little Pigeon Creek, near today's Gentryville. They sheltered in a three-sided "half-faced camp" of logs and brush. Tom, a skilled carpenter, soon began work on a cabin. His family and the few neighbors around helped.

Typically, writes Louis A. Warren in his account of Lincoln's boyhood, they'd fell some 40 logs, each a foot thick, for the sides. Men at each corner would set and notch them. Then more logs for the joists and loft, and clapboards and poles for the roof. Openings must be cut for window, door, and fireplace. Pioneer accounts said it could all be done in four days, a solid new home with the incense of green timber in the air.

Next came the chinking with mud and splints—work for Abe and Sarah. Stout pegs driven into a wall gave the boy a stairway to his loft bedroom, where he heard the howling of wolves and panthers that "filled night with fear."

Neither cougar nor wolf are seen there today, nor the clouds of passenger pigeons that roosted by the creek, nor the Carolina parakeets that tinged the woods with tropic finery. Yet the flavor of pioneer life remains at the Lincoln Boyhood National Memorial.

In the cabin of a living historical farm, a fire glows all day despite summer's heat. Matches were rare on the frontier. A boy might have to run to a neighbor for live coals to kindle a cold fireplace.

Without cold storage, milk fresh from the cow will not last the day. No great loss. The sour "blinky" will curdle into clabber. Outside, in a cloth bag hung from a limb, the final step is taking place; watery whey drips out, leaving cottage cheese. The park women, now busy at the fire, will serve some at the midday meal, with chicken, corn bread, potatoes, and pumpkin pie.

Pie in an open fireplace? Simple. Set a Dutch oven on a bed of coals, place more coals on the lid, and the pie inside soon spreads its aroma through the cabin.

The Lincolns had their pick of game. Abe, not yet eight, potted a turkey with his father's gun. Times have changed. "All we have," says one of the women, "is that little ol' sassy squirrel outside, and the park won't let us shoot that."

Another contrast. A century ago livestock wandered; the rail fence kept animals from the vegetables and cotton and flax and tobacco. Today the stock is penned. "If we let the cow loose," says one of the park's farmers, "we'd risk the same thing that happened to the Lincolns." Not far from the cabin he points to a patch of weeds—white snakeroot, which produces a poisonous alcohol. When pasture was poor, cows ate it. Their milk was poisoned. In 1818 "milk sickness" killed Abe's mother.

After a doleful year, Tom Lincoln married Sarah Bush Johnston, a widow with three children. Now the

Yoked to the land, young Lincoln knew the endless rounds still pursued at his Indiana home—pulling flax, driving the hayframe, milking, splitting rails. Though he "never learned... to love" many tasks, he swung an ax with zest, won repute as a master woodsman. Rail fencing, heavily used, was regulated by law; pioneers reduced legal jargon to plain talk: A sound fence was "horse high, bull strong, and pig tight."

COTTON COULSON

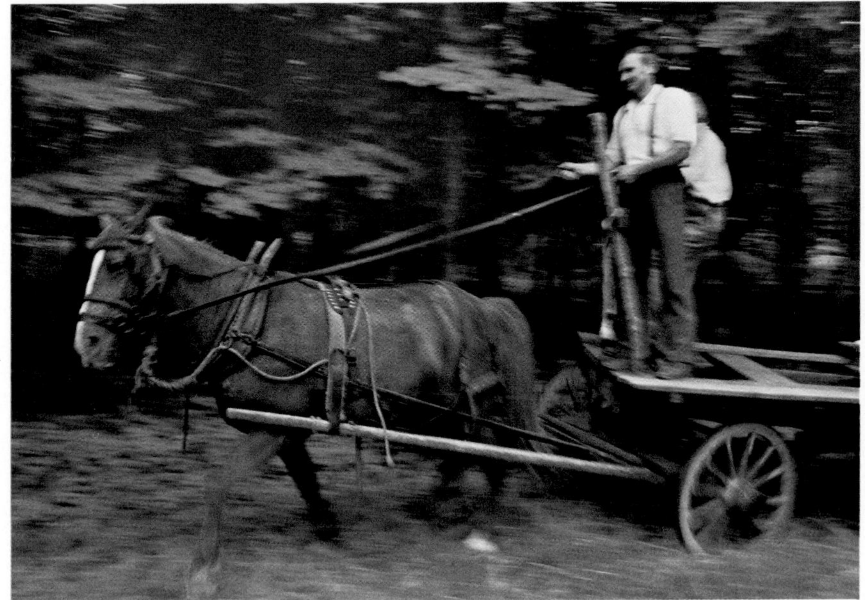

cabin brimmed with life. Tidy and bright, Sarah encouraged Abe in his learning. Chore work at times bored him. Some thought him lazy. One man who hired Abe complained that he was "always reading and thinking." People remembered his size—the schoolboy called "long shanks," the youth who "looked as if he were made for wading in deep water."

In 1830, the year Abe turned 21, Illinois lured the Lincolns. At first, pioneers had shunned the prairie. In this lovely desert of grasses—some so high a horseman could knot them above his head—there were no trees for shelter or fuel. And soil that wouldn't grow trees must be poor. But when men broke the sod, they discovered its riches. And the news got around.

The Lincolns spent a rough year near Decatur. Ague struck hard. Everyone knew this curse of fever and chills—from the severe "shakin agur" to the mild onset dubbed "the

Perched above the sluggish Sangamon, New Salem remembers its heyday on the Illinois frontier. At far right stands a replica of the store where Lincoln and a tippling partner sank into debt.

JAMES L. STANFIELD, NATIONAL GEOGRAPHIC PHOTOGRAPHER. LEFT: COTTON COULSON

slows." One remedy consisted of water and burnt gunpowder. Patients gagged. But, wrote one pioneer, as the Indian said, "No hurt, no cure."

Come spring the family headed southeast to Coles County—without Abe. On his own at last, he agreed to float a flatboat of cargo down the Sangamon, the Illinois, and the Mississippi to New Orleans. At New Salem, Illinois, the boat caught on a milldam, bow in the air. Lincoln shifted cargo to raise the flooded stern, bored a hole to run the water out, then bunged the hole and pushed on with his crewmates.

Months later he returned, to clerk in a New Salem store. So "the piece of floating driftwood," as he saw himself, came to rest in the log cabin village on the Sangamon.

Soon after, Lincoln bested the town bullyboy, Jack Armstrong, in a wrestling match. When volunteers mustered for the Black Hawk War in 1832, they elected Lincoln captain and his rival, first sergeant. The company never met the Indian foe.

Lincoln's six years at New Salem focused his life. Here, as he drifted through a variety of businesses and odd jobs without prospering, he turned to the study of law, ventured into politics, and was elected to the state legislature.

New Salem was born in 1829, dreaming of steamboats on the Sangamon. One steamer tried it; Lincoln helped pilot her back to safety, the stern wheel chewing mud. The Sangamon was no steamboat stream. New settlements siphoned off the town's trade. In 1840 it died. In time not a building remained.

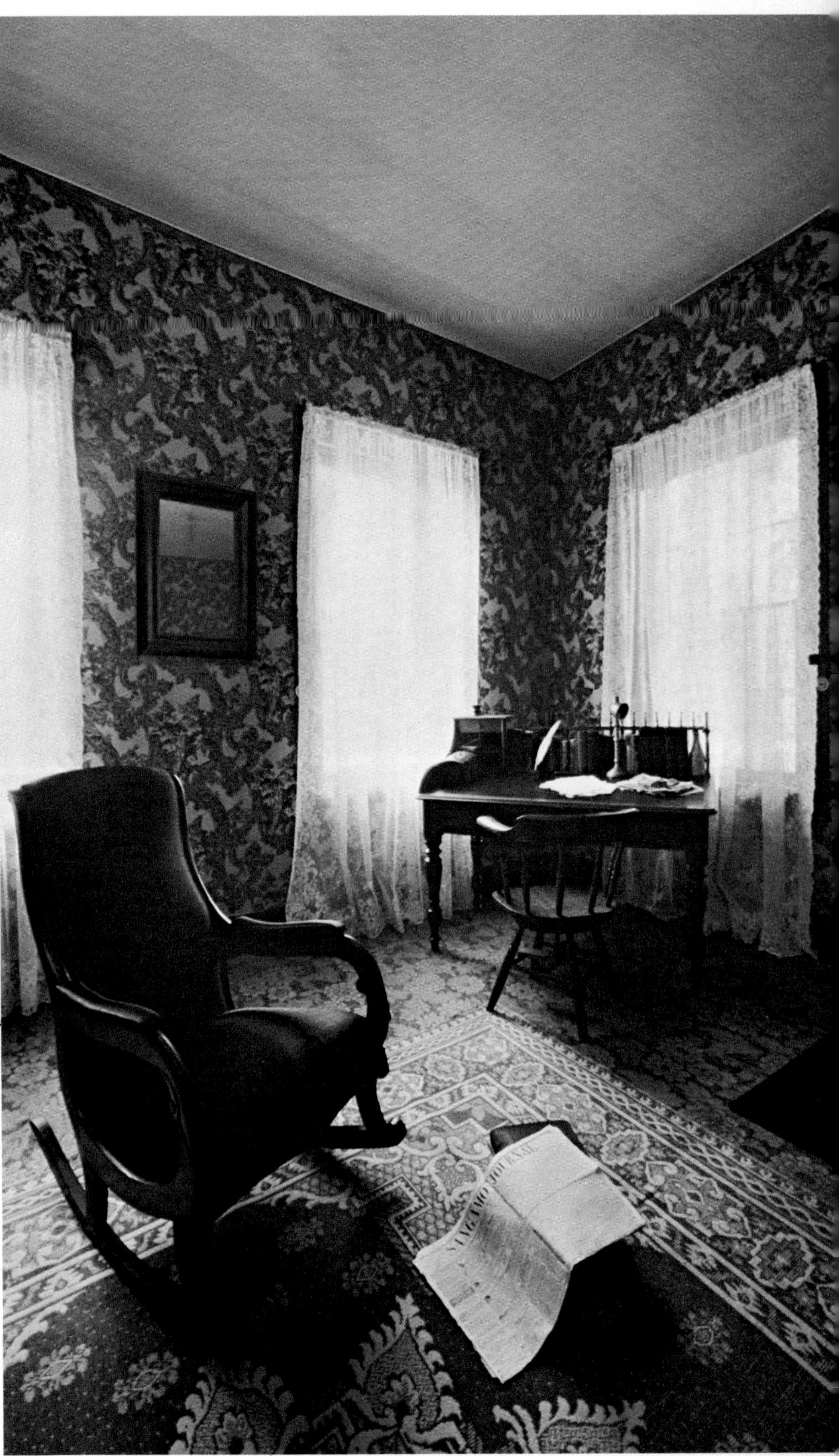

COTTON COULSON

Men in blue sound evening retreat at the Lincoln home in Springfield, Illinois. The horsehair rocker in his bedroom is a prized original. He sold many furnishings in 1861; some reached Chicago and fed the great fire of '71.

Today it stands again on its wooded bluff, a detailed re-creation of the village Lincoln knew. There on the banks the gristmill perches. Down the main street stand the two general stores which Lincoln partly owned. At Sam Hill's wool house, oxen tread the inclined wheel to power the carding mill. Nearby sits the vat in which Martin Waddell the hatter boiled his wool. His cabin has two rooms—one for the shop, the other for his wife, 13 daughters, and a son. A horse trainer, descended from sodbreakers named Hezekiah and Zadock, circles a clearing behind a green team of Morgans. It will take eight months just to teach them to go right and left, to "Gee!" and Haw!" Maybe more. One of the horses is dumb: "She won't look at you. A horse that won't look you in the eye isn't worth a damn."

Like the fragrance of a flower pressed in a book, the fading legend of Ann Rutledge hangs in the air here. When Ann died in 1835, the story goes, Lincoln lost the one true love of his life. He had boarded at her home, and may have fancied her. But hard evidence of a serious courtship points to a girl named Mary Owens. Despite her "unfortunate corpulency," he was ready for the altar. To his surprise, she wasn't.

We are strangers here in the past, never sure of our grasp. Yet there are moments. A cloud lowers on the village. In the darkened blacksmith's shop the forge spits up a shower of sparks, like a Fourth of July fountain. Outside, thunder and flying leaves, a deserted street. Rain blurs shapes, blurs time. Dim figures cluster on porches, waiting out the downpour. New Salem, relaxing on a Sunday afternoon.

Lincoln is to Illinois what sunshine is to Florida. Illinois invites us to courthouses on his law circuit, places where his kinfolk lived, towns that echoed to the thunder of the Lincoln-Douglas debates.

Above all, to Springfield. He had led the battle to make it the state capital, and there he moved in 1837, to rise from jack-of-all-cases lawyer to President-elect.

The town mingled urban boom and barnyard stench, a new capitol underway on the square, and hogs rooting up sidewalk planking. The streets were mud canals. Why not plant them to rice, asked a needling editor in the *Sangamo Journal.*

Politicians played rough. One challenged Lincoln to a duel in 1842. Unable to beg off honorably, Lincoln reluctantly accepted. Not until the parties reached the field of honor did friends head it off. The story improved with the years. Historian Paul M. Angle found one version in which Lincoln, asked to choose weapons, replied, "How about cowdung at five paces?"

Yankees and Southerners settled here. And passions lingered. In 1908 a race riot broke out. As a result, on the centennial of Lincoln's birth a national conference was called. It led to the creation of the National Association for the Advancement of Colored People.

The new statehouse of Lincoln's day is now the Old State Capitol, a Greek Revival gem of warm buff stone, whose mottled hues alter with changing light or rainfall. Its survival makes a fascinating story.

The state outgrew it and sold it to Sangamon County. In the 1890's the county needed more office space.

In the arena: A cloak marks Lincoln's legislative seat in Springfield's old capitol. Mementos of 1860 picture him and rival Stephen Douglas, and a hopeful view of the outcome. The Lincoln beard appeared after election.

NEW YORK PUBLIC LIBRARY. LEFT AND OPPOSITE: COTTON COULSON

Beams were laid through the lower stones and set on screw jacks. At the sound of a gong, workmen cranked each jack a quarter turn. Inch by inch the two-story structure, 123 by 89 feet, rose 11 feet. Beneath it went a new first story!

Outgrown again by the 1960's, it was resold to the state. Stone by stone, the building came down. Subsurface levels were built for parking and the state historical library. Above them, back came the old stones. The Old State Capitol stands again, two stories high, as in Lincoln's day ... the Supreme Court chamber where he argued 200 cases ... the House chamber where, as a candidate for the U. S. Senate, he spoke his famous paraphrase from the Gospel of Mark: "A house divided against itself cannot stand."

"We wanted the place to look as if the people had gone to lunch and would be back," says James Hickey, curator of the library's Lincoln collection. And so it does. Books lie open, cold pipes dribble tobacco ash on tables. And under the stairways stand the beds on which frugal clerks slept rent-free.

Across the square are the restored law offices of Lincoln and William Herndon. A tireless collector of Lincoln lore, Herndon professed to know a good deal about his partner's domestic life. If so, he learned it at a distance. He and Mary Todd Lincoln detested one another; he never set foot in the Lincoln home some five blocks from the office.

The Lincolns moved into the frame house with their infant son Robert Todd two years after their marriage in November 1842. There was joy and anguish in that house. Three sons were born in it; one died there. Mary, a highborn Kentucky belle, could sparkle with wit—and temper. Headaches tortured her. Domestic scenes contrast starkly. According to her enemy Herndon,

NEW-YORK HISTORICAL SOCIETY

FORD'S THEATRE
TENTH STREET, ABOVE E.
SEASON II .... WEEK XXXI .... NIGHT 196
JOHN T. FORD .... PROPRIETOR AND MANAGER
(Also of Holliday St. Theatre, Baltimore, and Academy of Music, Phil'a.)
Stage Manager .... J. B. WRIGHT
Treasurer .... H. CLAY FORD
Friday Evening, April 14th, 1865
BENEFIT!
—AND—
LAST NIGHT
OF MISS
LAURA KEENE

NATIONAL PARK SERVICE

The last act: A packed theater rings with laughter as Laura Keene and company romp through "Our American Cousin." In the Presidential box John Wilkes Booth, zealot of the lost cause, aims a derringer at Lincoln's head. A shot. The President slumps, mortally wounded. Twelve days later, so, too, the assassin, shot in a Virginia barn. Four plotters are hanged. Ford's stage goes dark. Today its footlights gleam again, and flag-draped Box 7 honors the leader who wrote an ideal ending for the tragedy of civil war: "With malice toward none, with charity for all."

GORDON W. GAHAN, NATIONAL GEOGRAPHIC PHOTOGRAPHER.
OPPOSITE: WILLIAM S. WEEMS

one neighbor told of seeing Mary chase her husband with a knife. And once, when the boys messed the parlor and she exploded, Lincoln "picked her up in his arms and kissed the daylights out of her. And she clung to him like a girl." Undone by tragedy, she lived out her years in the shadow of mental collapse.

The house is quiet today, though it, too, has a lived-in look: the newspaper spread by the rocker, the children's toys and puzzles. Touches of elegance, as well, befitting a lawyer of note: the formal parlor drapes of red velveteen, a strew of abalone shells edging the parlor floor.

Young visitors, with the candor fashionable these days, wonder aloud about the separate bedrooms of Mr. and Mrs. Lincoln. Well, says an official at the site, Lincoln liked to work at night—see, there's a desk in the corner of his bedroom. And besides, there's a connecting door between the bedrooms.

He entrained for Washington on the day before his 52nd birthday, "not knowing when, or whether ever, I may return." To lead a crumbling nation, he went, this soul of steel tempered in the wilderness. And after four years of agony, he had but five days to savor triumph, to turn to healing, before that dreadful night at Ford's Theatre.

The funeral train bore him across a mourning land, home to the prairie, to Springfield. There he rests in Oak Ridge Cemetery, with Eddie and Willie and Tad and Mary.

Why do we travel with Lincoln? Biographer Benjamin Thomas has written: "Lincoln saw his countrymen as inheritors of a trust. To them it had been given to make democracy succeed, to cleanse it of the hypocrisies that deprive it 'of its just example in the world.'" We travel with Lincoln because we must. We are on the same road.

SEYMOUR L. FISHBEIN

Taming the West

Cowboys eating trail dust to build cattle empires . . . railroaders uniting the nation . . . miners scratching for fortunes . . . sodbusters and cavalry pushing the Indians aside to fill up the country. Together they created cow towns and ghost towns—and a romantic legacy often bigger than the West itself.

JOE B. FRANTZ

You have to see the West to believe it. Even then you may doubt what you see.

It is a land of extremes. In places west of the Mississippi, temperatures in summer consistently top 100° F. and in winter threaten to drain the bulb at the bottom of the thermometer. Month after month of clear skies and no rain may be followed by a year's rain in 24 hours—transforming dry arroyos into torrential rivers, moving land and people out of their path as they rampage savagely.

Interminability, its very amplitude amplified by desert characteristics, marks the West. It is a long way between water holes. Across endless vistas, horizons 40 miles away, mirages resembling dancing waters hold out empty promises. But if its promise is fulfilled the West is, as one cowboy on the old ten-county XIT Ranch of Texas observed, "a grand place to view the stars."

The West is awesome today. What must it have been more than a century ago when it was largely unpeopled, a great void on the nation's map!

White men had advanced across the first third of the continent in some two centuries after the settlements at Jamestown and Plymouth. At that rate the other two-thirds would take 400 years more.

But this nation was settled by motion, by emotion, greed, revenge, restlessness. Who could have guessed that gold would be found at the far end of the continent, that railroads would reduce a trip from Omaha to the West Coast from a farfetched notion to a four-day ride, that a creature called cowboy would help to fill up the space between with longhorn cattle, that the military would remove the Indian barrier to white settlement?

In 1840, before all this hyperactivity broke loose, California had an amiable rancho-mission culture, Spanish flavored, with a trickle of foreigners from the United States and elsewhere. Among the most notable was John Augustus Sutter, born in Germany of Swiss parents. His scurrying life had included a shotgun marriage, four children, and debts that kept him always a fast step ahead of the law. In California he had become a Mexican citizen and by adroit borrowing controlled lands large enough to be worthy of his debts. In the Sacramento Valley he created almost his own nation—he called it New Helvetia—consisting of an adobe fort and all sorts of shops, fields, herds, orchards, and vineyards, along with a peasantry of Indians to support his baronial style. Most overland travelers to California tried to go by way of the fort, where Sutter proved as hospitable as a Swiss innkeeper.

Thus California lazed along, absorbing its trickle of Anglo-Americans, until one winter day in 1848 James W. Marshall found traces of "goald" in the tailrace of a mill he was building for Sutter on the American River. Realizing that hot-eyed money-lovers would soon invade his idyllic earldom, Sutter

"COMING THROUGH THE RYE" BY FREDERIC REMINGTON, NATIONAL COWBOY HALL OF FAME, OKLAHOMA CITY; PHOTOMONTAGE BY JAMES L. STANFIELD, NATIONAL GEOGRAPHIC PHOTOGRAPHER

HEYWOOD'S BUILDING

tried to keep the discovery a secret. But that kind of news won't keep. The fever spread—everywhere a ship docked, up and down the coast from Vancouver to Valparaiso, overseas to Hawaii, and eventually to both shores of the Atlantic. In a world of generally bad news, gold made the best news that many adventurous people had heard in a lifetime.

Sailors jumped ship, cowboys rode off from the herd, farmers left their fields. Away they went—the forty-niners—with zeal and faith, answering the call from beyond the 98th meridian. They sailed around the tip of South America, 14,000 miles fraught with freezing Antarctic winds or no winds, scurvy and dysentery, expense and danger. Or, in a trip half as long, they sailed to the Caribbean side of Panama and slogged across the Isthmus to cholera-ridden Panama City and a waiting list for Pacific ships.

Most tried it the short cheap way—overland. The busiest route was along the Platte River, over the Rockies, past Great Salt Lake, and across the Sierra Nevada. The rutted trails needed few markers other than the carcasses of oxen, broken wagon wheels, jettisoned furniture, and graves, graves, graves. People had accidents, women died in childbirth for want of sanitation and their babies for lack of mothering, scratches developed into major infections, Indians killed a share, others started too late in life, some froze to death, some starved. But more survived. And California filled like a boomtown.

WANTED

YOUNG SKINNY WIRY FELLOWS not over eighteen. Must be expert riders willing to risk death daily. Orphans preferred. WAGES $25 per week. Apply, *Central Overland Express, Alta Bldg., Montgomery St.*

Mail on horseback galloped between St. Joseph, Missouri, and Sacramento in April 1860, initiating the storied Pony Express. Bronze statue by Thomas Holland stands at the California end of the 2,000-mile relay. Faster than a speeding stagecoach, the service lasted a scant 19 months, until the newly completed telegraph began flashing instant mail.

LOWELL GEORGIA. ABOVE: PONY EXPRESS STABLES MUSEUM, ST. JOSEPH, MISSOURI

JAMES L. AMOS, NATIONAL GEOGRAPHIC PHOTOGRAPHER

Rails east, rails west—the twain shall meet at Promontory, near Utah's Great Salt Lake, Congress decreed. Annual reenactment again sets the ceremonial spikes that in 1869 united a nation. "The railway has so abridged time and space," said Leslie's Weekly *in 1870, "we have almost ceased to speak of the frontier." A lifeline for the West, iron rails split the domain of the Plains Indians. Belching "bad-medicine wagons" stopped along the way to disgorge loads of white settlers and supplies for a growing inland empire.*

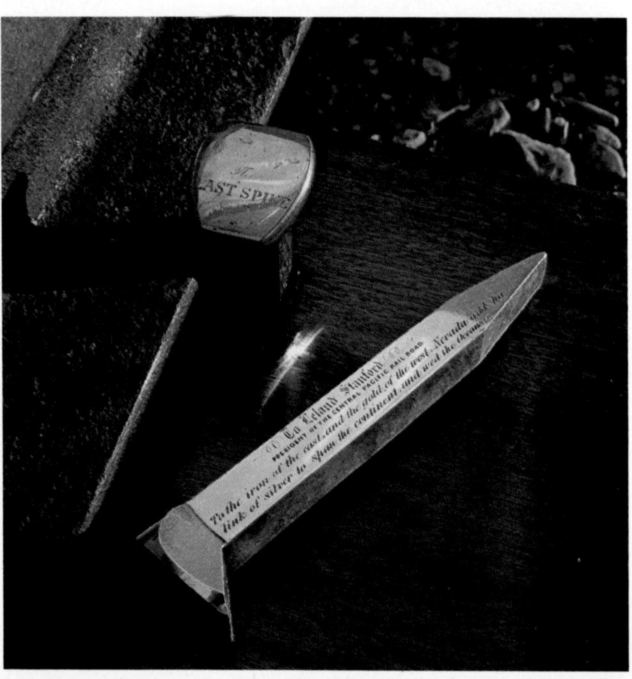

In 1848 California had about 20,000 persons other than Indians. When admitted to the Union two years later it had five times as many people, a burgeoning, brawling metropolis called San Francisco, and a host of hell-spawned mining towns with such evocative names as Delirium Tremens, Poker Flat, Hangtown, and Red Dog. Gamblers and saloonkeepers frequently formed the town leadership. Puritan morality had disappeared somewhere in the crossing of the Great Plains.

During the 1850's California continued to boom. What was happening there also occurred at various times in Colorado, Montana, Nevada, Arizona, South Dakota. Gold fever often led to silver strikes that promised equal wealth with more work and capital. One splendid feature of precious metals is that they are often found in remote places. Prospectors wandered into deserts, through high forests, up the sides of precipitous sierras, to areas where nothing grew and no one went. If a strike was made, the trails became roads and tents formed the nucleus for towns—Coloma, Placerville, Virginia City, Leadville, Cripple Creek, Bannack, Helena, Deadwood, and dozens more. If nothing happened, or the vein played out, people either found something else to do, moved on, or headed their creaky wagons back toward the morning sun. But success or no, permanent resident or round-tripper, they advertised the West. Here was unprecedented opportunity, and only the timid would stay home.

Since the 1840's politicians and entrepreneurs had dreamed of a railroad to the West Coast, but their dreams always foundered on sectional feeling in Congress. With the South out of the Union during the Civil War, Congress authorized two companies to complete the first transcontinental railroad. The Union Pacific would build from Omaha westward, the Central Pacific from Sacramento eastward. Awards of federal money and land would be based on miles of track laid.

Both roads built furiously. When in their haste to obtain the utmost federal subsidy they seemed likely to build right past each other, Congress stepped in to designate a trysting place.

Finally, on May 10, 1869, the day came for the wedding of the rails at Promontory, Utah. Symbolically, silver and gold spikes would be tapped into predrilled holes in a polished laurel tie at the spot where the two railroads united the nation. At every telegraph station in the United States an operator was alerted to receive the signal when yet another "last spike" took its sealing blow. Crowds at the stations would then raise a cheer befitting the last great thing that could possibly happen.

The ensuing ceremony cried for television. Union Pacific dignitaries from the East had arrived late. The weather was spring-wet and miserable, the site a sea of mud, the waiting crowd impatient.

At last the program began. As so often happens, too many speakers spoke too long. Then Leland Stanford, president of the Central Pacific Railroad, stepped up to hit the spike connected to the telegraph key. The onlookers became loud and unruly. Stanford, appropriately attired in a formal suit with a top hat, raised his mallet for the historic blow, slipped, and missed. The official account does not say that he fell sprawling in the mud.

But an alert telegrapher hit the key anyhow, and cheers resounded from the rockbound coast of Maine to the far Pacific shores. The nation had been joined. Golden California was now only days away from the money changers in Wall Street in New York or State Street in Boston.

And in between lay a region to be filled, with all the exploitive possibilities such a settling promised. The cheers were as much for profitable prospects as for the completion of the railroad itself.

But the railroads proved more than a triumph for financiers, inventors, and construction geniuses. They became the sinews that knit together the body of the West, performing functions that now are pursued by governments and travel bureaus.

Throughout Europe the railroads placed agents to contact people who might want to go to the New World. They helped the Bavarian farmer dispose of his holdings, arranged loans, conveyed him to his port of embarkation, saw that he got aboard ship, met him at port in the United States, installed him in a boardinghouse until the next train became available, and then saw him aboard for Nebraska or wherever else he wanted to go.

Once in the West, the new arrival again looked to the railroad for charts of available land and, if necessary, financing for the acreage he purchased. Meanwhile other railway employees scoured the world for crops that might grow successfully in this land of scant rainfall. Once settled in his sod house, the immigrant could look to the railroad to bring in mail-order catalogs and farm machinery, to haul his grain to market and see that he got a fair price. Railroads and settlers needed each other, could hardly exist without each other.

The advent of the railroad also helped spell the end of the Indian as an adversary to white settlement. Not only did the railroad fill former hunting grounds with people, but those people beat back the game — particularly buffalo — until Indians could no longer live off the land. The first Western passenger trains might be held up for hours while thousands — tens of thousands — of buffalo charged across the tracks. By 1890 the shaggy millions had been almost exterminated. Like the Indian, the buffalo became a ward of the federal government, rounded onto reservations, an endangered species.

Indians had hunted buffalo when they needed meat and clothing. White hunters killed for hides and for sheer sport. In some ways the hordes of buffalo hunters who infested the West in the 1870's and 1880's played a more effective role in subduing the Indians than the whole Western military.

One problem was the wastefulness of Americans wherever resources were plentiful. It happened to timber; it happened to good farmland. It happened to the buffalo. For every two hides recovered and shipped, three more lay rotting on the ground. The hunter rationalized, if indeed he thought about it at all, "With millions of buffalo, who's going to care if we shoot more than we need or can skin?" Only the Indian cared.

The Indians resisted the encroachment, with results that have colored Western history an indelible red. Taken together, the affrays between the Anglo-Americans and the Indians constituted a major war. Somewhere a fight was always going on, had recently been completed, or was about to break out.

OVERLEAF: *Grassy bluff recalls a century-old clash of cavalry and Indians in Montana's Custer Battlefield National Monument. Surrounding the invaders, Sioux and Cheyenne won the battle, lost the war. Stones now stand where Custer fell in a debacle that claimed all his 225 men.* NICHOLAS DE VORE III

GEORGE A.
CUSTER
LIEUT. COLONEL
BVT. MAJOR GENERAL
FELL HERE

A simple listing of all the skirmishes would run to several hundred pages.

Even passive persons were drawn in. Whites massacred Indians; Indians massacred whites. It required more forbearance than most men possess to calmly accept finding the cabin burned, the family mutilated, the stock run off. So the injured man struck blindly at the next Indian he could surprise, which in turn meant some other Indian had to retaliate or be branded a coward.

Geronimo, the terror of Apache country in Arizona and New Mexico, was just another tribesman when a party of raiding Mexicans killed his wife and children. His tribal council decided that, as Geronimo had suffered the greatest loss, he should lead the raid. He succeeded, but suffered other losses, so that he had to lead other expeditions until all his losses were compensated. By the time he "got even," he had become a leader of his tribe and a scourge of the Southwest, one of the last truly formidable fighters.

But the white man did not have to prove his courage by fighting Indians. Plenty of unprincipled people of his own kind hung around, getting in the way of orderly plans for progress. Miners fought miners over claims, railroaders fought railroaders for rights-of-way, cattlemen fought each other over water rights and fought sheep raisers over grass.

The cowboy story possesses the same accidental quality as the mining experience. The first cattle and horses were unloaded at Vera Cruz in the days of Spanish conquistadors. They drifted northward and westward, were brought into the future United States by explorers and priests such as Coronado and Father Eusebio Kino, and had waded the Rio Grande into Texas because the grass undoubtedly looked greener on the far shore.

In time Texas followed the Great Aberration out of the Union, leaving its cattle untended while its men fought for the Confederacy. When they returned they had a resource of possibly four million cattle and a ready market a thousand or more miles away, with neither highway nor railroad between.

An Illinois man in his twenties, Joseph G. McCoy had the answer. In one of the superior selling performances in American business history, he persuaded first railroad owners and then Texas cattlemen to support his scheme. He chose a site on the new Kansas Pacific Railroad, a former prairie dog stop called Abilene, so small that it sported only one saloon. Here McCoy built cattle pens and a drover's hotel. The new town soon boasted banking facilities, loading pens, dipping vats, watering tanks, and even a hell's half acre full of gamblers and "soiled doves." Abilene was ready to deal and to entertain the cattlemen. Texans drove their charges north to this newfangled railroad-cattle town, liked it, and Abilene became the first of a succession of storied American cow towns.

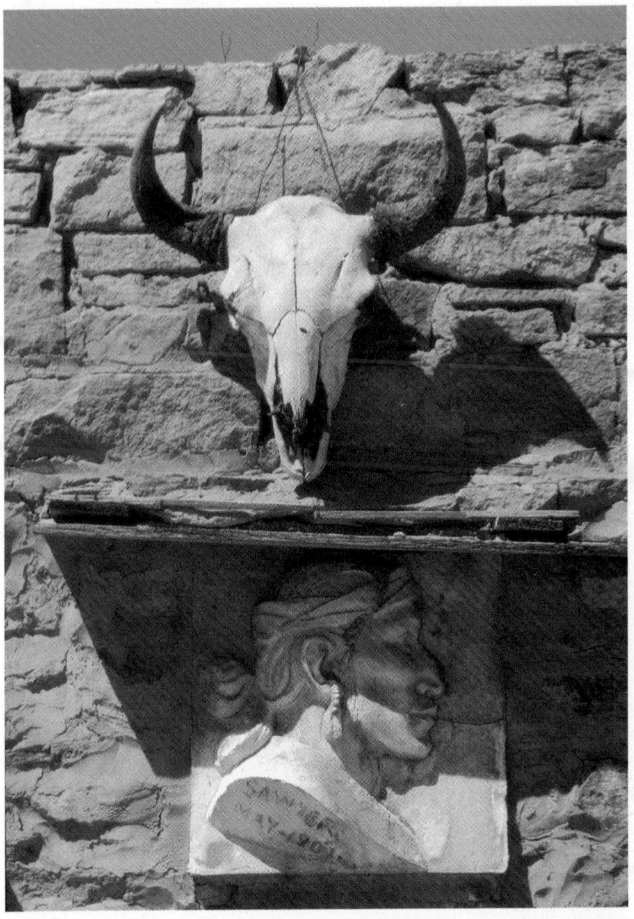

Bison skull and sand-cast profile of a young Navajo greet callers at century-old Hubbell Trading Post in Arizona. Amid harness, hardware, and goods traditional and modern, storekeeper and a Navajo woman set a price for her handwoven rug. Trade forged a peaceful link between Indian and white. The post also served isolated Navajo herders as a social center.

The $5 cost of a steer in Texas and a $50 sale price in the North and East meant a huge margin of profit. All sorts of men were attracted, men who didn't necessarily know a cow's horn from its hoof. The scheme was foolproof; take this year's crop of steers up the trail, sell them for a profit, return home to find that meanwhile the bulls and cows had renewed the herd, and then take next year's crop back up the trail. And so on and on. Unlike a mine, here was a resource that continued multiplying.

Like miners, cattlemen reached out to marginal lands that more careful men disdained. The federal government owned the grass, but gave cattlemen free rein to run as many head as they could afford on that public domain. And the ranchers increased, and the cattle thronged, and the profits swelled.

In his way the cowboy was as carefully caparisoned as if he were already playing a movie role: tight pants under leather chaps, roll-your-own cigarette pouch—his "makin's"—with its yellow string always hanging from his shirt pocket, bright neckerchief, hand-tooled saddle and holster with silver mountings. Most of these alleged affectations were functional, but to the outsider they were—and are—picturesque.

The frontier mythology has always depended on exaggeration, on covering lacks by overstating pluses. Certainly the West has done that with its battles and its heroes. It tends to exalt even antiheroes, to make them larger than life. Billy the Kid, a callow punk born in New York City, endures as a great recognizable name of the West. Calamity Jane, coarse and unfeminine, emerges in present-day glimpses as an attractive lass. Many of the reputed great lawmen—Wild Bill Hickok and Wyatt Earp, for instance—have dubious backgrounds as gunslingers on the wrong side of the law.

Probably the classic Western fight occurred at the O.K. Corral in Tombstone, Arizona, in 1881. One historian has dubbed the shoot-out "one of the most senseless acts of violence ever perpetrated on the frontier." Senseless or not, it seems to grow in public interest as the decades roll by. And Wyatt Earp, the hero or villain, depending on viewpoint, came out of the fight to be the subject of at least a dozen biographies.

Just as senseless was Lt. Col. George Armstrong Custer's notorious "last stand" at the Little Bighorn in Montana on June 25, 1876. In a burst of vainglory, Custer ignored his orders and allowed himself and his soldiers to be caught in a trap that led to the death of every last one of them. Yet many writers have treated Custer as the heroic figure in an inexorable Greek tragedy despite the fact that any West Point cadet in *any* era would have been dismissed from school for advocating such disastrous tactics.

Though its outsize ghosts refuse to lie quietly in Boot Hill, the lusty wide-open West that had room for such characters was rapidly disappearing.

Judgment day arrived in cattle country. By the middle of the 1880's, when the spreading networks of rails had ended the need for marathon cattle drives, too many cattlemen had overstocked the range. Drought and blizzard followed. Cattle died by the thousands. The myth of a bottomless well of profits died also.

By 1890 the grand era of the open range that typified the old Wild West had ended. Ranchers now purchased their land from the government, built barbed wire fences around it, and in some areas encouraged farmers to settle. As Badger Clark, the cowboy poet, said, "These ain't the plains of God no more, they're only real estate."

You'll find a tombstone, not a mine, friends warned. But Ed Schieffelin struck silver, named his claim "Tombstone," and founded a boomtown, soon a haunt of gamblers and gunslingers. Losers in a shoot-out at the O.K. Corral won a plot in Boot Hill. Courtroom (top) dealt more deliberate justice. "Too tough to die," Tombstone revives for fun its violent past.

LOWELL GEORGIA

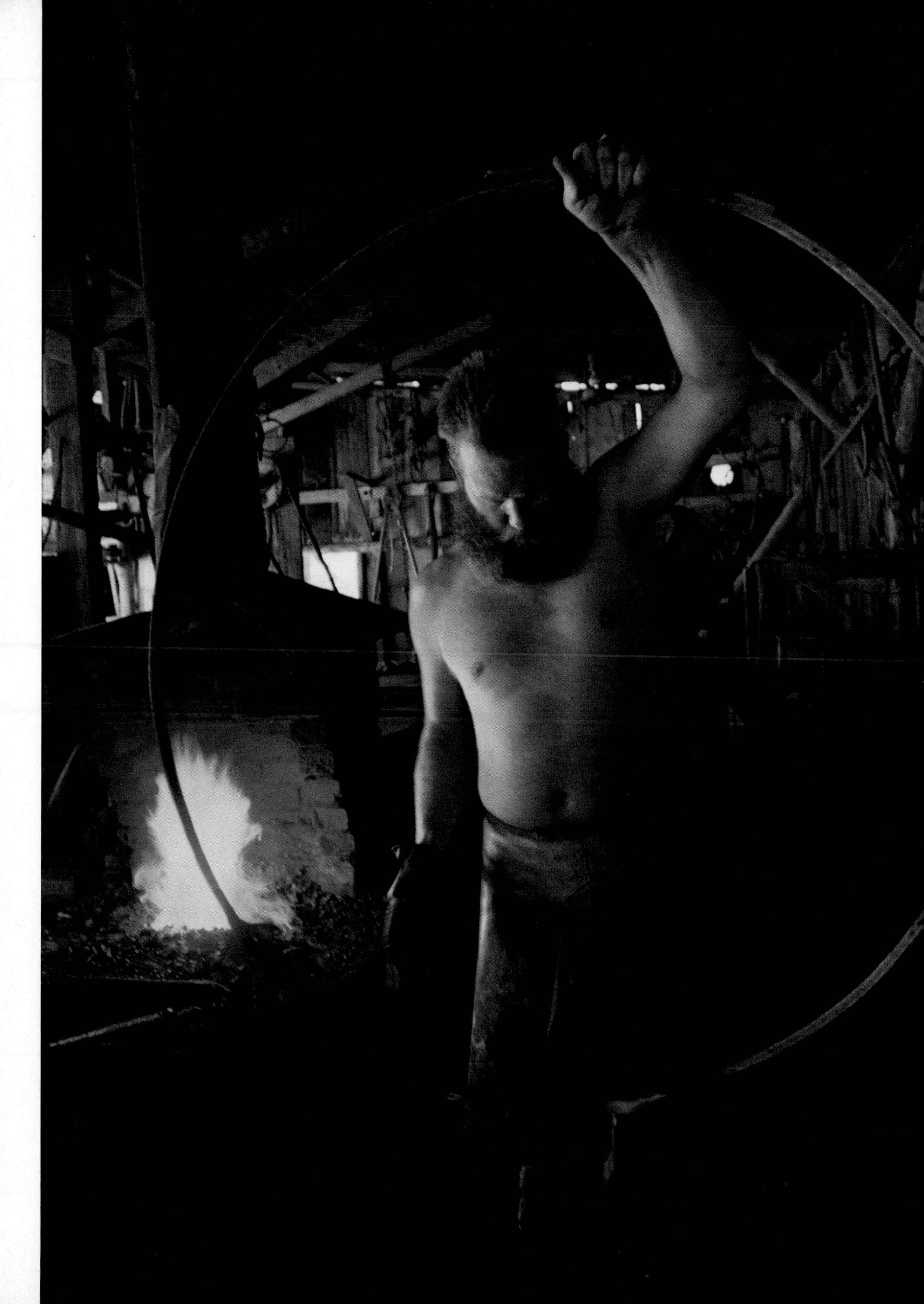

Gold Fever

The malady has no cure, though it is almost as old as sin and its cause is well known: soft, shiny, malleable, "saint-seducing" gold.

Gold fever has moved mountains and rivers, started wars, spurred bold journeys, woven a glittering thread through all man's history.

Today, a thousand feet below ground in the Colorado Rockies our guide, a fourth-generation miner, tells us, "There is *nothing* in the world more beautiful than a gold nugget." Lode, or hard-rock, mining is drilling, explosions, mucking, sweat, grime, danger. Until the ore-bearing rock hauled out by the ton is crushed and the ounces of precious metal extracted, there is no yellow gleam to impart a karat of glamor. "If it looks like 'gold' it isn't. It's probably iron pyrites, 'fool's gold.' The telltale sign of gold in this vein is a streak of purple fluorite."

Where do the beautiful nuggets come into the picture? From another kind of gold mining: placer mining. When Ed Grosh isn't working at or explaining lode mining to visitors at the Mollie Kathleen mine near Cripple Creek, he finds a gravelly stream rushing down from the Rockies and goes panning for gold as a pastime.

"Spring is best," he says. Freezing breaks rock seams in the mountains, and the thaw and rains wash down loose stuff that may include bits of gold, gold that looks the part. "You won't make a living at it—I say that from 18 years' experience—but it's a heck of a lot of fun."

You risk catching the fever that can be fun. At tour's end every visitor to the Mollie gets a chunk of purplish ore with a few invisible golden germs. As you ferret out old glory holes and ghost towns of the West, you meet people with symptoms. Sifting tailings beside rickety headframes of shafts abandoned as worthless a century ago. Hunkered over tin pans of mud with their feet in the icy Animas River in the San Juan Mountains, in Clear Creek west of Denver, in the American River and other Sierra Nevada streams where the epidemic flared.

The year: 1848. War with Mexico has ended. By treaty, gaining California and the Southwest, the American eagle stretches its wingspan sea to sea. Old glory-glutted Gen. Zachary Taylor is rolling toward the White House. Nine new towns take the hero's nickname, Rough and Ready, an echo of the times.

On January 24, a glint of yellow washed into a millrace hits the eye of James Marshall, working for John Sutter at Coloma, 50 miles by mule wagon from Sutter's fort.

Gold? GOLD!

Sutter tries to keep the lid on. A canny Mormon merchant named Sam Brannan has other ideas. He lays in supplies—picks, pans, food, mules that aspiring millionaires would need for the goldfields—and loudmouths the news. "GOLD! Gold from the American River!" And the epidemic is on.

Within two years some 80,000 fortune seekers pour into California. Shantytowns mushroom. Coloma first, with a population up to 10,000. Then all along the river bars of the Sierra foothills, sites linked now by scenic, serpentine California 49, the Mother Lode Highway.

Like many of the forty-niners, I touch base at San Francisco. A stop at the Wells Fargo History Room lets you ogle an enormous nugget of gold, admire one of the splendid Concord coaches that once hauled the ore, inspect reward posters for

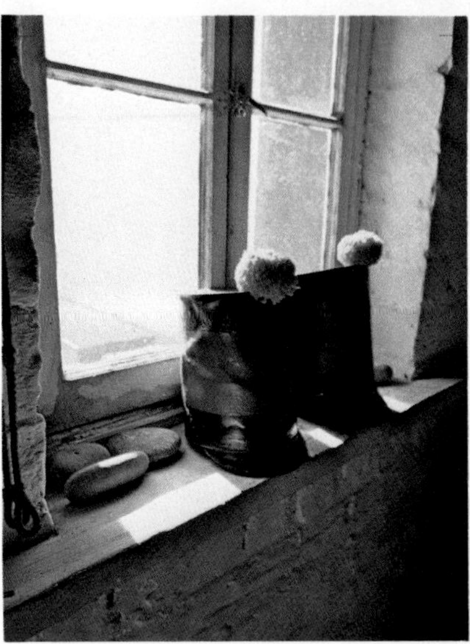

Gateway to eldorado, an adobe fort in Sacramento offered aid and shelter for trail-spent emigrants of the 1840's. Swiss trader John Augustus Sutter owned the outpost and some 48,000 acres; he ruled it with a military flair. Cannon guarded the bastions. Armed men drilled by day, stood sentry by night. Reveille of drumbeats summoned his Indian laborers to work wheatlands and tend stock. Unintentionally—by the prosaic act of building a sawmill upriver—Sutter set the fuse that exploded in a rush for gold. Hordes of forty-niners swelled California's citizenry and shattered Sutter's little empire.

LOWELL GEORGIA

BILLY CLANTON
TOM McLAURY
FRANK McLAURY
MURDERED
on the streets
of
TOMBSTONE
1881
TOM
McLAURY
Killed
Oct.26,1881

the likes of Black Bart who lifted some of it at gunpoint. And you can pick up an excellent map of the Mother Lode country.

For me, the beautiful mountainous setting of the gold rush is half its allure. Drought, not gold, fevers the tawny hills in the mid-1970's. A jack-rabbit lean as the times lopes up a roadside bank and away through the dry grass. Huge hoppers of newly-harvested sugar beets roll out of the Great Central Valley, veined with vital irrigation ditches.

The south fork of the American River at Coloma runs low. It has changed course through the years. The replica of Sutter's sawmill operates—on weekend afternoons—by electricity. Exhibits at the 230-acre state historic park recount the discovery of gold in California and explain various methods of mining. Restored buildings include a cabin that Marshall lived in, a blacksmith shop, and a Chinese store.

In most boomtowns, the feverish rush for wealth took precedence over such frivolities as sound dwelling places. Flimsy shacks of canvas and timber invited the second big event after the strike: the town fire. Columbia boomed in 1850, burned in 1854, rebuilt, burned again in 1857. Many structures built of brick or stone after the fires make Columbia the most tangible ghost town of the gold rush decade. Among them was a much-needed firehouse.

In the 1850's some 5,000 Chinese miners were working at nearby Chinese Camp. An 1856 dispute, over a rock rolled from one dig down onto another one, erupted into a full-scale tong war. The Sam Yap brotherhood mustered 1,200 men against 900 from the Yan Wo tong. The armies battled it out with picks, shovels, knives, clubs, and a few guns. Four men were killed, a handful wounded. Mail still shuttles through the Chinese Camp post office, ZIP 95309.

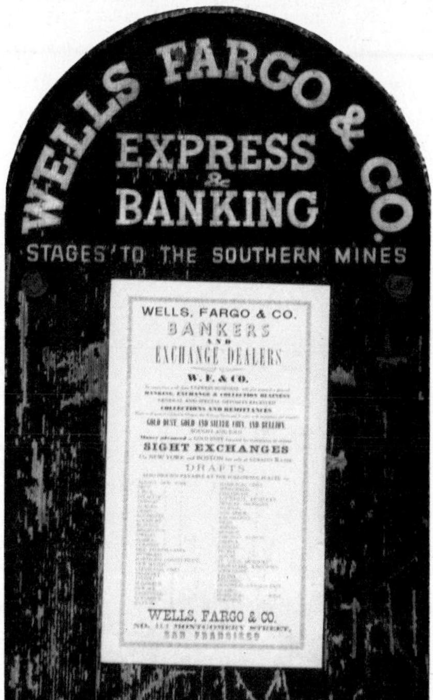

Wheel rims a smith, and vice versa, at Columbia, the "Gem of the Southern Mines" in California's Mother Lode. Vintage buildings of the state historic park include the Wells Fargo, whose stages hauled mail and miners in and gold out. Visitors can jolt down Columbia's dusty street in authentic gold rush style, behind huffing horses—riding shotgun for a few nuggets more.

OVERLEAF: *On a throne with a silver and gold lining sat "Queen of the Comstock," Virginia City, Nevada. Once a metropolis of 30,000 people, the town perches on the side of Mt. Davidson.*

LOWELL GEORGIA (ALSO OVERLEAF)

As gold fever peaked and waned in California, news from inland refueled it. In the gulches of western Nevada prospectors had been finding some gold and throwing away a lot of "damned blue stuff." In 1859 an assayer's report showed the stuff was silver, in amounts worth more than the gold.

A reverse stampede was on. From California men and mules streamed back across the Sierra, the formidable snow-capped barrier some had crossed but a few years earlier. An arterial highway now gentles what was successively a tortuous trail, a jolting wagon road, and the route of the transcontinental railroad.

A short detour over Donner Pass presses the history button, even on a sun-drenched day in August. No snow is in view, but snowsheds cover the train tracks that snake precariously along granite cliffs. You descend by scenic switchbacks. Sailboats skim the sparkling blue of Donner Lake; vacationers picnic in the state park that now marks the tragic wintering site of emigrants trapped by 20-foot snowdrifts.

A stiff crosswind blows off the Sierra into Nevada's Washoe Valley. Tumbleweeds roll. Hedges of Lombardy poplar sway like dancers. A dust devil spirals up from a quirky spot in a pasture. Winds and gilded sunsets over thirsty sagebrush hills have altered not at all since the Comstock Lode—richest silver strike of modern times—teemed with miners, stock merchants, saloonkeepers, gamblers, "hurdy-gurdy" girls.

And Mark Twain. After a "delirious revel" in silver mining, he came to the *Territorial Enterprise* in Virginia City, where he hit his stride in frontier journalism. Museums along the boardwalks of C Street entice with Twain-associated memorabilia: umbrella, marble-topped bureau, desk, antique typecases, printing presses brought round the Horn.

LOWELL GEORGIA

Bronze knob opens the walnut door of Graves Castle, bonanza-built mansion of a mine superintendent on Nevada's fabulous lode. Original furnishings from the world's far corners grace the opulent interior: Brussels lace curtains, hand-blocked wallpaper and gold-leaf mirrors from France, fireplaces of Carrara marble from Italy. . . . Perched uphill and upwind, Graves' home escaped the 1875 fire that razed the Virginia City business district and houses of 2,000. "Washoe zephyrs" blew so briskly over the divide that Mark Twain claimed he once saw a Chinese man flying an iron door as a kite.

The burgeoning city never lacked news: "political pow-wows, civic processions, street fights, murders, inquests, riots . . . a dozen breweries and half a dozen jails and station-houses in full operation, and some talk of building a church."

Beautiful St. Mary's in the Mountains and St. Paul's Episcopal are among century-old churches that still grace the town. A doughty Victorian, the Fourth Ward School yet strides the windy pass, panes rattling in the mighty zephyrs. Here a mansion, there a Miners' Union Hall. And saloons, saloons. You get your change in silver; one-armed bandits stand by like sharpsters of yore to lighten heavy pockets.

The Queen of the Comstock had a long reign; the Nevada lode was the nation's major source of silver until 1880. During those decades, important strikes and outsize rumors of gold and silver lured waves of fortune hunters to other Western states. In 1859 wagons rolling west bore the slogan "Pikes Peak or Bust!" Many of the signs got relettered to "Busted, by God!" But of the 100,000 hopefuls who toiled across the Great Plains to Colorado enough stayed to settle a new territory. Up and down the spine of the Rockies ghost towns retell the boom-bust mining saga.

Winches groan. Steel cables whine. Visitors snugged into a skip, or miner's cage, are lowered 1,000 feet into the Mollie Kathleen Gold Mine in Colorado. Here a miner-guide explains tools and methods used to extract ore in 1900. A tram car loaded with two tons of ore (opposite) is pushed along a slight decline to the shaft, where it will be raised to the surface in a skip. A system of bells is used to notify the operator above to hoist away. Mines in the Cripple Creek district, where gold was discovered in 1890, yielded $500 million before operations ceased in the early 1960's. The chunk of ore above, from the Mollie Kathleen, glows with iron pyrites—"fool's gold"—but also conceals perhaps three ounces of gold per ton of ore. Nuggets in the scale at left came from placers, stream deposits, some 40 miles from Cripple Creek. "Natural nuggets are like snowflakes," says Ed Grosh, "no two alike."

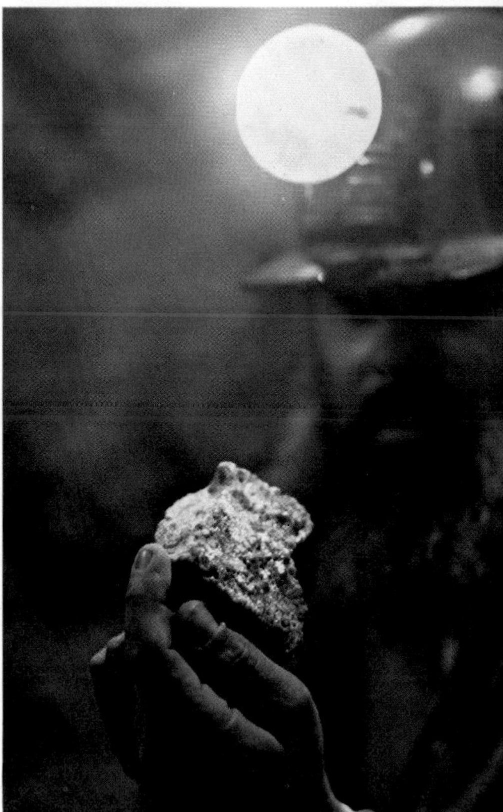

LOWELL GEORGIA

GRAND OPERA SEASON

OPERA HOUSE, CENTRAL CITY

Engagement Extraordinary

TUESDAY EVENING, SEPTEMBER 12, 1899,

The Celebrated

Lombardi Italian Grand Opera Co.,

OF MILAN, ITALY.

Direct from Successes at the

BROADWAY THEATRE, DENVER, IN

Verdi's Immortal Opera in four acts,

"Il Trovatore"

48 ARTISTS AND SINGERS 48

Special Scenery. Magnificent Costumes.

—Our Own Orchestra—

Cast of Characters.

Manrico - - Signor Juan Badaracco
Count de Luna - - Signor Pedro Galazzi
Leonora - - Signorina Adalgisa Rossi
Azucena - - Signorina Blanca Barducci
Inez - - Signorina Gilda Marchetti
Ferrando - - Signor J. Napoleone
Ruiz - - Signor P. Rataggi
Gypsies, Cavaliers, Women, Soldiers, Etc., Etc.

Synopsis of Acts.

ACT I.—Midnight in the Palace of Aliaferia.
ACT II.—Gypsy Camp.
ACT III.—Camp of Count de Luna.
ACT IV.—Prison Scene in Castle.

ARGUMENT OF

"Il Trovatore."

The opera opens in the palace of Aliferia, where Ferrando, a follower of the Count de Luna, relates to the servants how, some years before, the younger brother of the Count was supposed to be bewitched by an old gypsy. The sorceress was pursued, taken and burnt, but Azucena, the gypsy's daughter, actuated by revenge, stole the child with the intention of destroying it, with her mother. [illegible]

Seats on sale at Couch's.

Cultural diamonds like Central City's opera house glittered in many a rough minetown setting. On Colorado's gaslit stages stars of opera, drama, and melodrama played to nugget-tossing bonanza kings and roughhewn miners.

Stages went dark with the town's fading fortunes. Central City's opera house, built of granite in 1878, but then closed for years, was revived in the early 1930's. A month-long festival of sung and spoken drama in summer fills the refurbished landmark. Sale of memorial chairs helped finance the restoration. For $100 donation a patron could honor anyone: singer Patti, actress Bernhardt who once played Central City, the Redwood Fishers who took out the first marriage license issued in Denver.

LOWELL GEORGIA

"All aboard!" Two long toots of the whistle, a spurt of steam, and engine 478 chugs out of the Durango depot, wagging a tail of a dozen passenger-laden cars. Destination: Silverton, an old mining town 45 miles away. At a speed of 10 miles an hour, getting there is half the fun; the other half is getting back.

Rails only 36 inches apart thread two-million-acre San Juan National Forest, and hang on dizzying ledges above the rushing Animas River.

In 1868 the San Juan country was Indian-given to the Utes. In 1870 the word "gold" lured prospectors in and—the usual story—quickly forced the Indians out. Silver as well as gold plated the ribs of the San Juans. Completion of the railroad from Durango to Silverton in 1882 made it profitable to mine lower-grade ores.

Narrow gorges of the line give a close look at mountain wild flowers, glimpses of old mine shafts, fallen telegraph poles and wires, stagecoach stops. If you ride in an open gondola car, as I did, take a warm jacket. And goggles are an excellent idea. Nostalgia gets in your eyes.

There was one other stop. My last day in mining fever country—Central City, Colorado, it was—I was walking uphill to the parking lot, idly glancing in shop windows. Sun slanting in through the glass bounced off a stack of oversize tin pans, the kind I'd been seeing since the Sierra foothill towns. When the sun draws your eye so pointedly it's hard to turn away. I went inside. There's this rushing mountain stream I know. And come spring...

VERLA LEE SMITH

Into the past chuffs the iron horse Silverton. *Built in 1882 to haul ore from Silverton (silver by the ton) to Durango, Colorado, the narrow-gauge line now carries capacity loads of passengers. Engine 478, new in 1923, can pull no more than 12 cars up the cliff-hanging grades of the scenic San Juan Mountains. On the 90-mile round trip to yesterday the classy little locomotive corkscrews through the Animas River canyon, whose sheer walls expose Precambrian red granite and other rocks 600 million years old.*

LOWELL GEORGIA

The Cow Town

In Dodge City's Long Branch Saloon, Miss Kitty hands a gun to a customer and warns him that a murderous Indian is on his trail. The Indian arrives, the customer shoots him, and the saloon explodes with cheers. Then the gunslinger, a boy about seven years old, steps down from the stage to the table where his parents sit. And the nightly Long Branch Variety Show roars on, entertaining visitors with a froth of myth and misinformation.

Dodge City, "Queen of the Kansas Cow Towns," has a real past. But the city's visitors look at that past today through the flickering images of a once-popular television show, *Gunsmoke.* The saloon, itself a mock-up, has become a site that recalls a dual past: The Dodge City that saw a million head of cattle driven to its rail yard by the cowboys of a real West; and the Dodge City that inspired the long-running TV show about a fictional West.

The non-alcoholic saloon's "Miss Kitty" is a local woman portraying a TV actress who portrayed a fictional person. *Gunsmoke*'s principal character so hovers between reality and fiction that a scholarly book on Kansas cow towns lists him this way in its index: "Dillon, Matt: no police officer by this name ever served in early Dodge City. Sorry."

Mr. Dillon was too nice to be true, anyway. Real cow town lawmen were notorious disturbers of the peace. William Barclay ("Bat") Masterson, who in a long gunslinging career wore a badge in Kansas and Colorado, sometimes used his six-shooter to settle private grievances. In one Dodge City gunfight, stray bullets sprayed a doctor's office. Bat was arrested and kicked out of town.

Eastern newspapers, eager to find

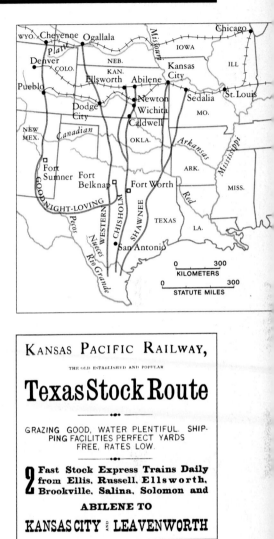

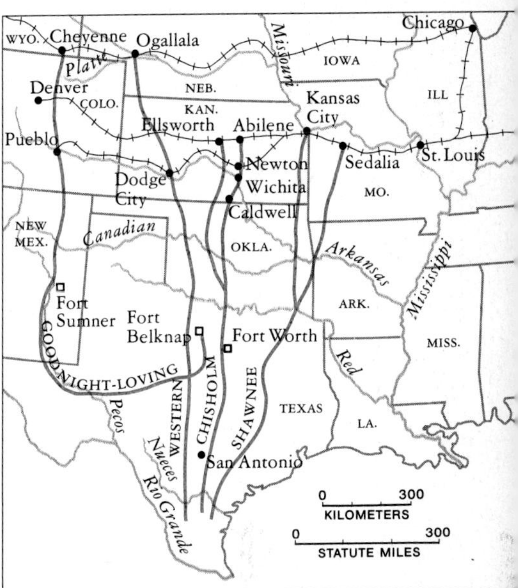

KANSAS PACIFIC RAILWAY,

THE OLD ESTABLISHED AND POPULAR

Texas Stock Route

GRAZING GOOD, WATER PLENTIFUL. SHIPPING FACILITIES PERFECT YARDS FREE, RATES LOW.

2 Fast Stock Express Trains Daily from Ellis, Russell, Ellsworth, Brookville, Salina, Solomon and

ABILENE TO

KANSAS CITY AND LEAVENWORTH

Longhorns, vanishing symbols of the West, make a comeback on a Texas ranch. Tenderer Herefords replaced the old tough breed, descended from Spanish strays and Americans' scrub cattle. After the Civil War some four million longhorns roamed Texas. Cattlemen there put us on the trail as a nation of beef eaters. "Pointed north," herds on the Goodnight-Loving Trail served beef-on-the-hoof to frontier consumers. Other hoof-carved paths led to railheads, where drovers prodding animals into cattle cars were dubbed cowpokes.

LOWELL GEORGIA. ABOVE: KANSAS STATE HISTORICAL SOCIETY, TOPEKA

Their guns aimed at entertainment, storefront cowboys blaze away in Dodge City, which lures more visitors than it ever did bad guys. A marshal of make-believe lights up at a mock-up of Front Street. In the real one (right) guns were banned but gambling was wide open — from "five-cent chuck-a-luck to a thousand dollar poker-pot" — and the mayor joined in "the giddy dance with the girls." An arrow-pierced skull is a relic of days when nearby Fort Dodge was commanded by George A. Custer. Dodge claims that its Boot Hill, now the site of city hall, was the West's first — a burial place for "the tainted," who "generally died with their boots on."

NICK KELSH. ABOVE: WESTERN HISTORY COLLECTIONS, UNIVERSITY OF OKLAHOMA LIB

the wild in the West, ballyhooed Bat into a killer with as many as 30 notches on his gun. Bat, who probably killed no more than four men, later admitted he had cashed in on false claims. He said he would buy a secondhand gun in a pawnshop, cut some notches on the butt, and then sell it to a wide-eyed collector.

Lawlessness was real and not very romantic. In the first three years following the Civil War, 1,035 people were killed in Texas alone. Only five murderers were brought to justice —and only one of them was hanged. In California mining camps, outlaws and renegade lawmen murdered miners for loot, Chinese for sport.

Young psychopaths like William ("Billy the Kid") Bonney killed to earn a reputation. John Wesley Hardin, son of a Methodist minister, was 15 years old when he slew his first man; he had gunned down 27 by the time he was 18.

Lynch mobs and vigilantes frequently lashed out with their own lawless justice. But law-abiding citizens, who called themselves "the better element," ultimately prevailed with grand juries and fair trials. Even in cow towns the law rarely came from the barrel of a gun.

The five main Kansas cow towns —Dodge, Abilene, Ellsworth, Wichita, and Caldwell—averaged one or two murders a cattle season during the 1865-85 span of the great Texas drives. In the few months James Butler ("Wild Bill") Hickok was marshal of Abilene, Kansas, two men were killed—both by him. One of them was his deputy, who strayed into Bill's wild fire.

Cow towns tried to confine their night life to a profitable, tax-paying district avoided by the better element. The law-abiding, then as now, did like to read about sin, though, and their lurid local newspapers did not disappoint them.

A Dodge newspaper reported on a Friday night south of the Santa Fe railroad tracks: "The boys and girls

. . . sang and danced, and fought and bit, and cut and had a good time. . . . Our reporter summed up five knock downs, three broken heads, two cuts and several incidental bruises."

On the ranges where the trails to the cow towns began, the fighting was not in fun. Cattlemen mobilized cowboy armies to war on homesteaders seeking to farm what the ranchers saw as their land. In New Mexico, warfare between rival cattlemen became so bloody that President Hayes removed the territorial governor and replaced him with Gen. Lew Wallace, a Civil War hero. He had to turn from his writing of *Ben Hur* to take on the task of governing the West's wildest realm.

The assassination of a judge and his eight-year-old son finally inspired the apathetic better element to begin a long, slow cleanup of the territory.

Such reform movements helped, but what most tamed the West was barbed wire. Perfected by Joseph Glidden, an Illinois farmer, the invention appealed at first only to homesteaders for fencing out cattle. Then along came a traveling salesman who would become a speculator known as "Bet-a-Million" Gates.

He began making his fortune one day in San Antonio, where he had doubting cowboys stampede a herd of cattle into a barbed-wire corral. The cows learned fast, and so did the cattlemen: The wire held and did the animals no harm. Production spiraled from 10,000 pounds in 1874 to 80 million in 1880.

And so the fencing of the West began. The raising and marketing of beef became a major industry, and cattlemen became businessmen. But

You'd never recognize the Long Branch Saloon in Dodge, Wyatt Earp! A respectable lady, "Miss Kitty" (opposite), runs it, and the cancan girls are not X-rated. But remember the old days, Wyatt? You (below) were at the original Long Branch (right), making a living as a faro dealer—and an assistant city marshal. Dodge has the cards, chips, and handcuffs in a museum now, along with a replica of the Buntline Special you got from Edward Judson. As Ned Buntline, he gave us the dime-novel "Western," which went thataway: from print to radio to screen to tube.

NICK KELSH. ABOVE: KANSAS STATE HISTORICAL SOCIETY, TOPEKA

the cowboy—always a boy, not a cattle-*man*—became a legend.

At $25 a month and keep, it was never much of a job. And yet, there was something about a cowboy... and there still is. Look in the reconstructed cow towns: kids of all ages and both sexes, walking through a cowboy past. They could have stayed home and savored other versions of the Old West in a Zane Grey novel, a John Wayne western, a rerun of *Gunsmoke* or *Bonanza.*

These pilgrims don't mind that the cow towns are cities now, full of people and places of the present. No matter that the past on display may be thin—a ramshackle building, a room full of old guns and badges. Here the past really happened.

In Dodge City, notorious Front Street has been eclipsed by a highway and urban renewal. Visitors—usually family posses—see a modern false front that screens souvenir counters and ticket takers. But Bat Masterson lived here—right here.

In Wichita, at a roundup of old local buildings called Cowtown, Girl Scouts act as guides. Their sweet recitations of outlaw tales may blur the bad old days. But Wyatt Earp walked here—right here.

In Abilene, Dwight D. Eisenhower is buried and hallowed. Strolling about his home or the Presidential library, patriotic visitors become inspired by the life of a hero. People, though, stray to Old Abilene Town, where they hear about a hard-drinking gunslinger named Hickok. Ike would understand. His own boyhood hero was Wild Bill. And Wild Bill drank here—right here!

THOMAS B. ALLEN

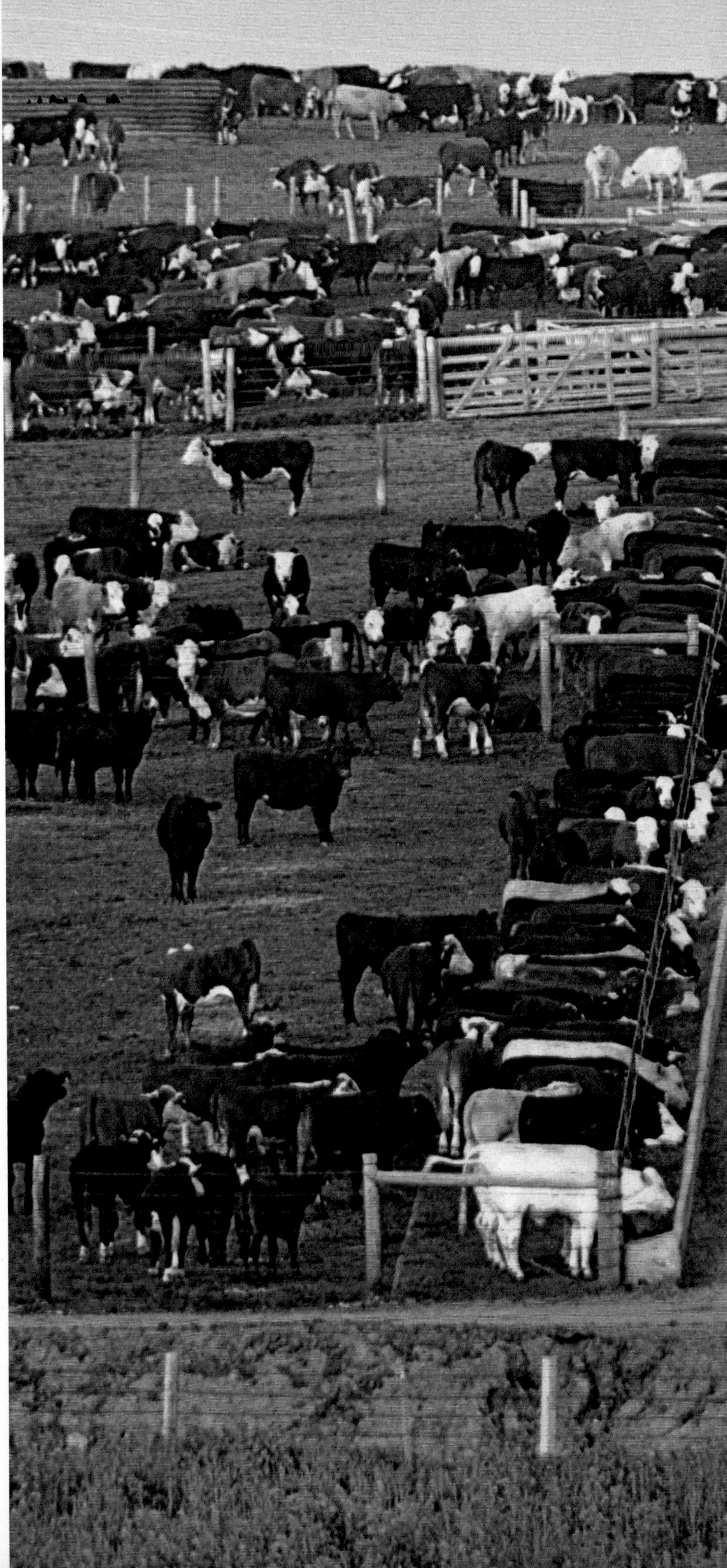

Cattle ignore a lone cowboy at a feedlot near Dodge City. No long trail-walks for them—just a trek to a trough, where about 140 days of effortless eating will produce some 400 added pounds.

NICK KELSH

Mechanizing a Nation

A land of plenty, and plenty of it. Born amid bounty, America grew up in the age of wondrous new machines made for abundance—they reaped it quicker, spread it around, created more and the hunger for more. From the fertile wilderness sprouted the giant of the Industrial Revolution.

BROOKE HINDLE

By the dawn of the 20th century the United States had become the largest republic in the world—and the oldest. In little more than a century it had swelled from a nation of some three million, clustered mostly along the Atlantic seaboard, into a continental power of 76 million, blessed with political freedom and vitality. And still it grew, devouring the natural riches of the land, transforming them by sweat and genius, daring and greed into mountains of material abundance. In countless ways life's burdens seemed lighter, though for many the process became merely a shifting of weight—the narrow horizons of farm life exchanged for the yoke of mine, mill, or factory.

In its swiftness and breadth the epic of America was a miracle of achievement. Like all miracles, this one defies analysis. But it can be appreciated. And so we savor the mementos of the past—the landfalls of the settlers, the rude cabins of the pioneers, the battlegrounds that trace the nation's struggles.

There is another side to the story, until recently the lightly regarded realm of the "hardware historian." But the growing field of industrial archeology views the relics of our technological past as historic monuments of meaning and grandeur—old canals, ghostly mining towns, plantations where iron, not cotton, was king, mills where smuggled secrets brought the Industrial Revolution to our land, and those battlegrounds of will where mind and hand combined to speed sound and light and then man himself through thin air. There is an exhilaration in feeling through the hands of the craftsman, in seeing through the eyes of the inventor. These feelings and these visions stand very close to the center of the American experience.

The beginning was a state of mind. Europeans perceived the New World as a land of plenty from which sailors returned pulling from their pockets rubies, diamonds, and pearls. Even when time shredded the myths, the facts remained fabulous. John Smith told of the vast sweep of Virginia, "as for the west thereof, the limits are unknown." Land signified wealth and status in Europe.

Before he sailed to New England, John Winthrop saw wood-starved men hacking at saplings. England was short of trees; poor folk shivered much of their lives. Beyond the sea, settlers faced great peril, but they could bask in warmth. There was wood to burn, acre upon endless acre. For clearing land, European felling axes proved clumsy and ill balanced. Within a century colonists crafted an ax so finely balanced that it tripled the woodsman's output. There was wood for houses and ships, and for the ravenous furnaces that smelted ore into iron. By the time of the Revolution, a third of Britain's ships were made in America. By then too, the Americans were producing as much iron as Britain. A colonial blast furnace consumed an acre of trees a day, and

DETAIL FROM "STEEL," MURAL BY THOMAS HART BENTON, THE NEW SCHOOL FOR SOCIAL RESEARCH, NEW YORK; PHOTOMONTAGE BY JAMES L. STANFIELD, NATIONAL GEOGRAPHIC PHOTOGRAPHER

iron plantations sprouted in the woodlands from New England to the Carolinas. These rural enclaves were a world apart from the urban infernos that cook our steel today.

Hopewell Village, not far from Reading, Pennsylvania, recalls that remote world. The ironmaster in his Big House ruled all. Deep in the forest colliers stacked mounds of cordwood, covered them with earth and leaves, set them slowly charring. Night and day the collier tended his pile, watching for a "live" fire; he was paid to make charcoal, not ashes. It was a grim life, lived in lonely forest huts. Even in the village the grinding tasks drove men to strong lubricant. To make a ton of iron, it took some 2½ tons of ore, 180 bushels of charcoal, and, it was said, a gallon each of whiskey and beer.

Atop the furnace, men loaded in layers of charcoal and limestone, and ore from nearby mines. Now the charcoal blazed. Its carbon and the ore's oxygen combined, forming carbon dioxide. The limestone flux drew out impurities, forming slag. Bellows powered by a waterwheel fanned the flames into a roaring blast. Finally the molten metal flowed out, into a main channel that fed smaller sand molds —like a sow feeding a litter of pigs.

Conestoga wagons trucked the pig iron to forges —such as Valley Forge, 18 miles southeast—where heat and hammer turned it into wrought iron, lower in carbon content, less brittle, ready for the smithy to shape into nails, horseshoes, wheel rims.

At Hopewell some liquid iron was cast into molds for pots, mill and farm implements, and, increasingly, stoves to replace wasteful fireplaces. Benjamin Franklin had known what we sadly rediscover today as we seek warmth in a new fuel crisis: Fireplace heat goes mostly up the chimney. He devised a much more efficient alternative, the Franklin stove. Of 80,000 stoves cast at Hopewell, many were similar to the Franklin design. Restored Hopewell Village displays a sampling of its cast-iron ware.

When Hopewell's ironworks died in 1883, it had outlived its time. Its techniques and achievements were those of colonial days, when technology rested upon processes passed on from generation to generation, with infrequent change or improvement. Preindustrial America used many tools and methods that had hardly changed since the Roman era. We can best experience this America at Colonial Williamsburg, where gunsmith, silversmith, weaver, and other artisans pursue traditional crafts with skill and authenticity.

The American Revolution launched the nation just in time to join a very different revolution which had begun a little earlier in England. This was the Industrial Revolution, a blending of new technology and economic organization that promised an outpouring of bounty far beyond even the fabled riches of the virgin continent. Despite its later start, the United States was first to realize that promise.

England had acquired a new power source in the steam engine, and learned to make cloth quicker and cheaper by mechanizing spinning and weaving in integrated factories. With coke, made from coal, the English could smelt iron without wood; by puddling molten iron and squeezing hot bars between rollers, they saved money and time in making wrought iron. England had discovered a magical money tree and took extraordinary pains to safeguard its secrets. She embargoed the export of the new machines and forbade emigration of mechanics who knew how to build and run them.

It did not work. Americans, always eager to adopt better means to satisfy their wants, pressed against the barriers. English agents broke open shipments marked as glassware or farm tools to find machinery parts. They intercepted America-bound voyagers carrying plans of prized industrial secrets.

Old Slater Mill in Pawtucket, Rhode Island, marks the site where Samuel Slater gave America a piece of his mind—memorized secrets of England's new cotton machines. The mill rose in 1793; today its exhibits trace the giant step from handicraft to mechanized textile factory. Slater's cane portrays Moses Brown, financier of the historic enterprise.

ABOVE: FRED WARD, BLACK STAR. OPPOSITE: MARIE-LOUISE BRIMBERG

A small mill on the Blackstone River in Pawtucket, Rhode Island, recalls the first major breach of English security and a beginning of the new machine production. Here America came to share one of England's greatest treasures.

What England had achieved was this: In the decade beginning in 1769, Richard Arkwright perfected his "water frame" for spinning strong cotton yarn, James Hargreaves produced the spinning jenny that could run several spindles at once, and Samuel Crompton's "mule" —combining frame and jenny—allowed a single worker to run as many as a thousand spindles. Arkwright linked the spinning to carding and roving machines that prepared the raw tangle of fiber, and applied water power to his system. English mills hummed with the magic of "perpetual spinning." At one such mill in Derbyshire, young Samuel Slater learned the system so well that he rose to superintendent while still an apprentice. News of Americans offering bounties for such knowledge lured him away. Posing as a farmer, he stowed his precious secrets where no British agent could find them—in his head.

In America the 21-year-old immigrant obtained the backing of the Quaker merchant Moses Brown —a benefactor of Brown University—and set to work in a mill by the Blackstone. From memory Slater reconstructed the intricate relationships for varying the machinery speed in the Arkwright system. He chalked plans on wood, and mechanics built the machines. When all was ready in December 1790, the river froze. Through the winter Slater spent bitter hours cracking ice to free the waterwheel. But America had its first successful cotton-spinning factory. In 1793 Slater built a new mill; it still stands, displaying early machines and the techniques that brought the enormous benefit of factory production to the new nation.

Slater's system replaced the old home spinning wheel. But weaving the yarn into cloth was still a cottage industry, done in homes on handlooms. The mill soon piled up a surplus of yarn; the local weavers were overwhelmed. A worried Moses Brown wrote to Slater that "thee will spin all my farms into cotton yarn." In time the remedy arrived as an additional "borrowing" from abroad—but in a different method of technological transfer that came to be frequently used. Rather than import the expertise, Americans themselves went off to study and memorize new machines. Thus the entrepreneur Francis Lowell, of Boston, studied power looms in England. When he came back, the gifted mechanic Paul Moody translated Lowell's memory into machinery and made it work. At Waltham, Massachusetts, all the steps were combined for the first time, creating the "strange Yankee phenomenon . . . that took your bale of cotton in at one end and gave out yards of cloth at the other, after goodness knows what digestive process." The Waltham factory has not survived, but the old Slater Mill preserves later versions of the power loom.

Textiles swiftly became a growth industry, and Slater grew with it. At Manchester, New Hampshire, he helped to establish the Amoskeag Manufacturing Company, which eventually became the largest cotton factory complex in the world. It stretched a mile and a half along the Merrimack River, produced enough cloth every two months to wrap the earth in cotton. Some of the buildings remain—modernized factories with a variety of products, enclosed by the antique facade of mighty Amoskeag of the late 19th century.

Just as England's ingenious "mechanics" were inventing the cotton machines, James Watt presented her with a new source of power to drive them. An instrument maker by training, Watt was asked to repair a Newcomen steam engine. He

The electrifying rivalry of Alexander Graham Bell and Thomas Alva Edison changed our lives—and household budgets. Bell's telephone spoke first; Edison improved it. Edison fathered the phonograph, set it aside as a "mere toy." When Bell's aides refined it, Edison took up the race. Here he rests with his brainchild after a 72-hour spurt in 1888.

AMERICAN TELEPHONE AND TELEGRAPH COMPANY.
OPPOSITE: EDISON NATIONAL HISTORIC SITE, WEST ORANGE, NEW JERSEY

studied it, experimented, then designed his wonderful condensing engine. In the earlier Newcomen engine, steam was condensed in the cylinder, creating a vacuum, and atmospheric pressure drove the piston down. With each cycle, heating and cooling wasted energy; the clumsy rig was good for little except pumping water out of mines. Watt's engine, using the direct force of steam pressure, cut heat loss and boosted power. Easily converted to rotary motion, it became an integral part of England's Industrial Revolution. American textile makers saw little need for it at the time; the land was veined with rushing streams. Falling water remained the prime mover of American industry until the 1860's.

Yet Americans could hardly resist dreaming of ways to use the remarkable device. Thus John Fitch in 1784, strolling a dusty Pennsylvania road as a horse and carriage clattered by, dreamed of owning "a carriage without the expense of keeping a horse." Why not a steam engine to propel a carriage? Fitch, a mechanic and jack of many trades, foresaw great difficulty in achieving his dream, however, and turned to building steamboats. But not many years later, an awed Philadelphian wrote of seeing a "waggon go through our Street without Horses.... I look forward to having a Carriage that I can wind up and set agoing as I do my watch, without trusting my Life to ... drunken Coachmen or perhaps wild horses." Oliver Evans, inventor of an automated flour mill and a high-pressure steam engine, had fitted wheels to his newly designed steam dredge. Steam power drove it through the streets and into the Schuylkill River—and dredged Philadelphia's harbor!

By then, John Fitch had built three steamboats, had run one more than 2,000 miles on a commercial schedule on the Delaware River, and had titled himself "Lord High Admiral of the Delaware." In 1803 a New Orleans steamboat with an Evans engine ran ashore. An inspired entrepreneur attached the engine to a saw and piled up a fortune before local hand sawyers burned the mill down. But the idea took hold. Stationary steam engines spread down the rivers from the Eastern cities. Britain had the know-how and the capital that would have made the introduction of steamboats much easier there. Even Robert Fulton, despite his own ingenuity and the skills available to him, succeeded only after he imported a British engine—with a license from Parliament. On the Hudson River, Fulton brought the steamboat to the point of practical utility.

Why did it happen here? No other nation had a greater need. The population was spread out; roads were primitive. Americans struggling with the untamed land in 1800, observed historian Henry Adams, "seemed hardly more competent ... than the beavers and buffalo which had for countless generations made bridges and roads of their own."

The steamboat converted fine river systems into great internal highways. Yet the steamboat was not enough. Canals were cut, and roads and bridges were built. But that was not enough. When England developed the steam railroad, America swiftly imported the new technology. The first locomotives used here came from England, beginning in 1829, but they were not designed to cope with the curving, rickety American railroads. Parts of the *Stourbridge Lion,* brought in 1829, and the entire *John Bull,* an 1831 import, are at the Smithsonian Institution. In 1830 Peter Cooper built for the Baltimore & Ohio the experimental *Tom Thumb.* A replica is at the B & O Railroad Museum in Baltimore, where a historic depot and roundhouse reflect the spirit of early railroading.

"Americans take to this little contrivance, the railroad, as if it were the cradle in which they were born," wrote Ralph Waldo Emerson. Unlike vehicles on river or road, trains could run in the rain or snow, and, before long, in the gloom of night. For economy and speed Americans built more powerful locomotives. They accepted sharper curves, steeper grades; construction was cheaper that way. They built with vast energy and in incredible profusion: 9,000 miles by *(Continued on page 366)*

Greenfield: Henry Ford's Americana

"American history comes to life" at Greenfield Village. A time-lapse panorama spreads before us, from frontier home to village green, from birch canoe to airplane, from craft shop to brick factory. Here on 260 acres in his native Dearborn, Michigan, Henry Ford mass-reproduced his American dream.

With money and doggedness he strove for the real thing, the relic, not the replica. The chair in which Lincoln was shot is *the* rocker from the theater in Washington. A Maryland home, circa 1650, was moved here with the bones of two brothers buried in its garden. Independence Hall was not for sale; Ford built an identical twin. From Dayton, Ohio, came the Wright brothers' shop. There is Ford's birthplace, too. And the Henry Ford Museum preserves—with fine collections of decorative and mechanical arts—an archive of 14½ million items about the pioneer automaker.

Ford opened the village in 1929 to honor Thomas Edison. He bought Edison's abandoned laboratory in Menlo Park, New Jersey, restored and stocked it, dug up carloads of Jersey clay, even a junk pile. Inventing, Edison had said, requires "imagination and a scrap heap."

Here it stands, with its phials and jars and test gear, the nation's first industrial research lab. The 19th century's greatest invention, wrote the philosopher Alfred North Whitehead, "was the invention of the method of invention." If so, the grandest of Edison's creations is the Menlo Park laboratory itself.

MARIE-LOUISE BRIMBERG

It lit without a match, glowed without flame—a "beautiful light, like the mellow sunset of an Italian autumn." The account of Edison's incandescent lamp thrilled the land in 1879; thousands jammed Menlo Park. Among the first to enjoy the new light were Sarah Jordan's roomers. None more deserving. For they manned the devoted "insomnia squads" that Edison drove night and day. Should one oversleep, a mechanical "corpse reviver" noised him awake. But Edison could also revive weary souls in the wee hours with food and drink, with small talk and music from an organ installed in the lab. The Jordan house and a historic bulb are aglow at Greenfield Village.

Partly deaf, Edison tested a telephone by feel. When a needle rigged to a vibrating receiver pricked his finger, it set him on the path to his most original invention—the phonograph (top).

MARIE-LOUISE BRIMBERG

Ford heralded the future, yet revered the past. He despised the farm chores he was born to, yet devotedly restored his farm home—and never, amid all his multimillions, shed his country style. A $1.50 fiddle, the first he owned, and a parlor organ remember the musicales he loved. He preached education, but not book learning. Learn by doing was his text. He tinkered with timepieces; at a bedside bench he made them tick with tools shaped from knitting needles and corset stays. He "read" engines, and in 1896 crafted his quadricycle, steered by tiller, without brakes or reverse gear. Seeing things is better than reading about them, he said. These are at Greenfield Village, for all to see.

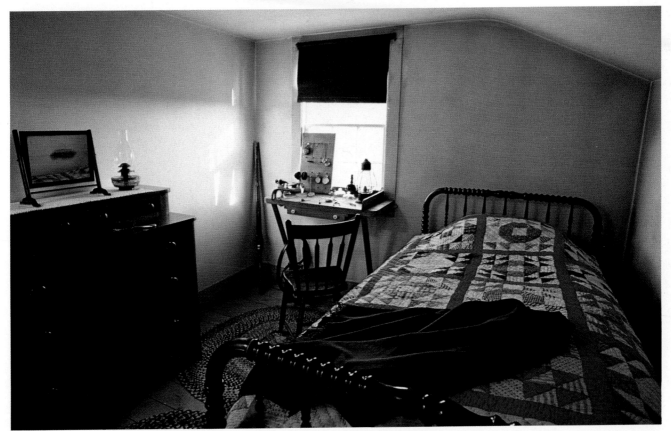

MARIE-LOUISE BRIMBERG

Horse-drawn sleigh nears the Wright home and cycle shop at Greenfield Village. Winter slowed the bicycle business—time for Wilbur and Orville to stock up, tend to paper work, experiment. Any future in horseless carriages? Never, says Wilbur. "Be easier to build a flying machine." They know that the lowered pressure on a curved surface slicing through air will lift weight. They study airfoils rigged to a balance wheel on a speeding bike. They try gliding—a costly, risky venture. They build a boxlike wind tunnel (opposite); in it they test 200 wing surfaces. With hard, reliable data, they shape wings, body, engine, controls. Then . . .

MARIE-LOUISE BRIMBERG

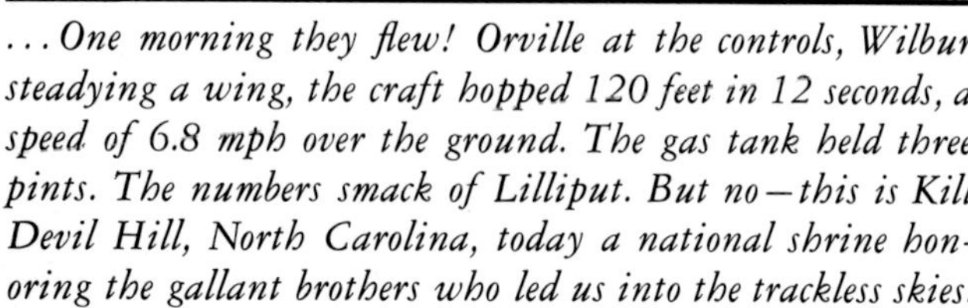

. . . One morning they flew! Orville at the controls, Wilbur steadying a wing, the craft hopped 120 feet in 12 seconds, a speed of 6.8 mph over the ground. The gas tank held three pints. The numbers smack of Lilliput. But no—this is Kill Devil Hill, North Carolina, today a national shrine honoring the gallant brothers who led us into the trackless skies.

1850, and 30,000 by 1860, knitting Northeast and Midwest in time to be a decisive factor in the Civil War. By 1869 a bond of steel tied the continental nation together. Now industry envisioned a national market, an open door to large-scale production.

Meanwhile, a revolutionary new way of making things had evolved, which the British dubbed "The American System of Manufacturing." Its development was, in fact, peculiarly American. To sense the change, consider a gunsmith at Williamsburg, working in the old way. He shapes each part and fits them all together. Should a part fail, he must shape a new one and custom-fit it. Now pour his skill into machines, each turning out a component part in precise measure. No longer must a trigger be individually filed and fitted. They are all interchangeable. Spares can be stockpiled. When workers could assemble a product from interchangeable parts, the foundation was laid for mass production.

Tradition ascribes the beginnings of the system to Eli Whitney. In 1798 he turned from a failing cotton-gin business to make muskets. Whitney promised much, produced little. To sustain government support, he staged a demonstration in 1801 before President-elect Jefferson and other officials in Washington. Out on a table he dumped a helter-skelter collection of pieces for musket locks. Selecting at random, he put together a lock, the pieces fitting precisely. The officials marveled. We now know that Whitney never quite attained interchangeability. For the demonstration, yes. But studies of his production muskets reveal telltale marks of the old way—filing and fitting for individual pieces. Yet he dramatized the goal that others would reach.

By 1820 John Hall was certainly using interchangeability at Harpers Ferry to make the breechloading rifle he designed. The historic town in West Virginia today bears witness to an America faltering in Civil War. Though Hall's armory is

LIBRARY OF CONGRESS

gone, Harpers Ferry also lives in history as a landmark in America's march to greatness. So does Springfield Armory in Massachusetts, where Thomas Blanchard devised a lathe that carved the complex form of a wooden gunstock from a pattern. The armory museum exhibits his pioneer machine.

From guns to wooden clocks to brass clocks, production soared, prices plummeted—with scarcely a tinge of regret for the sacrifice of hand finish and workmanship. The American System surged on, to new products, new industries, including the basic one that embodied Eli Whitney's desire to "form the tools so the tools themselves shall fashion the work"—the machine tool industry.

In colonial America, Franklin had found electricity a parlor game and gave it some of the characteristics of the modern science. Later the American artist-turned-inventor, Samuel F. B. Morse, found the magnetic spark that wrought the marvel of instant communication far beyond the reach of eye or voice. In 1837, the very year his telegraph began to pulse, the electric dynamo came into practical use—for electroplating. For decades most of the world's dynamos were used to produce plated silverware or to coat iron with rust-resistant nickel, zinc, or tin.

In September 1878, Thomas A. Edison journeyed to Connecticut to inspect a promising new use for the dynamo. He watched, enraptured, as current from the dynamo shot across a gap between carbon electrodes to spark a blinding electric arc lamp. At his laboratory in New Jersey, Edison had meshed minds and money and skills, producing inventions as needs were presented. He strove not primarily for new understanding, but for inventions that offered new services and stimulated new markets. When he gazed at arc lights in Connecticut, he saw beyond the streets of Paris, beyond John Wanamaker's store in Philadelphia, already brilliantly arc-lighted. Edison saw into the home of everyman.

For that the arc-light system would not do. Its lamps were bright, but few in number. They were wired in series, one after another in line. One switch controlled all. If one lamp blew, all went dark. Back at his laboratory in Menlo Park, he set forth his grand vision, obtained financing, put his men to work. He would wire his lights in parallel, to permit many switches on a circuit. He would design a power station. He would devise a suitable incandescent bulb. Its filament must use little current and give long service before burning out. News that the "wizard" had embarked on a quest for "electric candles" created a sensation; stocks of gaslight companies flickered in gloom

Edison's seemingly haphazard search for the right filament—a carbonized thread, found in October 1879—projects the popular view of a lone inventor puttering through trial and error. It is a mythical view. The Edison National Historic Site in West Orange, New Jersey, which preserves his laboratory complex—along with a replica of the world's first motion picture studio, the "Black Maria"—provides some three-dimensional reality. Edison pioneered in industrial research. Of the more than 1,000 patents he was granted, most resulted from the teamwork at West Orange and the earlier Menlo Park laboratory.

A few years before the triumph of the light bulb, Edison joined a historic contest. The telegraph (its name derived from the Greek for "far writing") had enjoyed a huge success. Now the race was on to bring forth its offspring, the telephone ("far speaking"). Many took *(Continued on page 376)*

"Rocking gallows" frame swings out, another body drops to its chassis, another Model T hits the road. Seventeen years after Ford road tested his quadricycle, he engineered the revolution of moving assembly at Highland Park, Michigan.

FORD ARCHIVES, DEARBORN, MICHIGAN

Biltmore: Monument to a Gilded Age

Marble and bronze whirl in the air, pause at a landing where the circle is squared, loop upward again. Biltmore's Grand Staircase soars in mingled splendors—the high style of French Renaissance, the majestic vistas beyond the mullioned windows, the chandelier bejeweled with Edison's bright new idea.

Biltmore is a fringe benefit of the new ideas that industrialized America. "Commodore" Cornelius Vanderbilt's fortune grew with the steamboat and railroad. Telegraph, telephone, electric light—all were entwined with the vast Vanderbilt empire, which swelled to some $200,000,000. In the Gilded Age splurging of the late 19th century, Vanderbilts pioneered in palace building on Manhattan's Fifth Avenue and in Newport, Rhode Island.

George Washington Vanderbilt, youngest son of the third generation, sited Biltmore amid the lofty grandeur of the Blue Ridge at Asheville, North Carolina. For this stone fantasy, architect Richard Morris Hunt borrowed inspiration from the Renaissance chateaus of the Loire Valley. It opened in 1895 after 1,000 men labored five years. Scientific forestry and dairy farming—with more workers and a bigger budget than the U. S. Department of Agriculture had—gave the 125,000-acre estate a purposeful air.

Most of the land is now in Pisgah National Forest. Vanderbilt heirs still run the dairy—and Biltmore, too, welcoming tourists to its treasure-filled rooms, its beguiling labyrinth of walks and gardens.

VICTOR R. BOSWELL, JR., AND LARRY D. KINNEY, BOTH NATIONAL GEOGRAPHIC STAFF

Across its lofty plateau Biltmore sweeps 780 feet from carriage house to swimming pool terrace, a facade of Indiana limestone combining pavilions, miniature flying buttresses, clusters of pinnacles and gables and Gothic chimneys. The gray slate roof crowned an area greater than that of any other building in the land. Architect Hunt took pride: "the mountains are in scale with the house."

George Vanderbilt's education consisted mainly of field trips, the world his classroom. He traveled with tutors, learned eight languages, honed a taste for art and literature. His library, paneled in Circassian walnut, reflects a well-heeled connoisseur of both. Among the 20,000 books are a first edition of Milton's Paradise Lost *and a volume containing a lock of Lord Byron's hair.*

Before the master's study, a carved monk signals "Quiet."

VICTOR R. BOSWELL, JR., AND LARRY D. KINNEY, BOTH NATIONAL GEOGRAPHIC STAF

Merrily, merrily, merrily, merrily, life is but a dream. *Gently the rounds began at Biltmore—breakfast in the Palm Court, under the oak-ribbed windows, a bower of palm and fern, a chatter of parrots, a fragrance of fresh flowers delivered through a trapdoor in the sunken marble floor.*

How many for dinner? 20, 40, 60? The table will expand, with damask chairs to spare. No need to shout; superb acoustics enable diners at head and foot to converse as if tête-à-tête. The Norman Banquet Hall is filled with conversation pieces: rare Flemish tapestries, rugs from Persia and from carcasses of Alaska brown bears, an organ loft opposite the triple fireplace, a ceiling that arches 75 feet above the floor.

These are among 22 rooms or areas visitors see, the grandest of Biltmore's 255 rooms.

VICTOR R. BOSWELL, JR., AND LARRY D. KINNEY, BOTH NATIONAL GEOGRAPHIC STAFF

part; Edison contributed an improved transmitter. But the telephone rested most heavily on the work of Alexander Graham Bell. His success was not the result of a lifetime study of electricity, but of a compelling sense of need. He had inherited a family vocation in communication—teachers seeking to convey the gift of speech to the deaf.

One outdistanced rival remarked that if Bell had known more of electricity, he would have been unable to invent the telephone. Indeed, the invention required knowledge of the ways of sound, and called for hunt-and-try mechanical efforts which a scientist seeking greater understanding of electricity might have disdained. In the mid-1870's Bell achieved "conversation *viva voce* by telegraph": Air vibrations of speech struck a sensitive membrane, or diaphragm; movements of the diaphragm varied an electric current in proportion to the air waves; at the other end a receiving diaphragm translated the current into the vibrations of speech. Bell won one of the world's most valuable patents, and exultantly predicted that "wires will be laid on to houses just like water or gas—and friends converse . . . without leaving home." His earliest telephones are on view at the Smithsonian Institution.

The product that most dramatically fulfilled American success in mass production and in the outpouring of bounty bore little relation to electricity, or to obvious need. This was the automobile. In the 1890's, when Henry Ford entered the field, the internal combustion engine had evolved in Europe, and Americans were producing automobiles.

Ford, possessed of a special sensitivity to the "way to wealth" for himself and the American people, left his engineer's job in an Edison power company to make a good, lightweight car. Soon he was on the trail blazed by the American System of Manufacturing. He simplified the product, made standardized parts as cheaply as possible, linked all the steps in an integrated factory. In 1913 he introduced the moving assembly line, the pre-eminent model of mass production. In 1908, the first year of the famous Model T, Ford turned out less than 6,000. Price: $850. In 1916 he produced 577,036. Price: $360. Mass production and mass marketing turned the auto business into the "archetype" of the 20th-century consumer industry, "among the first to create a necessity out of a luxury."

Though the best expression of Ford's methods may be found at the present River Rouge plant in Dearborn, Michigan, a visitor can sense the nature of his world and his work at his shop, preserved in nearby Greenfield Village. Despite his celebrated comment—"History is bunk"—the village and the adjoining Henry Ford Museum display his sense of the continuity of history.

An industry of the still further future was heralded in 1903, the year that the Ford Motor Company was born. On a North Carolina beach the bicycle mechanics Wilbur and Orville Wright flew a biplane, powered by a 12-horsepower engine, in four separate trials on the morning of December 17. The last and longest spanned 59 seconds and 852 feet. The Wrights then took lunch, washed the dishes, and walked four miles to wire the news home to their father in Dayton, Ohio. A Virginia newsman heard of the wire and offered the story to 21 newspapers. Most deemed it unfit to print. The next morning only three papers in the United States announced the birth of the air age. The meaning of the Wrights' achievement dawned very gradually.

The world's first flying machine went into exile in an English museum as controversy embroiled the inventors. At last, in 1942, the Smithsonian Institution granted full recognition, and today the Wrights' *Flyer* holds its place of primacy there.

The quest for novelty, for abundance, goes on. Yet, already, the United States has created a horn of plenty more magical and more real than any imagined in the past. The costs, too, have been beyond any foreseen: pollution, frightening energy and resource depletion, a challenge to the human spirit.

But they who industrialized America bequeathed more than the bounty and the costs. In their record of problems solved we find also a guide for problem solving, the tools and imagination for coping with the realities of this world. Will we use them?

"I lift my lamp beside the golden door!" Revolution wrought her radiant symbols: 1776 sparked the light of liberty; the Industrial Revolution flung wide the door to opportunity. And the yearning millions streamed through, to share the burdens and fulfill the promise of both.

EDWIN S. GROSVENOR

Freedom's Capital

"There is no new thing to be said about Lincoln," observed Homer Hoch, one of the congressmen from Kansas, in 1923. "There is no new thing to be said of the mountains, or of the sea, or of the stars. . . . But to the mountains and sea and stars men turn forever in unwearied homage. And thus with Lincoln."

The Union he preserved numbered only 36 states, North and South. Today, in silent symbolism, 36 marble pillars enwrap the classic temple of the Lincoln Memorial in Washington, D. C. From its cool depths the Great Emancipator looks down on a crowd come to pay him homage—and almost seems about to speak. For half a century the stirring sculpture by Daniel Chester French has spoken silent volumes to millions of visitors. More people pause here than at any other shrine in this city of memorials to a nation's heroes. Inscribed above the statue is one of the reasons why: "In this temple, as in the hearts of the people for whom he saved the Union, the memory of Abraham Lincoln is enshrined forever."

Wherever an American may live, the city of Washington in the District of Columbia is a second hometown. History echoes through the chambers of government. The laurels of valor rest on mighty monuments and on the simple stones of Arlington National Cemetery just across the Potomac River. Mementos from every generation fill museums. And swaths of green parkland interweave the quiet shrines and busy buildings to offer respite to tired feet and crowded minds.

In these pages the city sits for its portrait. And beside the Potomac it waits to welcome Americans home.

WILLIAM S. WEEMS

WILLIAM S. WEEMS

"Who are the Congress? Are they not the Creatures of the People...?"

George Washington

With his words and deeds, George Washington firmed the foundation of the nation that calls him father. With his hands he laid the cornerstone of the Capitol that has housed legislatures for most of America's two centuries. From offices in other buildings, lawmakers gather here—the several hundred representatives in this south wing chamber, the hundred senators in a similar hall of the north wing—to propose, debate, and perhaps enact.

Visitors to either chamber take seats in a gallery above the main floor. Each guest must first obtain a pass, given without charge by the visitor's own representative or either senator. For major debates, the gallery fills quickly and people are turned away. Many go instead to public hearings of committees and subcommittees, where no passes are needed and much of the real work of Congress gets done.

As the nation has grown, so has its Capitol. By Civil War times—when some rooms saw duty as bakery, hospital, and barracks—a low wooden dome had been replaced by this soaring vault of iron. On its lantern stands a bronze *Freedom,* often mistaken for an Indian maid because of eagle plumes in her hair.

Her back to the Washington Monument, *Freedom* faces the Library of Congress. Burned in 1814, begun anew with Thomas Jefferson's 6,487 books, the nation's bookshelf now bulges with some 20 million volumes and millions more manuscripts, photographs, maps, pieces of music. Nearly two million people visit each year, some to search out the past in the main building's quiet and cavernous reading room.

WILLIAM S. WEEMS

"May none but Honest and Wise Men ever rule under This Roof"

John Adams

It was cold and lonely in the big unfinished mansion as President Adams penned those words to his absent wife. Now, from a marble mantel in the State Dining Room, the graven hopes of America's second President speak anew to his successors. The columned residence at 1600 Pennsylvania Avenue has been the home of every Chief Executive since Adams moved in in 1800.

Little more than the stone shell remains from his day. Flames lit up the clouds on an August evening in 1814 as British redcoats burned the mansion to celebrate the capture of Washington. A timely downpour doused the blaze, and soon the task of rebuilding was begun. For years it was called the "President's House" or "President's Palace." Gradually its painted sandstone exterior gave it the name known around the world: the White House.

Visitors are welcomed—often by the hundred—at an east gate daily (except Sunday and Monday) for a tour of stately rooms on the first floor. Second and third floors house the First Family and guests.

Amid the silent cannons and riotous azaleas of neighboring Lafayette Park, Gen. Andrew Jackson salutes the mansion he occupied from 1829 to 1837. Sculptor Clark Mills had never met Jackson, never taken art lessons, never seen an equestrian statue—and never been taught that a man and a rearing horse in bronze would topple without extra support. His tour de force has stood since 1853, one of the few statues of its kind in the world.

"We the People of the United States, in Order to form a more perfect Union...and secure the Blessings of Liberty"

Preamble to the U.S. Constitution

WILLIAM S. WEEMS

With those words, the Preamble to the Constitution begins. By the last of its five sheets of parchment, it has sketched in a government of, by, and for the hundreds of millions of Americans who have lived under it. Among its innovations: a Supreme Court unlike any other. The highest tribunals of most other nations were created to settle disputes and points of law—but this one, as it has evolved, can rule on the law itself, striking down Presidential directives and acts of Congress, upholding rights guaranteed by law, even interpreting the Constitution.

The Supreme Court has known many homes—second-floor rooms over an open-air marketplace in New York, Independence Hall in Philadelphia, even private homes in Washington while the Capitol's old north wing took shape. The Court shared the Capitol with Senate and House from 1801 to 1935. Today, behind this magnificent pillared portico, the Chief Justice and eight Associate Justices meet to uphold the motto blazoned on its pediment: "Equal Justice Under Law."

From October through June the Court alternates about every two weeks between public sessions and closed-door workdays. At any season, visitors may tour the building, admire a pair of five-story elliptical spiral staircases, and view the cornerstone laid by Chief Justice Charles Evans Hughes in 1932. "The Republic endures," he said, "and this is the symbol of its faith."

The Court has been called the nation's conscience—and the National Archives its memory. In a muraled rotunda a family peers at hallowed charters of freedom: the Declaration of Independence, the Constitution, and the Bill of Rights, sealed in helium under special glass and filters. At closing time—and if danger looms—the documents are lowered, cases and all, into a vault 20 feet below.

EQUAL JUSTICE UNDER LAW

"Oh! I have slipped the surly bonds of Earth"

John G. Magee, Jr.

All who have piloted a craft into the air know the joy distilled in *High Flight,* a poem by a student airman of 1941. And all who visit the new National Air and Space Museum sense some of that excitement. For here winged history hovers in time.

WILLIAM S. WEEMS

In this newest of the Smithsonian Institution's 12 exhibit centers, millions peer into the space-scarred Apollo 11 module and relive the electric moment in 1969 when Neil Armstrong took "one giant leap for mankind." Many gaze up at the *Spirit of St. Louis* and remember when Charles Lindbergh soloed the Atlantic in 1927. But few recall the day of Orville Wright's first flight in 1903—in that rickety rig of spruce and muslin, the *Flyer.*

Dubbed the "nation's attic," the Smithsonian awes visitors with such wonders as the Hope Diamond, the original Old Glory, white tigers and giant pandas in its zoo, gowns of the First Ladies, rarities beyond counting, art treasures beyond description. Allow a week to see its best.

"The last full measure of devotion"

Abraham Lincoln

Words from a distant Gettysburg field of battle echo as a timeless requiem. In life the nation's fallen heroes served us to the fullest, fighting our wars and guiding our course through the perilous waters of peace. They gave us their lives—and now we give them our homage, bright as flame, enduring as stone and bronze.

"I could stay up here forever," President John F. Kennedy said on a grassy knoll in Arlington National Cemetery as he gazed across the Potomac at Washington, D. C. Millions have climbed that knoll to view his resting place, drawn by the flame his widow ignited and by the spark he kindled in human hearts.

A combat photograph translated into metal and stone, the Marine Corps War Memorial displays the colors nearby. And beneath a 50-ton marble tomb, flanked by comrades fallen in World War II and Korea, a doughboy of World War I finds eternal peace in the Tomb of the Unknowns. Guards keep an unending vigil over this "American Soldier known but to God."

WILLIAM S. WEEMS

> "I have sworn... eternal hostility against every form of tyranny"
>
> *Thomas Jefferson*

In 1800 Benjamin Rush of Philadelphia opened a letter and read these words by the author of the Declaration of Independence. Today Thomas Jefferson's impassioned denunciation of oppression "over the mind of man" encircles the great classical rotunda of the Jefferson Memorial. Its design recalls Monticello, home of the third President, a hundred miles away in the Virginia foothills. And the quotations carved in its panels recall the soaring intellect of the man who stands in bronze, 19 feet tall at its center.

Stately Ionic columns streak the Tidal Basin at the monument's feet as workers erect a temporary concert stage. In April the pool's grassy banks burgeon with the powdery pink of cherry blossoms. Under hundreds of trees given to the nation by Japan in 1912, visitors stroll on winding walks and watch couples puff and pedal past in the basin's fleet of paddleboats. Concerts, a parade, and the crowning of a queen draw hundreds of thousands to an annual rite of spring, the Cherry Blossom Festival.

Nearby, the Lincoln Memorial shimmers in the Reflecting Pool, a ribbon of water stretching toward the lofty obelisk of the Washington Monument. An elevator ride to the top of the 555-foot-high spire reveals a breathtaking panorama, from Capitol to White House, from shady gardens to museums crammed with wonders—and to sites filled with special memories.

An August day in 1963. From the Lincoln Memorial, black leader Martin Luther King, Jr., electrified with hope an army of civil rights demonstrators. "I still have a dream.... I have a dream that one day every valley shall be exalted, every hill and mountain shall be made low, the rough places will be made plain, and the crooked places will be made straight...."

The kind of dream that has kept Freedom's Capital strong.

WILLIAM S. WEEMS

Index

Text references appear
in lightface type,
illustrations in **boldface**.

Type composition by National Geographic's Photographic Services. Color separations by Colorgraphics, Inc., Forestville, Md.; Graphic Color Plate, Inc., Stamford, Conn.; Progressive Color Corporation, Rockville, Md.; J. Wm. Reed Company, Alexandria, Va. Printed and bound by Fawcett Printing Corporation, Rockville, Md. Paper by Boise-Cascade Paper Group, Portland, Oreg.

Library of Congress CIP Data

National Geographic Society, Washington, D. C. Book Service.
Visiting Our Past.

(World in Color Library)
Includes bibliographical references and index. 1. United States—History. 2. United States—Description and travel—1960- 3. Historic sites—United States. I. Boorstin, Daniel Joseph, 1914- II. Title.
E178.N19 1977 973 77-21828
ISBN 0-87044-003-9

Acknowledgments and References

Like the pieces in a giant jigsaw puzzle, the nation's historylands each have their own colors to add to the whole, their own story to tell. As we assembled this portrait of America's past and visited the sites that enshrine it, we studied the works of many authors and sought the guidance of many authorities. Though we cannot name all those who helped us, we do offer our thanks to the National Park Service and to the scores of curators, guides, information officers, and state and local historical societies who provided background, answered questions, and verified facts about the sites we included in this book. The writers, editors, and researchers are especially indebted to Duncan Morrow of the National Park Service and to Ruth Boorstin for their invaluable assistance.

Several libraries and museums were especially generous with their help and facilities. We are grateful to the people of the National Geographic Society Library, the Library of Congress, and the Smithsonian Institution for their expert assistance.

Among books of broad scope, we found these to be particularly useful: *The Americans: The Colonial Experience, The Americans: The National Experience, The Americans: The Democratic Experience,* and *The Landmark History of the American People* (two volumes), all by Daniel J. Boorstin; *The Americans: A Social History of the United States 1587-1914* by J. C. Furnas; *The Colonial Experience* by David Hawke; and the individual state volumes of the American Guide Series, some dating from a Work Projects Administration program begun in the 1930's, others available today in modern revisions.

For details on foothold settlements, we consulted *The Eyes of Discovery* by John Bakeless; *Narratives of Early Virginia, 1606-1625* by Lyon Gardiner Tyler; *Colonial Virginia* by Richard L. Morton; *Tidewater Towns* by John W. Reps; *Captain John Smith* by Bradford Smith; *The Three Worlds of Captain John Smith* by Philip Barbour; *Life Along the Hudson* by Allan Keller; William Bradford's *Of Plymouth Plantation 1620-1647; Mourt's Relation: A Journal of the Pilgrims at Plymouth; Saints and Strangers* by George F. Willison; and *The Puritan Oligarchy* by Thomas Jefferson Wertenbaker.

Among our sources for the colonial section were *A Brief and True Report for the Traveller Concerning Williamsburg in Virginia* by Rutherfoord Goodwin; *A Window on Williamsburg* by Taylor Lewis, Jr., John J. Walklet, Jr., and Thomas K. Ford; *Colonial Williamsburg: Official Guidebook; Here Lies Virginia* by Ivor Noël Hume; *The Byrds of Virginia* by Alden Hatch; *Cities in the Wilderness* and *Myths & Realities: Societies of the Colonial South* by Carl Bridenbaugh; *The Great Plantation: A Profile of Berkeley Hundred and Plantation Virginia from Jamestown to Appomattox* by Clifford Dowdey; *Plantations of the Carolina Low Country* by Samuel G. Stoney; *Charleston in the Age of the Pinckneys* by George C. Rogers, Jr.; *South Carolina: A Bicentennial History* by Louis B. Wright; *Records of the Moravians in North Carolina* (four volumes); and *Old Salem in Pictures* by Frances Griffin.

References for the Revolutionary War period included *Encyclopedia of the American Revolution* by Mark M. Boatner III; *Rebels and Redcoats* by George F. Scheer and Hugh F. Rankin; *A New Age Now Begins* by Page Smith; *The War of the Revolution* by Christopher Ward; *The Boston Massacre* by Hiller B. Zobel; *The Minutemen and Their World* by Robert A. Gross; *Diary of Independence Hall* by Harold D. Eberlein and Courtlandt Van Dyke Hubbard; *A Rising People: The Founding of the United States 1765-1789,* a collection from the American Philosophical Society, The Historical Society of Pennsylvania, and The Library Company of Philadelphia; *Benjamin Franklin* by Carl Van Doren; the multivolume biographies of George Washington by Douglas Southall Freeman and James Thomas Flexner; *George Washington Diaries* (four volumes) edited by John C. Fitzpatrick; *Jefferson and His Time* (five volumes) by Dumas Malone; *Monticello* by Frederick D. Nichols and James A. Bear, Jr.; *The Jeffersonian Cyclopedia* (two volumes) edited by J. P. Foley; and *Thomas Jefferson: An Intimate History* by Fawn Brodie.

Details on American expansion came from a number of sources, among them *The Year of Decision: 1846* by Bernard DeVoto; *Lewis and Clark: Partners in Discovery* by John Bakeless; *The Maritime History of Massachusetts* by Samuel Eliot Morison; *New England and the Sea* by Robert G. Albion; *Seafaring America* by Alexander Laing; *Freedom's Ferment* by Alice Felt Tyler; *The People Called Shakers* by Edward Deming Andrews; *Bishop Hill* by Olov Isaksson and Sören Hallgren; *The Original Journals of the Lewis and Clark Expedition 1804-1806* edited by Reuben G. Thwaites; *The Oregon Trail Revisited* by Gregory M. Franzwa; *The Gathering of Zion* by Wallace Stegner; *The Great Platte River Road* by Merrill J. Mattes; *The Road to Santa Fe* by Hobart E. Stocking; and *The Life and Times of Junípero Serra* (two volumes) by Maynard J. Geiger.

For background on the era of the Civil War, the books we turned to included *The Civil War and Reconstruction* by J. G. Randall and David Donald; *The American Civil War* by Peter J. Parish; *The Confederacy* by Charles P. Roland; *The Civil War* (three volumes) by Shelby Foote; *A Centennial History of the Civil War* (three volumes) by Bruce Catton; *Natchez* and *Plantation Parade* by Harnett T. Kane; *Antebellum Natchez* by D. Clayton James; *A History of the Old South* by Clement Eaton; *Lincoln's Youth: Indiana Years* by Louis A. Warren; *Abraham Lincoln* by Benjamin P. Thomas; *"Here I Have Lived": A History of Lincoln's Springfield 1821-1865* by Paul M. Angle; and *Lincoln's New Salem* by Benjamin P. Thomas.

Insight on the taming of the American West was gleaned from *Exploration and Empire* by William H. Goetzmann; *Prospector, Cowhand, and Sodbuster,* a publication of the National Park Service; *Sutter's Fort: Gateway to the Gold Fields* by Oscar Lewis; *Gold and Silver in the West* by T. H. Watkins; *Mining Frontiers of the Far West* by Rodman W. Paul; *The New Eldorado* by Phyllis F. Dorset; *Great Gunfighters of the Kansas Cowtowns* by Nyle H. Miller and Joseph W. Snell; *Frontier Violence: Another Look* by W. Eugene Hollon; *The Cattle Towns* by Robert R. Dykstra; and *Burs Under the Saddle* by Ramon F. Adams.

Sources for the age of mechanization included *America's Wooden Age* edited by Brooke Hindle; *Edison* by Matthew Josephson; *Scientific Technology and Social Change* (Readings from *Scientific American); From Know-How to Nowhere* by Elting E. Morison; *Bell* by Robert V. Bruce; and *Those Inventive Americans,* published by the National Geographic Society.

It is impossible in this space to list separately the hundreds of booklets, brochures, and pamphlets we consulted. We gratefully acknowledge this invaluable body of reference provided by historic sites across the nation, and we thank the staff members who supplied it to us.